JUST DEAL WITH IT!

JUST DEAL WITH IT!

Funny Readers Theatre for Life's Not-So-Funny Moments

Diana R. Jenkins

TEACHER IDEAS PRESS
Portsmouth, NH

Teacher Ideas Press
A division of Reed Elsevier Inc.
361 Hanover Street
Portsmouth, NH 03801-3912
www.teacherideaspress.com

Offices and agents throughout the world

Library of Congress Cataloging-in-Publication Data
Jenkins, Diana R.
    Just deal with it! : funny readers theatre for life's not-so-funny moments / by
Diana R. Jenkins.
        p. cm.
    ISBN 1-59158-043-9 (acid-free paper)
    1. Children's plays, American. 2. School children—Juvenile drama.
3. Schools—Juvenile drama. I. Title.
PS3610.E54Ju7 2004
812'.6—dc22   2003019954

Editor: Suzanne Barchers
Production Coordinator: Angela Laughlin
Typesetter: Westchester Book Services
Cover design: Susan Geer
Manufacturing: Steve Bernier

Printed in the United States of America on acid-free paper

10 9 8 7 6 5

For Mom and Dad
with love and appreciation

Contents

Introduction

"Mama! Mama!"

Okay, so I only had one line. And my paper bonnet wouldn't stay on my head. Still, my dramatic debut as a living doll made first grade memorable—and inspired a lifelong love of the theatre.

It's been many years since my last performance. (Unless you count my experience as a teacher. There wasn't a dry eye in the room when I did my imaginary deathbed scene. My "last" words: "Spell the best you can . . . Hack! Cough! Gurgle!") However, I'm still enjoying the benefits of having read, watched, and performed in plays throughout my school years.

Being involved in theatre is a valuable experience for any child. It improves language skills such as listening, reading, speaking, and even writing if children get involved in creating their own plays. Theatre also encourages appreciation of storytelling and literature and develops understanding of concepts like plot, character development, and story line. Most importantly, theatre builds self-esteem and character.

Using theatre in your classroom can be complicated, time-consuming, and labor-intensive. Fortunately, there's an easy way to get the benefits of "regular" theatre without all the complications—readers theatre!

What Is Readers Theatre?

In readers theatre, actors read their lines instead of memorizing them. Other aspects of staging are kept simple, too. While costumes, props, sets, or movement can be part of a readers theatre performance, they are not necessary. In other words, a readers theatre production doesn't have to be a big production, so to speak. Programs can be pulled together fairly easily, and students can feel relatively comfortable and unstressed as they perform. (So can their teachers!)

Preparing for Readers Theatre

You have to decide what works best for your students, but here are a few suggestions to get you going:

Always read a play yourself before you use it. This will allow you to determine if it's appropriate for your particular group. (It's a good idea to do this with the supplemental reading, too.) Think about which students can handle the more difficult roles and which ones need less challenging parts. Note any vocabulary your students might find difficult so you can go over the words before having students read the play.

Make copies of the script you want to use. You'll need as many copies as there are parts, plus an extra copy for you. (You might want to go ahead and run off a few extras just in case. Kids have been known to lose things!) In each copy, except your own, highlight one character's lines to make it easier for the actor to follow along. Since scripts will see a lot of use, it's worthwhile to put them in binders or folders so they'll last. (Students can help with these tasks.)

Getting Started on Readers Theatre

Reading cold can be a terrifying experience, so give students time to preview the script, too. Then let them read the play aloud from the safety of their desks. To involve more students, you can change casts for each scene. This also gives you a chance to see who might best fit each role if you are planning to perform the play for a live audience.

Don't hesitate to have students read the same play several times (on different days). As students become more and more familiar with a play, you can work with them on fluency and expression. Suggestions for delivery are included in the introductory material to each play. Discuss these suggestions, and encourage students to think about how to incorporate them into their performances.

Many students tend to read in a stiff, robotic manner even after reading through a script several times. For students who have particular trouble with poor expression, try echo reading. You read a line with good expression and ask the student to repeat it exactly as you said it. Usually it takes several tries before the student can let go of his robot voice and speak the line naturally. Echo read a few lines until the student has the idea. (You'll know he has it when his face lights up with pride at how good he sounds!) Then let him develop his own style for the rest of his part.

After the initial reading, move students from their desks to the front of the classroom. Traditionally, readers theatre is performed on a bare-bones set. Actors usually sit on stools in a semicircle or other simple arrangement throughout the play. The narrator is often placed to one side with his script on a lectern or other stand. In some performances, actors sit with their backs to the audience, then face front when participating in a scene. You'll probably want to start your students out with basic staging like this. Later, you can allow students to gesture, stand, move around, and enter and exit if you wish, but remember that movement is not usually necessary.

Performing Readers Theatre

Readers theatre can be an enjoyable and educational addition to your classroom, but performing in front of an audience is what theatre is all about. Nothing is more frightening, exhilarating, rewarding, and fun! To prepare for a live performance, rehearse the play until students feel comfortable enough to take their noses out of their scripts, look up once in a while, turn to other characters, and read their lines fluently.

Costumes and props can be used if you wish, but like movement, they are not essential. You may find, however, that students ask for them, especially for "real" plays. If you decide to use costumes and props, don't introduce them too early in the rehearsal process as they tend to distract students from improving their performances.

A class of younger students makes an appreciative—and not-too-threatening—first audience. When your group feels comfortable, try more challenging audiences like students of the same age, parents and grandparents, or even other adult audiences at places like nursing homes or club meetings.

You may want to work up several of the plays in this book so that you can involve more students and present a longer program. While you rehearse with the cast of one play, other groups can work on their plays. They might sit together informally in the back of the room and read through their scripts together. Or they could work on making props, costumes, or backdrops, if you are including these extras in your performance. Once they have some experience with theatre, students could work on writing their own scripts for later programs.

Because actors read their lines instead of memorizing them, you'll find that student absences aren't as devastating in readers theatre as they can be in "regular" performances. However, it's a good idea to choose understudies for major roles and have them rehearse with their group a time or two. If you are putting together several plays, you can have the cast of one play understudy another, watching and even participating in rehearsals.

Readers Theatre and Writing

Even if you're just getting started, you can use readers theatre to improve your students' writing skills. Encourage students to rewrite lines or add new ones to the script. When lines are interrupted, have students write out what the character would have said if he were allowed to finish speaking. (This is a good way to avoid those obvious pauses where a character stops talking before he's actually interrupted. The actor can continue on with the line he's written until the next speaker butts in.) Ask students to write alternate endings to the plays and share them with the class.

Creating their own readers theatre scripts is a great writing activity for students. To start out, have students write scripts based on familiar stories like folk tales, fairy tales, and myths. Pose questions that push students to add new twists to these old stories. (Whatever became of the cow that Jack sold for three beans? What if Beauty turned into a beast? What would happen if the Three Pigs took the Big, Bad Wolf to court?) Students might also enjoy writing plays based on favorite television shows or movies.

After students have written several derivative scripts, encourage them to come up with fresh ideas and original characters. They might find it easiest to do this by brainstorming in small groups. After an idea session together, students can then leave the group and write their plays independently. Or the group can stay together, collaborating on a play as someone serves as the secretary, writing by hand or typing on a computer.

The Benefits

Make readers theatre a regular activity in your classroom, and you'll be amazed at the results. Students won't just improve their academic skills—they'll grow as people. A good performance takes hard work, so students learn how to meet a challenge and work toward a goal. They also gain social skills like cooperation, teamwork, and appreciation of others as they work together to put on a good show. And they get a real sense of accomplishment from their personal achievements as well as the group's success. This *genuine* self-esteem—the kind that comes from really accomplishing something—can have a powerful impact on every aspect of a child's life!

1

Alcatraz Junior High

Summary

Jason feels that his school is like a prison. The teachers are guards, the principal is the warden, and his best friend, Wink, is his cellmate. It's like Alcatraz Junior High—and Jason can't take it any more!

Costumes/Props/Sets

All characters can wear contemporary clothing. Striped shirts for the "prisoners" would add some humor.

Actors can be seated on stools onstage. If desired, the performance area could be decorated in a prison theme, with crepe paper bars on a window, pictures of Alcatraz, and the like.

Except for a note in the last scene, props are not essential. Students and Mrs. Keaton could carry textbooks if desired.

Presentation

The play can be performed with actors seated throughout or they could enter and exit as needed. In the locker-room scene, actors could mime the fight and Coach Parker arriving and taking Roger out.

Supplemental Reading

George, Linda. *Alcatraz*. New York: Children's Press, 1998.
Oliver, Marilyn Tower. *Alcatraz Prison in American History*. Springfield, New Jersey: Enslow Publishers, 1998.

Cast of Characters

Narrator

Jason

Wink, his cellmate and friend

Mrs. Keaton, English teacher
Cafeteria Lady
Aimee
Chris
Roger
Principal Stevens
Teacher One
Teacher Two
Coach Parker

Alcatraz Junior High

Scene One

Narrator: *(to audience)* Out in San Francisco Bay, a mile from the nearest land, there's an island made of solid rock. And on that island there's a prison called "Alcatraz." Maybe you've heard of it.

Jason: Of course, we've heard of it. It's supposed to be the toughest prison in the world, home to the most dangerous criminals known to man, yadda yadda yadda.

Narrator: Actually, Jason, the prison has been closed since 1963. Now it's just a tourist attraction.

Wink: I wonder if they have a gift shop.

Jason: Who cares?

Wink: Well, I was just wondering what they'd sell in a gift shop there. Tin cups? Cakes with files baked in them? Pajamas striped like—

Jason: Whatever!

Narrator: *(to audience)* For years, Alcatraz Prison was called "The Rock." It was known the world over as the worst, the meanest, the roughest—

Jason: Yeah, yeah, yeah! Everybody thinks that there's no place as tough as Alcatraz Island, but it's not true. I know because I'm a prisoner in the worst penitentiary on earth!

Wink: What are you talking about?

Jason: I'm talking about Central Junior High, of course.

Wink: Here? Our school?

Jason: Yes, our school. They treat us like prisoners, Wink.

Wink: Oh, come on, Jason. It's not that bad.

Jason: Oh yeah? Have you forgotten what happened to us this morning?

Wink: When?

Jason: When we took those books to the office for Señora Delgado.

Wink: I remember the books . . . .

Jason: Okay, let me refresh your memory. We dropped off the books—

Narrator: Hey, wait a minute. That's my job.

Jason: Go ahead then.

Narrator: *(to audience)* Jason and Wink dropped off the books and headed back to their

---

classroom. They were just walking down the hall, minding their own business, when Mrs. Keaton, the English teacher, came along.

Jason: Mrs. Keaton . . . also known as . . . the Queen of Grammar.

Mrs. Keaton: Why aren't you boys in class?

Jason: We just did an errand for Señora Delgado.

Mrs. Keaton: Oh, really?

Wink: Yes, ma'am.

Mrs. Keaton: Where's your pass?

Jason: Well, uh, let me see . . . here it is!

Mrs. Keaton: This doesn't look like Mrs. Delgado's signature.

Wink: It is, Mrs. Keaton. Really!

Jason: You can ask her yourself.

Mrs. Keaton: Hmph! I'll be sure to do that. Now you boys stop loitering about the halls, wasting time, and get back to your class.

Jason: We weren't loitering! You stopped *us*, Mrs. Queen . . . I mean, Mrs. Keaton.

Mrs. Keaton: You weren't counting on that, were you? You thought you'd just slip right by me, didn't you? Well, I'm not easily fooled.

Wink: No, ma'am.

Jason: Can we get back to class now?

Mrs. Keaton: Right away!

Narrator: Mrs. Keaton watched as the guys continued down the hall and around the corner.

Jason: Like she thought we might try to escape.

Wink: She was just doing her job, I guess.

Jason: Well, I hate it! I hate the way they treat us around here. We have to do what they tell us and go where they want us and—

Wink: That's what they're supposed to do, Jason.

Jason: We're not little kids. We don't need to be guarded, do we?

Wink: *(sighs)* I don't know. Anyway, it's not as bad as you say.

Jason: It is too! Wake up and smell the coffee, Wink. We are prisoners in Alcatraz Junior High!

Scene Two

Narrator: Jason and Wink had exactly the same schedule.

Jason: Yeah, we're like cellmates here at the Rock.

Narrator: They were best friends, too, so Jason felt that he had to make Wink understand the reality of their situation. Whenever he got the chance, Jason pointed out the prison-ish . . . prison-like . . . prisony . . . he made sure that Wink noticed how their school was like a prison. Like when they lined up for lunch . . . .

Jason: If we had some tin cups, this would be just like a prison chow line.

Wink: What do you mean?

Jason: Well, we're standing in a ridiculously long line with these stupid trays that they're going to fill up with inedible slop that we'll only get three minutes to—

Roger: Move it!

Jason: Hey!

Narrator: Every day Roger cut in the lunch line. Since he was twice the size of Frankenstein's monster, everybody was afraid to do anything about it.

Roger: You have something to say to me, shrimp?

Jason: No, sir. I mean, of course not. You go right ahead.

Narrator: After Roger got his food and moved out of earshot, Jason turned to Wink.

Jason: See? This place really is a prison! And Roger is the top dog. You know, the biggest, meanest inmate who bosses around all the other prisoners.

Wink: Roger's just a big bully who picks on people who are smaller than he is.

Jason: Isn't that what I just said?

Wink: Not really.

Cafeteria Lady: Hold out your tray please. *(disgusting plop as food hits tray)*

Jason: Man! When are we going to get some decent grub around here?

Cafeteria Lady: I beg your pardon?

Jason: Uh . . . never mind. Mm-mmm, this gruel looks yummy!

Scene Three

Narrator: Later, Jason got another chance to make his point when the guys were rushing to the Band room.

Wink: *(panting)* How are we supposed to get all the way from one end of the building to the other in three minutes?

Jason: *(panting)* It's just part of their plan to break us, Wink. They make it impossible for us to get to Band on time, and then we get punished for being tardy. It's a power trip, Wink, a mind game they use to control the prisoners.

Wink: Hey, look! Mr. Day isn't waiting outside the door to catch us.

Narrator: That *was* pretty amazing. Mr. Day was always right there, standing guard with a big pad of tardy slips.

Jason: He must be inside, ready to pounce.

Narrator: Jason and Wink dashed into the room and found that Mr. Day wasn't inside either. They got their instruments, took their seats, and waited with the other kids.

Aimee: Where is he?

Chris: He's never late.

Roger: And he's never absent.

Narrator: For a while, everyone just sat around and talked. Some people even practiced a bit.

Jason: See, Wink? Everything is going just fine. We're doing great without a guard.

Wink: I guess.

Narrator: But things gradually got a little louder. And wilder. Roger started "accidentally" hitting people with his trombone slide.

Roger: So sorry! Sorry again! Did I hit you? Sorry!

Narrator: Two guys played keep-away with Aimee's flute.

Aimee: Give it back! Give me my flute! Hey, give it!

Narrator: A tuba rolled down the risers and crashed onto the floor with this huge trainwreck noise.

Chris: Oops!

Aimee: Give me my flute right now!

Roger: Oh, man! Did I hit you? I'm ever so sorry!

Narrator: Flutes flew. People shouted. Windows rattled. Furniture tipped over. Finally, a person of authority appeared at the door.

Aimee: The principal!

Jason: You mean: the warden!

Principal Stevens: Everybody settle down right now!

Narrator: Things got deadly quiet.

Jason: Of course! The warden likes to punish infractions with long bouts in solitary.

Wink: You mean detention?

Jason: Whatever.

Principal Stevens: Mr. Day is ill. Since we couldn't get a sub for this period, I will be supervising you. This will be a study hall for today. Put away your instruments, clean up this mess, and get to work. Now.

Narrator: Everyone did as the warden . . . I mean, principal, ordered.

Wink: See, Jason? We *did* need somebody to take charge.

Jason: It's not like anything really happened. We were just having fun.

Wink: Oh, sure.

Scene Four

Narrator: After Band, Jason and Wink had to hurry to make it to Math, all the way back at the other end of the building.

Teacher One: Boys! Slow down!

Jason: Why is that teacher yelling at us? She (he) doesn't even know us.

Wink: I guess we are going kind of fast.

Jason: We have to go fast or we'll be late. Come on. Hurry it up!

Aimee: Hey, run me down, why don't you?

Wink: Sorry, Aimee!

Teacher Two: You boys! No running in the halls!

Jason: You're not the boss of me, buddy (lady)! And furthermore, I'm tired of all the ridiculous rules around this place. I'm not going to take it anymore.

Narrator: Yeah, sure. Like you really said that.

Jason: Well, I wanted to say something like that. I just didn't have time to stop and talk.

Chris: You guys are going to be late again!

Jason: No, we're not! Move it, Wink!

Narrator: At that moment, Jason turned to look at Wink. Just for a second! Unfortunately, that was the second that Mrs. Keaton stepped out into the hall. Jason ran smack-dab into her, knocking her books to the floor.

Mrs. Keaton: What in the—

Jason: Oh, I'm sorry, Mrs. Queen . . . Mrs. Grammar . . . Mrs. Keaton . . . Let me pick those up for you.

Mrs. Keaton: This is why we ask you not to run in the halls.

Jason: I wasn't running.

Mrs. Keaton: Don't talk back to me!

Jason: I'm not. It's just that I wasn't really running. Not very fast, anyway. I mean, we don't have much time to get to class and . . . uh . . . I'm sorry, Mrs. Keaton.

Mrs. Keaton: Be more careful in the future, young man. I could have been seriously injured by your rash actions. You wouldn't want that, would you?

Jason: Yes, ma'am. I mean, no, ma'am. I mean, yes, I'll be careful because, no, I wouldn't want anyone to get hurt.

Mrs. Keaton: Very well. Quit loitering about and get to your class.

Jason: But we weren't—

Wink: Yes, ma'am! We're on our way right now.

(Bell rings.)

Jason: Rats! We're tardy again. It's all Mrs. Keaton's fault!

Wink: No, it's not. We should have listened to the teachers who told us to slow down.

Jason: Hey, suck up to the guards if you want to, but I'm keeping my spirit alive, man!

Wink: Whatever.

Scene Five

Narrator: As that day wore on, Jason's hatred for Alcatraz Junior High grew until it ate away at his guts like acid.

Wink: That is disgusting.

Jason: I can't take this place, Wink! The rules! The constant supervision! The orders! The total lack of freedom! How will I ever survive my whole two-year sentence?

Wink: Oh, come on, Jason!

Jason: It's terrible here.

Wink: Brother!

Jason: It is! In Math, Mr. Bacon got on my case when he saw I was doodling instead of starting the assignment. Like I was going to get anything done in the last ten minutes of class.

Wink: I got half the homework finished.

Jason: So?

Wink: I'm just saying—

Jason: And in Study Hall—the real Study Hall—Ms. Presley was mad when she checked our assignment books and found out that I wasn't using mine. What does it matter if I use the stupid assignment book as long as I get my assignments in?

Wink: Actually, haven't you forgotten to do some assignments?

Jason: Maybe a few.

Wink: A few!

Jason: And in English, the Queen of Grammar patrolled the aisles while we took our test. It was like she was scared that somebody might cheat. Who could with her breathing down our necks?

Wink: Isn't that the—

Jason: Don't you get tired of it all, Wink? All the rules? And people watching your every move and ordering you around?

Wink: Yeah, sometimes. But you have to have rules, Jason. And people to make sure everybody follows the rules.

Jason: You just don't get it.

Wink: We'd better get to P.E. class.

Jason: Gee, I hope they let us walk around the exercise yard for a few minutes.

Wink: Huh?

Jason: Like in prison. It's a joke.

Wink: Oh. I think we're playing basketball today. Or maybe alley soccer.

Jason: The point is, we're playing whatever we're told to play. Because we have no rights here at The Rock.

Wink: Give me a break!

Narrator: Jason and Wink reached the locker room and started to change for class. Jason kept trying to make Wink understand that he was a number, not a name, at Alcatraz Junior High.

Jason: Just look at how they make us wear these P.E. uniforms, Wink. We all look alike in these things. It's like we're not even individual people.

Wink: I like the uniforms.

Jason: Oh, man! You're totally brainwashed!

Narrator: The guys were all dressed and ready to head to the gym, when Roger took a step backwards and ran right into Jason.

Roger: Hey, watch it, you idiot!

Jason: You backed into me.

Roger: Don't get smart with me, little guy.

Narrator: Before Jason knew what was happening, Roger slammed him up against a locker and started punching him. It was all Jason could do to keep his arms up to protect himself.

Wink: Don't worry, Jason. I'll save you!

Jason: Hey, where are you going?

Narrator: Wink ran out of the locker room, while everyone else just stood around and watched Roger pound on Jason. Luckily, Wink found Coach Parker who got Roger off of Jason and hauled him to the office.

Wink: Are you okay?

Jason: Yeah, I think so. Thanks, Wink!

Wink: Sure. Isn't that what cellmates do for each other?

Jason: Funny.

Scene Six

Narrator: Later, Coach Parker stopped the guys in the hall and told them that Roger was suspended.

Coach Parker: And, Jason, I'm really sorry you had that trouble. I got all involved in changing the basketball net at the far end of the gym where I couldn't hear anything. I should have been in the locker room.

Jason: That's okay, Coach.

Coach Parker: No, it's not. It's my job to watch out for you guys. Believe me, I'll be on guard in the future.

Jason: Uh . . . thanks!

Coach Parker: See you tomorrow!

Wink: Gee, Prisoner 2738904531479, why didn't you tell him that you don't need a guard?

Jason: *(mumbles)*

Wink: What was that? I couldn't hear you.

Jason: Maybe I changed my mind, okay? Maybe we do need some people in charge. Maybe. Sometimes. Now and then. Maybe.

Wink: *(laughing)* Right.

Narrator: The guys went into Social Studies class and took their seats. A few minutes into the period, the teacher turned to write something on the board. That was when Wink tossed Jason a note. Jason opened it up and read:

Wink: Tunnel finished. Breaking out tonight. Are you with me?

Narrator: Ha! Good one!

Jason: Yeah.

Wink: I thought so.

Narrator: Things aren't so bad here at Alcatraz Junior High. Are they?

Jason: No, I guess not. Not with a cellmate like Wink!

2

And Then There's Muriel

Summary

No one is more negative than Muriel! Just once, Alexis would like to see Muriel have a positive attitude about something. She comes up with several schemes to get Muriel to change, but nothing seems to work. Is Muriel a hopeless case?

Costumes/Props/Sets

All performers can wear contemporary clothing. Muriel's clothing should be odd in some way. She could wear something outrageous or mismatched. Her hair should be messy and tangled.

A glass half full of water is needed for the first scene. In Scene Five, Alexis and her friends display "Muriel for President" signs.

Stools or chairs in a semicircle can serve as seats for the Narrator, Alexis, and her friends. Later Mrs. Edelstein and the Extra Students can enter and gather around. Muriel can enter and exit as needed.

Presentation

Muriel has a dreary, whiny, obnoxious voice. She sits slumped over, and she often sighs. She blows her nose often in an annoying way. Keiko is cheery and optimistic. Brody is pessimistic, but not nearly as much as Muriel.

Supplemental Reading

Park, Barbara. *Rosie Swanson: Fourth-Grade Geek for President*. New York: Random House, 1991.

Cast of Characters

Narrator

Alexis

Muriel
Keiko
Brody
Erin
Faisal
Heath
Mrs. (Mr.) Edelstein
Extra Students

And Then There's Muriel

Scene One

Narrator: They say there are two kinds of people in this world. There are optimists—the people who always look on the bright side. You give an optimist half a glass of water, and something like this happens . . . .

Alexis: Here, Keiko.

Keiko: Ah, some nice, refreshing water! Thanks, Alexis!

Narrator: Then there are the pessimists. Those are the people who tend to look at things more negatively. Give a pessimist half a glass of water, and you'll get this kind of reaction . . . .

Alexis: Have some water, Brody.

Brody: Hey! This glass is half empty!

Narrator: See? Optimists and pessimists!

Alexis: And then there's Muriel.

Narrator: *(sighs)* Yes, then there's Muriel.

Alexis: So really there are three kinds of people in the world: optimists, pessimists, and Muriel.

Narrator: Give Muriel half a glass of water and you'll get a reaction . . . well, maybe it's better if you see for yourself.

Alexis: Hey, Muriel, here's some water for you.

Muriel: But this glass is practically empty. What, like maybe there are three swallows in there? Why didn't you give me a full glass? You hate me, don't you? Everybody hates me.

Alexis: No, no, I don't hate you.

Muriel: Well, then what's the deal? Has someone already been drinking this water? Oh, no! This glass is covered with germs, isn't it? Why, I bet this water is swimming with bacteria. I can't drink after anybody else. I have a very sensitive constitution, you know. I figure I'm going to die young. Like any day now. *(blows nose)*

Keiko: Oh, I bet you're going to live a good, long life, Muriel.

Brody: *(muttering)* Or not.

Muriel: Hey, is there something swimming around in this water? What is that?

Alexis: Give me that glass! *(drinks)* See? Perfectly safe!

Muriel: I think you just swallowed a fly.

Other Kids: Ew!

Alexis: No, I didn't. (*looks uncertain and burps*)

Muriel: Did that taste like a fly?

Other Kids: Ew!

Alexis: No!

Muriel: You know, Alexis, flies are covered with deadly germs.

Alexis: So?

Muriel: So it's been nice knowing you.

Alexis: Muriel, have you ever been positive about anything in your entire life?

Muriel: Of course, I've been positive. Do you think I'm a total loser or something?

Alexis: Tell me, when have you ever been positive?

Muriel: Right now.

Alexis: No, you're not!

Muriel: Yes, I am. I'm positive that you just swallowed a fly.

Alexis: Aaaargh!

Muriel: You hate me, don't you? (*blows nose*)

Scene Two

Narrator: You can see why everybody found Muriel a little annoying.

Alexis: (*mocking*) You're one of those optimists, aren't you?

Narrator: Maybe. Anyway, Alexis decided that Muriel had to change.

Alexis: Once, just once, I want to see Muriel have a positive attitude about something.

Brody: Like that will ever happen.

Alexis: It's not impossible.

Faisal: Look, Alexis, we've all known Muriel for years. She has always been totally, completely, utterly . . . Muriel.

Heath: Yeah, she'll never change.

Keiko: Anybody can make a change for the better.

Erin: Muriel isn't just anybody! She's Muriel!

Heath: Yeah, Muriel the Moper!

Brody: Muriel the Moody!

Faisal: Muriel the Morose!

Erin: Muriel the . . . muh . . . muh . . . muh-whiny!

Alexis: I don't care how muh-whiny she is! I agree with Keiko: anyone can make a change for the better. Even Muriel!

Narrator: *(mocking)* You're one of those optimists, aren't you?

Alexis: Maybe. So—are you guys going to help me?

Brody: How are you going to get Muriel to be positive?

Alexis: Well, I've been thinking. Maybe *we* are part of Muriel's problem.

Erin: You're joking, right?

Alexis: No, I'm not. Think about it! When Muriel is whining about something, what do we do?

Heath: Plug up our ears.

Brody: Moan in pain.

Keiko: Try to talk her out of it.

Faisal: Beg her to stop.

Brody: Wish for death.

Alexis: In other words, we give her all kinds of attention for her negative attitude.

Faisal: I get it! In a way, we're just encouraging her to be . . . Muriel!

Keiko: So all we have to do is quit reacting to her when she's negative.

Alexis: Right!

Brody: Is it nice there on your dream world?

Alexis: Come on! It's worth a try, isn't it?

Keiko: Sure!

Faisal: I guess.

Erin: Okay.

Heath: We can try it.

Brody: It will never work.

Scene Three

Narrator: The next day, the kids got right to work on "Operation Muriel."

Alexis: *(to audience)* I thought of that. Every great plan has to have a name.

Narrator: You know, a lot of bad plans have names, too.

Alexis: I thought you were an optimist.

Keiko: Here comes Muriel!

Alexis: Okay, everybody ready?

Keiko: Ready!

Others: *(with no enthusiasm)* Yeah, sure, right, etc.

Alexis: Good morning, Muriel!

Muriel: Not really. The air is just full of pollution this morning. I can feel it. Microscopic particles of poisonous chemicals are working their way into every fiber of my body, damaging my cells, wrecking the functions of my vital organs, and making my nose itch. *(blows nose)*

Alexis: *(turns away towards others)* So what's up with you guys?

Others: *(look at each other)*

Alexis: I *said,* "What's up with you guys?"

Erin: Nothing.

Alexis: *(waits a moment)* Hey, isn't it a beautiful day?

Keiko: It sure is!

Faisal: Actually, I think my nose is itching, too.

Alexis: *(hissing)* No, it isn't.

Faisal: But . . . oh, yeah . . . my nose is totally not itching. And . . . and it's a beautiful day.

Muriel: *(blows nose)* At least it's sunny.

Others: *(gasp)*

Alexis: Yes, it is! And isn't that great, Muriel?

Muriel: Yeah, I wouldn't want rain on my last day on earth.

Keiko: What do you mean?

Alexis: *(whispering)* Don't encourage her.

Muriel: Well, you may not realize how very delicate I am. This air is slowly poisoning me. I'll be lucky to make it through the day. So I'm just glad to feel the warmth of the sun on my face one last time.

Alexis: *(turning away)* So, Brody, what are you doing this weekend?

Brody: Nothing.

Alexis: Oh. How about you, Keiko?

Keiko: I'm going to clean my room. I just love doing that!

Alexis: Uh-huh.

Muriel: I like to keep my room clean.

Alexis: You do? That's so interesting, Muriel.

Muriel: I'm terribly allergic to dust. The doctor says that I am the most allergic patient he has ever had. He says I'm so allergic that I shouldn't come to his office unless it's an emergency. He's very afraid that I might be exposed to some kind of deadly allergen while I'm there, so he thinks I should stay home as much as possible.

Brody: It sounds like he's allergic to you!

Muriel: You might be right, Brody. He seems okay when I first go into his office, but by the time I leave, he always looks flushed. Wait a minute. He hates me, doesn't he? My doctor hates me.

Alexis: Hey, Erin, how are things with your baby sister?

Erin: She's driving us nuts!

Alexis: *(hinting)* You mean—because she's so cute?

Erin: She looks like an evil dwarf!

Alexis: *(whispering)* How about demonstrating a positive attitude?

Erin: Oh. Heh, heh. Just kidding. She's as cute as a button.

Alexis: That's nice.

Muriel: Babies have all kinds of germs that they spread all over the place.

Alexis: Hey, Faisal, you sure did a good job on that history test.

Faisal: Uh . . . thanks.

Muriel: And babies always have something oozing out of them somewhere, don't they?

Heath: That's disgusting!

Muriel: Yes, it is.

Alexis: But you love babies anyway, don't you, Heath?

Heath: Well . . . uh . . . .

Muriel: How about the way babies slobber all over the place? That is so unsanitary.

Brody: Yeah, I hate that.

Alexis: Brody!

Muriel: You really don't know what a baby might have drooled on. There could be baby spit on almost anything anywhere, just sitting there, reeking of bacteria.

Alexis: Hey, anybody seen any good movies lately?

Muriel: And what about diapers? Talk about germs! Why, who knows—

Alexis: Stop it, Muriel! Just stop it! Babies are cute! And sweet! They're not just some kind of germ factories, leaking putrid goop and spreading disease.

Faisal: Ew, Alexis.

Heath: That's sickening.

Erin: Yuck!

Muriel: If she's going to be so negative, maybe we should just ignore her.

Brody: Good idea, Muriel. Let's all move over there.

Alexis: Aaaaargh!

Scene Four

Narrator: So "Operation Muriel" wasn't working too well.

Alexis: Which wasn't my fault! Everybody was supposed to help me.

Heath: We helped.

Faisal: Yeah, we ignored Muriel.

Alexis: Right. Let me explain something. When you're ignoring someone that means you don't talk to them!

Brody: Gee, thanks for clearing that up.

Alexis: You guys were no help whatsoever! You kept talking to her all the time. And couldn't you have at least *tried* to act positive yourselves? You know, set a good example?

Erin: You didn't say we had to do that.

Alexis: Well, duh! I didn't think I had to explain the obvious.

Brody: Hey, wait a minute. You didn't follow your own plan. You yelled at Muriel. Yelling is not ignoring, is it? And it certainly isn't a good example of positive behavior, either.

Alexis: Well, it doesn't matter anyway because now I have a new plan.

Keiko: I knew you would think of something!

Heath: So what's your plan, Alexis?

Alexis: I've been thinking a lot about why Muriel is the way she is.

Erin: And?

Alexis: I think that Muriel has low self-esteem. She feels like everybody hates her.

Brody: Well? Everybody *does* hate her.

Keiko: That's not true! I like Muriel.

Faisal: She's just so obnoxious.

Alexis: So people don't like to be around her. She senses that, I'm sure, and it makes her feel bad about herself. That just makes her more and more negative. If we all make her feel good about herself—you know, build her up a little bit—then she'll develop a better attitude.

Keiko: That's a great idea! Don't you guys think so?

Heath: I guess.

Erin: We can try it.

Faisal: Okay.

Brody: It'll never work.

Alexis: Are you going to help or not?

Brody: Okay, okay.

Faisal: Here comes Muriel right now.

Alexis: Hi, Muriel!

Keiko: Hi, Muriel!

Other Kids: *(without enthusiasm)* Hi, Muriel.

Muriel: Hi. *(blows nose)*

Alexis: Your hair really looks cute today.

Muriel: It does?

Alexis: Yep, that style looks great on you, Muriel.

Muriel: Are you talking about *my* hair?

Alexis: Yes. I said that it looks cute.

Muriel: My hair?

Alexis: Yes, Muriel, *your* hair is cute. Isn't it, you guys?

Keiko: It is so cute! You have such cute hair. Right, Brody?

Brody: Yeah. Sure.

Muriel: My mother always says that my hair is like a rat's nest. I've never actually seen a rat's nest, but I don't think rats' nests are cute at all so I don't know why you're saying my hair is cute. Unless it's a joke or something. Are you guys making fun of me? You hate me, don't you?

Alexis: No, Muriel, we don't hate you.

Brody: *(muttering)* Speak for yourself.

Alexis: We really like your hair.

Keiko: Yeah, it's just so . . . so . . . so . . . .

Faisal: You!

Muriel: It is?

Brody: Oh, it's definitely you.

Heath: It has you written all over it.

Faisal: *(laughing)* You, you, you!

Erin: *(laughing)* Totally you!

Brody: *(laughing)* It's almost frightening how you it is!

Alexis: What he means is—

Muriel: I know what he means. He's making fun of me. You're all making fun of me. I'm used to it though. Everybody hates me.

Alexis: No, we don't, Muriel. We like you.

Muriel: Why?

Alexis: Well . . . uh . . . because . . . we . . . .

Muriel: Don't overwork your brain, Alexis. If you think too hard, you can blow out your brain cells.

Alexis: But, Muriel . . . .

Muriel: I have to go. I have a doctor's appointment, and I want to get there early so I can talk to the receptionist. She likes to be kept up-to-date on my health. *(exits)*

Brody: I told you it wouldn't work!

Scene Five

Narrator: They say there are two kinds of people in the world—

Alexis: Yeah, yeah, yeah. Optimists and pessimists.

Narrator: I'm talking about two other kinds of people. There are the quitters, and then there are the people who never give up. And Alexis wasn't a quitter!

Alexis: That's right! I never give up. Never!

Narrator: So for the next few days, Alexis wracked her brain trying to come up with a new plan to change Muriel.

Alexis: Yeah, I probably blew out half my brain cells.

Narrator: And finally she got a fantastic idea.

Alexis: Muriel for class president!

Heath: You must be joking!

Erin: Are you nuts?

Alexis: No, I'm not. This is the best idea ever, you guys. If Muriel is elected president, she'll have to stop thinking that everyone hates her.

Brody: But how in the world are you going to get people to vote for Muriel?

Alexis: It won't be easy, but we can do it. First, somebody has to nominate her.

Keiko: I will!

Alexis: And then somebody has to be her campaign manager. That'll be me, I guess.

Brody: Well, okay, but I was really, really hoping to get that job.

Alexis: And then we'll make signs and talk to people and all that.

Faisal: I don't know, Alexis.

Alexis: Oh, come on! It'll be fun.

Erin: Right.

Alexis: Okay then, it'll be a challenge.

Keiko: And a really nice thing to do.

Faisal: Well, okay. We'll try.

Alexis: Great! This will work, you guys. I know it will.

Narrator: A few days later, Mrs. Edelstein stopped work early and asked for nominations for class president. Muriel's campaign team was ready.

Mrs. Edelstein: All right then. We have Edward, Aimee, and Pat. Are there any more nominations?

Keiko: *(waves hand)*

Mrs. Edelstein: Yes, Keiko?

Keiko: *(as friends wave "Muriel for President" signs)* I want to nominate Muriel.

Extra Kids: *(laugh)*

Mrs. Edelstein: Class! Is there a second to Keiko's nomination?

Alexis and Friends: *(look at each other then all say)* Second!

Extra Kids: You're joking! Funny! Yeah, right! etc.

Mrs. Edelstein: Class! Settle down. Muriel will be our fourth candidate for—

Muriel: No, I won't! They're just making fun of me, Mrs. Edelstein.

Alexis: No, we're not!

Muriel: They planned this just to humiliate me.

Mrs. Edelstein: Is this true?

Alexis: No! Yes! What I mean is, we did plan it, but we're serious about it. We really want Muriel to be president.

Mrs. Edelstein: Why? I mean . . . isn't that nice?

Muriel: *(to Alexis)* I'm not as stupid as you think I am.

Alexis: Muriel, we're sincere about this. We made all these signs for you. And I'm going to be your campaign manager. And we're going to talk to everybody and convince them that you'd be a great president.

Extra Kids: Yeah, right! Sure! etc.

Muriel: And what were you going to say to people, Alexis? How were you going to convince them to vote for me?

Alexis: Well . . . uh . . . you see . . . .

Muriel: That's what I thought.

Alexis: Give me a minute! I can't think as fast as you can, Muriel.

Brody: That's why she can't run for president herself, Muriel. Because she can't think fast enough to be in charge of anything. Right, Alexis?

Alexis: Huh? Oh, yeah . . . you're a quick thinker, Muriel. That's one reason why you should be president.

Heath: Yeah, and you're really organized, Muriel. A president has to be organized.

Erin: Right! And you know about a lot of things. Like germs. And viruses. And diseases. A president has to be knowledgeable like that.

Muriel: *(blows nose)*

Faisal: And clean. A president should be very clean, and that's you, Muriel. Clean is your middle name!

Muriel: Actually, my middle name is Leona, but I get your point.

Keiko: And you never do anything to hurt people. You're nice. I want a nice president.

Muriel: *(looks at Brody)* Well?

Brody: Uh . . . uh . . . you should be president because . . . your hair is cute!

Muriel: *(smiles a little)* Nice try, Brody. Okay, I'll do it.

Alexis and Friends: *(cheer)*

Mrs. Edelstein: Well, then. Candidates, you have one week to campaign. The election will be next Friday.

Scene Six

Narrator: If you're an optimist, you're thinking that Muriel was elected class president by a landslide. If you're a pessimist, you believe that Muriel lost big-time. The truth is: Muriel lost, but not as badly as you'd think.

Alexis: She got eleven votes. Can you believe it? Eleven whole votes!

Brody: I think Mrs. Edelstein miscounted.

Keiko: Yeah, I bet Muriel got more votes than that!

Brody: Right.

Faisal: The real question is: Did this whole thing change Muriel?

Erin: Yeah. Or is she still . . . well, Muriel?

Heath: Here she comes now. And she doesn't look happy at all.

Alexis: Hi, Muriel.

Muriel: Hello.

Keiko: Are you okay?

Muriel: I lost the election. I knew I would lose. Everybody—

Alexis: Don't say it! Don't say that everybody hates you because it's not true, Muriel.

Muriel: I wasn't—

Alexis: Look, Muriel. Eleven people voted for you! Eleven! Think about that.

Muriel: I have, and—

Alexis: I don't know why you can't have a positive attitude once! Just once!

Muriel: I was going to say that everybody worked so hard on the campaign. Even though I didn't win, I feel lucky to have friends like you guys.

Alexis: Oh.

Brody: Gee, that sounded pretty positive. Didn't it, Alexis?

Alexis: Yeah, it did.

Keiko: People *can* change.

Brody: Yes, they can. I hope you've learned a lesson about that, Alexis.

Alexis: Hey! I was the one who . . . never mind! So, Muriel. Do you want to go to the park with us?

Muriel: Is that outside?

Alexis: Well, yes.

Muriel: I don't know. I'm quite delicate, you know.

Faisal: Come on, Muriel.

Erin: You should get out a bit and enjoy Mother Nature.

Muriel: I think I'm allergic to nature.

Alexis: Give it a try, Muriel.

Muriel: We-e-ell, okay.

Others: Great! Fantastic! etc.

Muriel: Is there any grass in this park? You know, I can't touch grass or walk on any grass or just get near to grass because I am terribly allergic. I'm so sensitive that—

Others: Muriel!

Muriel: But I'm sure I'll have a lovely time anyway. Let's go!

3

Boss of the World

Summary

After years of being bossed around by Janice, Lily can't take it any more. She enlists the help of her friends in teaching Janice a lesson, but things don't turn out quite the way she planned.

Costumes/Props/Sets

All actors can wear contemporary clothing.

A semicircle of stools can be arranged for the actors, with a stool for the Narrator slightly off to one side, and another for Mr. Washington off to the other side.

Presentation

Mr. Washington has a bossy tone in general, but he speaks sweetly to Janice. In Scene One, he pretends to point to Group One and Group Two. The actors in this play form Group Three. Grant is scared of Janice and speaks to her in a high, nervous voice. Janice is very domineering. She speaks quickly, in clipped tones, and she doesn't give people a chance to resist. She sounds superior and even venomous at times.

In Scene Six, when the kids are teasing Janice, they should emphasize the "in" syllable of each word.

Supplemental Reading

Cohen-Posey, Kate. *How to Handle Bullies, Teasers, and Other Meanies*. Highland City, Florida: Rainbow Books, Inc., 1995.

Cast of Characters

Narrator

Lily, who is tired of Janice

Alvin

Mariah
Phoebe
Nick
Grant
Mr. (Mrs.) Washington, Social Studies teacher
Janice, the "Boss of the World"

Boss of the World

Scene One

Narrator: Everyone agrees that Janice is smart.

Lily: She's probably the smartest kid in school.

Alvin: She can do huge math problems in her head.

Mariah: And she can read like the wind.

Lily: Face it, Janice is good at everything.

Narrator: The problem is that Janice is kind of bossy.

Lily: "Kind of bossy"? Janice thinks she's the Boss of the World!

Phoebe: She's a dictator.

Nick: And a tyrant.

Grant: And she hurts people's feelings with her insults. I mean, she just crushes them until their hearts are broken into bits. Then she stomps all over the bits until they're pulverized. Pulverized!

Lily: Are you okay, Grant?

Grant: Yes, of course I am! I just hate it when she does that to people. Other people, you know. She doesn't really bother me.

Narrator: For some reason, teachers just love Janice. Maybe they're so impressed with her big brain that they miss the fact that she has a teeny heart.

Grant: A heart made of stone! And it's cold, man, cold.

Lily: Relax, Grant.

Narrator: Teachers are always putting Janice in charge of things. And Mr. Washington, the Social Studies teacher, is no exception.

Mr. Washington: Listen up, people! I expect these Revolutionary War projects to be stupendous. I didn't buy these huge pieces of plywood for you to glue down a few plastic soldiers and some grass. Understand?

Students: Yes, sir.

Mr. Washington: The first thing your group needs to do is decide on the historical event you'll be re-creating. Let's get that accomplished today please. Group leaders, keep everybody focused.

Janice: Sure, Mr. Washington.

Lily: *(to Mariah)* He hasn't announced the leaders. Why does she assume she's one of them?

Mariah: *(to Lily)* Come on, Lily. You know he's going to pick her.

Mr. Washington: *(pointing to imaginary groups)* Steven, you'll be the leader for Group One. Rosario, you lead Group Two. And Janice?

Janice: Yes, Mr. Washington.

Mr. Washington: *(pointing to actors)* You lead Group Three, okay?

Other Kids: *(moan)*

Mr. Washington: Is there a problem?

Other Kids: No, sir!

Mr. Washington: Then get to work.

Janice: Okay, everybody, notebooks out! Sometime today, people. Move it, move it, move it!

Lily: *(to Mariah)* I'm so tired of her.

Janice: What was that, Lily?

Lily: Nothing, Janice! *(muttering)* Oh, high and mighty queen!

Scene Two

Narrator: Janice runs Group Three like she usually runs things—with an iron fist!

Janice: Phoebe, you bring the aluminum foil. Do not crumple it up! We want to have a nice, reflective quality to the water.

Phoebe: Okay.

Janice: Write it down in your notebook so you won't forget.

Phoebe: I can remember.

Janice: I don't believe your tiny brain can retain that much information. Write it down.

Phoebe: I'm writing, I'm writing!

Janice: Listen up, Grant.

Grant: *(in a high nervous voice)* Yes, ma'am?

Janice: You need to—

Lily: Wait a minute! Mr. Washington said we should decide on an historical event first.

Janice: It's decided.

Lily: You mean *you* decided! It's a group decision, Janice. Isn't it, you guys?

Others: *(mumble, afraid to disagree with Janice)*

Lily: What a bunch of wusses! Listen, Janice, we all get a say in this project.

Janice: Very well. Let's vote on it. All those in favor of my idea, raise your hand.

Narrator: Every hand shoots up into the air—except for Lily's.

Lily: But you don't even know what her idea is!

Narrator: All the hands drop.

Janice: We're doing the Boston Tea Party.

Narrator: The hands shoot up again.

Janice: The Boston Tea Party it is! Now, Grant, you need to bring some wood, glue, and cloth to make the ships.

Grant: Yes, ma'am. It would be my pleasure. Great! I'm your man!

Janice: Write it in your notebook.

Grant: Sure will! I'm doing it right now. Don't you worry—I won't forget.

Janice: And I know it's tough, but could you try to be a little less stupid?

Grant: Okay. Let me write that down . . . .

Narrator: Janice goes on issuing orders until the whole project is planned out.

Janice: Everybody bring everything tomorrow, and we'll get started. Got it?

Others, except Lily: *(dully)* Got it.

Janice: Lily?

Lily: You know, you're not the boss of me.

Janice: Maybe we should ask Mr. Washington about that.

Lily: Okay, okay. I'll bring my stuff.

Scene Three

Narrator: Lily has spent years being bossed around by Janice, and she's sick of it. At lunchtime, she lets her frustrations out.

Lily: That stupid Janice! She makes our lives miserable. We should stand up to her, you guys.

Nick: How do you stand up to a bulldozer?

Lily: By sticking together. If we do that, we can put Janice in her place.

Grant: But you know how she is, Lily. She has a—

Lily: A heart like stone! I know, Grant. But we don't have to take her abuse. I mean, this is America, you guys! Land of the free.

Alvin: And home of the chickens.

Lily: Look, it won't be that hard. We just don't cooperate.

Nick: What do you mean?

Lily: Well . . . like tomorrow we all "forget" to bring our stuff.

Grant: *(terrified)* But she'll be mad! She'll be really mad!

Lily: So? Don't you guys want to be free of her power?

Others: Yeah, sure, etc.

Lily: So . . . are you with me?

Others: *(excited)* Yeah! We're with you!

Scene Four

Narrator: The next day, everybody in Group Three comes to Social Studies with . . . nothing!

Janice: All right, people! Let's start by putting all our materials on the table. Go ahead. This table here. Put your things on this table. Now! Are you people deaf? Or just stupid?

Lily: I guess we're stupid because we don't know what you're talking about.

Janice: I'm talking about the materials for our project. Phoebe, where's the foil?

Phoebe: Oh, yeah. The foil. I forgot.

Janice: You forgot? Didn't you write it down like I told you?

Phoebe: Yeah, but then I forgot my notebook.

Janice: What about the rest of you? Where are the things you were supposed to bring?

Mariah: I forgot.

Alvin: Me, too.

Lily: I guess I did, too.

Nick: My dog ate it.

Janice: Grant?

Grant: I . . . I . . . I . . . .

Janice: Funny, people. Fortunately, I am a natural leader who knows how to handle this kind of situation.

Lily: Oh, really?

Janice: Really. Just watch me. *(yells)* Mr. Washington! Mr. Washington!

Nick: Stop, Janice. We'll get in trouble.

Janice: Perhaps you should have considered that before. *(louder)* Mr. Washington!

Mr. Washington: Really, Janice. Couldn't you walk over and speak to me like a human being instead of calling me like a dog?

Janice: I'm sorry, Mr. Washington. I hope you know that I have nothing but the utmost respect for you, and I will never do that again.

Mr. Washington: Thank you, dear.

Janice: I suppose I was just upset because we're having a problem here.

Narrator: So Janice tells on everyone, and surprise, surprise, Mr. Washington takes her side and punishes the rest of the group.

Mr. Washington: Since you people didn't come prepared today, you can all write reports on your historical event.

Janice: That would be the Boston Tea Party, sir.

Mr. Washington: What a good idea! I bet you thought of that, didn't you?

Janice: Yes, sir.

Mr. Washington: All right, people! Get to work! I expect those reports on my desk tomorrow.

Alvin: Gee, thanks, Lily.

Lily: I didn't know that would happen!

Scene Five

Narrator: The next day everybody in Group Three comes with a report on the Boston Tea Party—and the materials for the project.

Lily: Hey, you guys, I want to talk to you while Janice is busy sucking up to Mr. Washington.

Nick: We don't need any more of your big ideas, Lily.

Lily: Listen—we can still defeat Janice!

Phoebe: No, we can't.

Nick: If we try anything, she'll just tell on us.

Lily: Don't you people have any self-respect at all?

Mariah: Not really.

Alvin: Very little.

Grant: I'll have self-respect when Janice tells me to have self-respect.

Lily: Well, be a bunch of pansies if you want, but I'm going to do something.

Janice: What's all the chatter over here? Why aren't you working, people?

Lily: *(sweetly)* We were just waiting for you to tell us what to do, Janice.

Janice: What a good idea. You surprise me, Lily. Okay then! Let's start with the water. Phoebe, lay the foil down.

Lily: Here let me help you, Phoebe. I'll hold one end and you hold the other.

Narrator: Lily grabs the foil and "accidentally" moves her end towards Phoebe's end.

Janice: Watch it, you morons! You're crumpling the Boston Harbor! Pull the other way, Lily.

Narrator: But Lily pulls just a little too hard . . . .

Janice: You ripped it!

Lily: Oh, I'm so sorry.

Janice: I don't suppose you had the sense to bring an extra piece, did you, Phoebe?

Phoebe: Uh . . . no.

Janice: I didn't think so. Well, we'll just have to do that part tomorrow. In the meantime, let's make the ships. Where are the materials, Grant?

Grant: Right here, oh, group leader. I even carved the wood into the shape of little boats.

Janice: Not bad, Grant.

Grant: Oh, thank you, thank you, thank you!

Janice: Please! I've asked you to control your stupidity.

Grant: Sorry.

Janice: Okay, everybody help paint these ships. Chop-chop!

Narrator: After the painting is finished, Lily gets out the tea she was supposed to bring.

Lily: Look, Janice, I brought the tea. Let me open the package and show you.

Janice: That's not necessary. I have seen tea before.

Narrator: But Lily tears open the box with such force that the tea "accidentally" falls out. All over the newly painted ships.

Janice: You clumsy oaf! Look what you've done!

Lily: I'm so sorry, Janice. I'm sure it won't take long to pick those little pieces of tea off each and every boat.

Janice: Everybody get picking! Once the tea is removed, we'll probably have to repaint the ships. Thank you, Lily, for your total incompetence.

Lily: Gee, Janice. I'm glad you're not angry.

Narrator: Class is over by the time the tea is cleaned up and the ships are repainted. Janice is steaming mad!

Janice: I can't believe that this is all we've accomplished today. What a bunch of losers! I expect you to work doubly hard tomorrow and get twice as much done. Capisch?

Others: Sure! Of course! etc.

Janice: And Lily? Try to bring your brain tomorrow, okay?

Lily: Okay! Hopefully it'll be back from the cleaners by then.

Janice: *(upset)* You are so not funny. This is a serious project, a major part of our grades. Try to stay focused, okay?

Lily: Relax, Janice. Don't let a few little setbacks freak you out.

Janice: I'm not freaking out! *(calmer)* I'm not. Now get out of my way and let me out of this freak show before I'm late for Band.

Scene Six

Narrator: Group Three is way excited about how easily Lily got to Janice. It's all they can talk about at the lunch table.

Alvin: And the great thing is that there's nothing she can tattle about.

Mariah: Yeah, you were brilliant, Lily.

Lily: And just think: I did that all by myself! If I had a little help . . . .

Nick: I'm in!

Alvin, Phoebe: Me, too.

Mariah: We'll all help you, Lily.

Grant: Well . . . I . . . uh . . . .

Lily: Aren't you tired of how she treats you, Grant? She's always calling you stupid.

Grant: I am stupid.

Lily: No, you're not! You just act that way.

Grant: Thanks, Lily. I think.

Lily: Are you going to help or not?

Grant: Okay. I'll do it.

Lily: Great! Now listen, everybody. I have some ideas.

Narrator: The next day, Group Three puts Lily's plan into action. First, Nick and Phoebe wrinkle the new piece of foil as they put it into place.

Janice: I'm surrounded by idiots! Well, that will just have to do.

Narrator: Then everybody pretends to have trouble putting the masts and sails on the boats. Janice is so unhappy with their sloppy work that she does all of it over herself.

Janice: I have never worked with such inept, incapable, incompetent, inadequate idiots!

Lily: You left out intelligent.

Nick: And incomparable.

Alvin: What about incredible?

Janice: Shut up! You're driving me crazy!

Lily: Don't you mean insane?

Janice: Are you doing this on purpose?

Lily: You mean—intentionally?

Janice: You are, aren't you? You're trying to make me nuts. Is this some kind of plot, Grant?

Grant: I . . . uh . . . .

Janice: Speak, Grant!

Grant: Uh . . . arf?

Others: *(laugh)*

Janice: So! You're in on it, too. Very well. You people leave me no choice. Mr. Washington!

Lily: You know he hates that. Go over and talk to him like a human being, why don't you?

Scene Seven

Narrator: While Janice marches across the room and tries to get Mr. Washington's attention, Group Three goes to work.

Lily: Quick! Spread the glue. Where's the . . . stick them all over. Here! Put the box in her pack.

Nick: *(loudly)* Oh, hi, Mr. Washington.

Mr. Washington: Janice tells me that you people are not cooperating. What's the problem?

Lily: We just don't agree with her ideas, Mr. Washington. She's ruining the whole project.

Janice: *I'm* ruining it? You must be joking!

Lily: I'm sorry, Janice. But you can only take realism so far.

Mr. Washington: Perhaps you don't understand the . . . Oh, my stars! Are those real, live fish?

Alvin: No, they're real dead fish.

Lily: We tried to tell her it wasn't a good idea, Mr. Washington. But Janice said that there were fish in the Boston Harbor so we had to have fish!

Janice: What!

Lily: She brought this box of dead minnows from the bait shop.

Mariah: And she made us glue them down.

Janice: I did no such thing!

Lily: Okay, she didn't really *make* us. But she did suggest it very strongly.

Mr. Washington: Janice, I'm afraid I have to agree with your friends. Dead fish are just not appropriate for a school project. They . . . they smell!

Janice: But, Mr. Washington . . . .

Mr. Washington: It doesn't look like the glue has dried yet, Janice. Just take the fish off.

Janice: Me?

Lily: Why don't you put them back in the box, Janice?

Janice: What box?

Nick: The box you put in your backpack.

Janice: There is not a box in my pack! See?

Narrator: Janice rips open her pack, and there's the bait box sitting right on top of her stuff.

Janice: Ew! My pack is going to smell like fish!

Mr. Washington: Just scrape off the foil and throw everything away. The box, too.

Lily: Good idea, Mr. Washington. Too bad we'll have to start all over. But Janice didn't mean to ruin everything. We know she didn't, don't we?

Others: Of course not! Oh, no! etc.

Janice: *(yelling)* I did not ruin the project!

Mr. Washington: Calm down, Janice. Just clean everything up, and get a fresh start tomorrow.

Janice: But, Mr. Washington—

Mr. Washington: Looks like trouble in Group One. I'd better go check.

Janice: Mr. Washington! Mr. Washington!

Lily: Well, get busy, Janice.

Janice: Handle dead fish? I don't think so! You people made this mess, so you can clean it up.

Lily: You heard Mr. Washington. He said for you to do it.

Janice: Listen, people, I am in charge here, and I—

Lily: Not any more you're not! We're all tired of you ordering us around, Janice, and we're not letting you get away with it anymore. From now on, this group is a democracy. All those in favor of Janice cleaning up this mess?

Narrator: Every hand shoots up . . . well, except Janice's, of course.

Lily: Fish duty it is! Get to work, Janice.

Narrator: Janice cleans everything up, but she shoots dagger-eyes at everybody as she does it.

Grant: *(to Lily)* She looks awfully upset.

Lily: So?

Mariah: That was a pretty mean thing to do.

Lily: She treats us all like . . . like slaves! And she's so insulting. We had to teach her a lesson.

Grant: It just doesn't seem right, lying like that.

Lily: Just wait and see how much better our lives are without the Boss of the World. You guys will be thanking me then.

Scene Eight

Narrator: For couple of days, everything goes smoothly. Janice says nothing while the other kids discuss their ideas and work together on the project. If someone asks her to paint something or glue something or whatever, she does it without a peep.

Grant: *(to Lily)* I think Janice's feelings are hurt.

Lily: You said she has a heart of stone. How can she have feelings?

Grant: Everyone has feelings, Lily.

Phoebe: We were awfully rough on her. I bet she feels terrible.

Lily: I bet she feels like getting revenge. I just know she's plotting something.

Grant: Her heart is too crushed for revenge.

Alvin: Yeah.

Lily: I'm telling you: she's going to try and get us back.

Narrator: On the day that the projects are due, everybody wonders if Lily was right about Janice getting revenge. When they walk into the Social Studies room, their project is gone!

Nick: Where did it go?

Lily: Where do you think?

Janice: Hello, Group Three. Hmmm . . . isn't something missing here?

Lily: Where's our project, Janice?

Janice: How should I know?

Grant: Oh, please, Janice, please give it back! Please! We are so sorry for what we did to you!

Lily: We don't need to apologize to her.

Janice: Of course not. So you set me up and lied about me and made me look like an idiot in front of the teacher. What could be wrong about any of that?

Grant: It *was* wrong, and we are so, so, so sorry!

Lily: Stop that, Grant.

Grant: *(whimpers)*

Lily: I said stop!

Janice: Goodness! Who's ordering people around now?

Lily: Just give us back the project, Janice.

Janice: What makes you think that I have anything to do with this?

Lily: Because you're a big, stinking—

Phoebe: Lily! Stop!

Alvin: Just face facts, why don't you? She wins.

Mariah: We need that project or we'll flunk.

Lily: Oh, all right. You win, Janice.

Janice: What is it that I win? I hope it's a nice, big apology.

Grant: We are really sorry, Janice.

Phoebe: Really, really sorry.

Nick: Please accept our humble apologies.

Mariah: Please, Janice!

Alvin: We are the sorriest people on earth!

Janice: And so honest, too. What about you, Lily?

Lily: *(clipped)* Sorry.

Janice: There now. That wasn't so hard, was it?

Lily: So where's our project?

Janice: I haven't the foggiest idea.

Lily: What? I'm going to clobber you!

Mr. Washington: What's all this noise about?

Lily: Janice hid our project so we can't turn it in. She's trying to make us all flunk!

Mr. Washington: Come now, Lily. Does that really make sense? It's a group project. If you all flunk, then Janice will, too.

Grant: Oh, yeah.

Nick: Of course.

Phoebe: What were you thinking, Lily?

Lily: Well, then what happened?

Mr. Washington: I thought it was the best project by far, so I put it on display in the library. Good job, Group Three!

Janice: See? I told you I didn't take it. I would never play such a cruel trick on you guys. No matter how much you hate me.

Mariah: We don't hate you, Janice.

Grant: Yeah, Lily is the one who—

Lily: Zip it, Grant!

Janice: *(near tears)* Whatever. I don't care.

Scene Nine

Narrator: Mr. Washington lets the whole class go to the library to see Group Three's Boston Tea Party on display. While everyone's looking at the project, Lily keeps her eyes on Janice.

Grant: She looks so sad, doesn't she?

Lily: Yeah, so? What am I supposed to do about it?

Grant: Come on, Lily. You know what to do.

Lily: But . . . I . . . oh, all right.

Narrator: Lily works her way around the room and pulls Janice to one side.

Lily: I want to apologize for the dirty tricks we played on you. I mean . . . apologize for real.

Janice: *(surprised)* You do?

Lily: Yes, I do. We were really mean, and it wasn't right to treat you that way.

Janice: I suppose you were trying to make a point. I know I can be a little overpowering at times.

Lily: A little! Are you kidding? I mean . . . yes, a little.

Janice: I suppose I can forgive you.

Lily: Thanks. Hey, our project really is fantastic, isn't it?

Janice: Of course it is.

Lily: And do you know why it's so great?

Janice: Because—

Lily: I'll tell you why. It's because we all worked together on it, Janice. We talked about things. We put our heads together. We helped each other out. We weren't just a bunch of robots following one person's orders. Can't you see that?

Janice: Well . . . it is the best project I've ever worked on.

Lily: Our teamwork made it that way! You don't have to boss people around and insult them to get good results. And everybody likes you better when you don't act like the Boss of the World.

Janice: They do?

Lily: Yes! So could you just tone it down a little?

Janice: Maybe. I suppose I could. I'll try.

Narrator: The rest of Group Three nervously joins Janice and Lily.

Mariah: Hi. Are you okay, Janice?

Janice: Fine, thank you.

Alvin: Great!

Grant: We don't want you to feel bad, Janice. Not at all. Not one little bit. We would hate that.

Nick: Hey, you guys, doesn't our project look great?

Lily: Fantastic!

Alvin: Janice, those little crates you made look great.

Janice: Why, thank you.

Grant: Yeah, they're the best things in the whole scene. Yessirree! So realistic! Just the best—

Janice: *(irritated like usual)* Grant! Please! Must you be so . . . *(notices everyone looking at her)* humble? My crates aren't nearly as good as your ships.

Grant: Really? *(clears throat and speaks normally)* Really?

Janice: Really.

Lily: So, Janice . . . got any ideas for a good science fair project?

4

Call Me Mr. Euclid

Summary

The first period Math class is happy to learn they're having a substitute teacher. Houston is especially excited about the situation because he likes to make life rough for subs. But it turns out that Mr. Euclid isn't your ordinary sub!

Costumes/Props/Sets

The students should wear contemporary clothing. Mr. Euclid should be dressed more formally with a tie and blazer. Mrs. Pembroke's hair should be disheveled, with forgotten pencils stuck in it. Her clothing can be mismatched and incorrectly buttoned.

A wastebasket is needed for Scene Two. There should be a plan book, textbook, worksheets, and a seating chart on the teacher's desk. Students need math books, paper, and pencils. If the performance area does not already have an intercom speaker, a mock-up could be hung on the wall or placed on the teacher's desk.

Desks should be arranged in rows like a classroom, with a desk to one side for Mr. Euclid. Problems may be written on the chalkboard if desired.

Presentation

Mr. Euclid speaks in a dignified way until he becomes annoyed with Houston. Mrs. Pembroke is frazzled and confused.

In Scene Five, the other students are scared of Mr. Euclid, but they still think that Houston's antics are funny. They try to hide their smiles and giggles. In Scene Six, Mr. Euclid uses a high-pitched voice when speaking to the principal.

Supplemental Reading

Coville, Bruce. *My Teacher Is an Alien*. New York: Minstrel Books, 1989.
Gilson, Jamie. *Thirteen Ways to Sink a Sub*. New York: Avon Camelot, 1999.
MacDonald, Amy. *No More Nasty*. New York: Farrar, Straus & Giroux, 2001.
Pinkwater, Jill. *Mr. Fred*. New York: Dutton Children's Books, 1994.

Cast of Characters

Narrator

Houston, who enjoys tormenting substitute teachers

Ming

Jake

Bonni

David

Ruby

Alonso

Mr. Euclid, a new substitute teacher

Mrs. Pembroke

Mr. Stephano, the principal (offstage voice)

Call Me Mr. Euclid

Scene One

Narrator: Every single morning, day after day, week after week, the students in first period Math walked into the classroom to find Mr. Franklin writing problems on the board.

Houston: Every morning!

Narrator: And every single morning, Mr. Franklin insisted that everybody get right to work on the first problem.

Ming: Even if the bell hadn't rung yet!

Houston: *(in a stuffy imitation of Mr. Franklin)* I have been here working hard since 7:00 a.m. An extra minute or two of learning isn't going to kill you. Why in my day—

David: *(entering)* Mr. Franklin is absent! Mr. Franklin is absent!

Houston: You're joking.

David: I was buying my lunch ticket at the office window, and I heard Mr. Stephano tell the secretary that Mr. Franklin won't be coming in today because he's a little under the weather.

Houston: Hey . . . do you know what that means?

Alonso: It's an idiom, Houston. It means that Mr. Franklin is ill.

Houston: I know that! What I'm saying is that we're going to have a sub.

Ming: Wow! That's right.

Jake: I wish I'd known Mr. Franklin was going to be absent. I wouldn't have bothered doing my homework.

Mrs. Pembroke: *(entering)* Excuse me, boys and girls. Is this Room 312?

Bonni: No, it's not.

Mrs. Pembroke: I didn't think so. *(leaves)*

Ruby: I love having a sub.

Houston: Yeah, it's fun to get them all confused. *(Mr. Euclid enters behind Houston)* There's nothing like tricking a sub into calling everybody by the wrong names. Or how about when you get them on the wrong page in the book? It's so easy to get them flustered! Not that I *like* to see them cry.

Mr. Euclid: *(clears throat)* Is this Room 321?

Alonso: Yes, it is.

Jake: Are you our sub?

Mr. Euclid: Your sub? . . . Why, yes! Yes, I am. Would you all please be seated?

Houston: *(muttering)* Couldn't someone have told me he was back there?

Bonni: Sorry!

Scene Two

Narrator: Mr. Euclid made himself right at home at Mr. Franklin's desk.

Mr. Euclid: Now let's see what information your teacher has left for me. Hmmm . . . seating chart . . . plan book . . . textbook with the current page marked. You *are* on page 56, aren't you? *(looks at Houston)*

Houston: Yes, sir.

Mr. Euclid: According to the seating chart, your name would be . . . Houston.

Houston: Yes, sir.

Mr. Euclid: I see that Mr. Franklin has a little star by your name, Houston. I wonder what that means. Oh, yes, I see. It stands for "troublemaker."

Houston: Me? A troublemaker?

Mr. Euclid: And here are some further notes. "Watch this boy like a hawk." "Nothing but trouble." "Wild and undisciplined."

Students: *(start to laugh, realizing that Mr. Euclid is joking)*

Mr. Euclid: "Has driven ten teachers into early retirement." "Probably responsible for the sinking of the Titanic."

Houston: Real funny!

Mr. Euclid: Well, Houston, I trust that all of that is behind you now. You won't be causing any further problems, will you?

Houston: I didn't do anything in the first place!

Mr. Euclid: Of course not. Now, class, let's open your books to—

Houston: You're not a real teacher, are you?

Mr. Euclid: Wh-why do you say that?

Houston: Well, for one thing, you look too young to be a teacher.

Mr. Euclid: Why, thank you, Houston.

Houston: And you didn't even tell us your name. That's what teachers always do first!

Mr. Euclid: Teachers are all different, Houston. But you are correct: I should introduce myself. I am . . . Pythagoras Euclid.

Students: *(laugh)*

Houston: Should we call you "Pie" for short?

Students: *(laugh)*

Mr. Euclid: *(with quiet force)* You may call me "Mr. Euclid." Now open your books to page 56.

Students: *(comply)*

Scene Three

Narrator: It turned out that Mr. Euclid made the kids work even harder than Mr. Franklin had. They had to do problems on the board, plus an extra worksheet, and homework in their books.

Alonso: I never thought I'd say this, but I miss Mr. Franklin!

Ruby: Yeah, he never loaded us down like this.

Houston: And he was never rude like this Pie Guy.

Jake: What do you mean? When was he rude?

Houston: How about the way he treated me at the beginning of class?

David: He was just joking.

Ming: Yeah, I thought he was funny.

Houston: Well, I didn't. And if I ever have him for a sub again, I'm going to get him back.

Alonso: Calm down, Houston. I'm sure Mr. Franklin will be back tomorrow.

Narrator: But the next morning, the students walked into class and found Mr. Euclid behind the teacher's desk again.

David: Oh, man! Look at all those worksheets!

Houston: Well, I'm not going to sit still for another day like yesterday. I'm getting out of here.

Ming: What are you going to do?

Houston: You'll see.

Mr. Euclid: Everyone, turn in your homework and get started on these worksheets.

Narrator: Soon all the students were working quietly at their desks, but they watched Houston.

Bonni: *(whispering to Alonso)* What do you think he's going to do?

Alonso: I don't know.

Mr. Euclid: No talking!

Mrs. Pembroke: *(entering)* Excuse me. Is this Room 213?

Mr. Euclid: Sorry, no, it's not.

Mrs. Pembroke: Of course not. *(leaves)*

David: Who is that lady?

Ruby: I don't know.

Mr. Euclid: I said: No talking!

Houston: *(moaning and clutching stomach)* Ooooh! O-o-o-ow! Oh, man!

Mr. Euclid: No moaning either.

Houston: But I'm sick, Mr. Euclid. Really sick.

Mr. Euclid: I doubt that.

Houston: Can I go to the bathroom?

Mr. Euclid: No.

Houston: But I'm going to puke my guts out. I can feel everything churning, churning, churning around in there.

Mr. Euclid: What a shame.

Houston: Mr. Franklin is going to be really upset if I throw up on this carpet. That's one thing Mr. Franklin hates. He says to never, never, never—

Mr. Euclid: Oh, all right.

Houston: *(starts to get up)*

Mr. Euclid: You may put the wastebasket right next to your desk, just in case.

Houston: What?

Mr. Euclid: Just be certain that you don't miss. Now, everyone, get back to work.

Houston: But, Mr. Euclid. . . .

Mr. Euclid: But what?

Houston: Well . . . I just think . . . shouldn't I . . . never mind.

Mr. Euclid: How about getting to work?

Houston: *(muttering)* How about shutting your piehole?

Mr. Euclid: What was that?

Houston: Nothing.

Jake: *(whispering to Houston)* Ooh, you really showed him!

David: *(whispering)* Yeah, he's real scared of you.

Mr. Euclid: Quiet!

Houston: *(waits a bit, then whispers to friends)* He'd better not be here tomorrow—or else!

Scene Four

Narrator: But Mr. Euclid was back the next day with even more worksheets piled on his desk.

Alonso: Again?

Ming: My brain is so stuffed with math that I can't . . . can't . . . can't . . .

Bonni: Think?

Ming: Yeah, that's it.

Houston: Man, that guy is making our lives miserable.

Jake: He's just doing his job, I guess.

Houston: And I'm going to do my job. I've cracked many a sub before—and I can crack the Pie Guy, too. Just watch me.

Mr. Euclid: Students, take your seats and get started on the problems on the board. Once you've finished those, you can start on today's worksheets.

(Students work for a moment. Houston begins to hiccup and continues to hiccup while talking.)

Houston: Mr. Euclid . . . Mr. Euclid . . . Mr. . . . Euclid!

Mr. Euclid: Yes, Houston.

Houston: I . . . have . . . the . . . hiccups!

Mr. Euclid: I hadn't noticed.

Houston: Could . . . I . . . get . . . a . . . drink of water?

Mr. Euclid: No. If you hold your breath for a couple of minutes, the hiccups will stop.

Houston: Thank . . . you . . . Mis . . . ter . . . Eu . . . clid. *(holds breath)*

Students: *(watch)*

Houston: Hey, it worked. Thanks, Mr. Euclid. Thanks a million!

Mr. Euclid: You're welcome. Now everyone get back to work.

Houston: Yes, sir. *(hiccups)* Oh no . . . maybe . . . if . . . I . . . got . . . some water.

Mr. Euclid: You are not leaving this classroom. Get to work. Now!

Mrs. Pembroke: *(entering)* Excuse me. Is this Room 123?

Mr. Euclid: Ma'am, we're on the third floor.

Mrs. Pembroke: This school has three floors?

Mr. Euclid: Yes, it does.

Mrs. Pembroke: No wonder I can't find my room. *(leaves)*

Houston: I . . . could . . . help—

Mr. Euclid: Quiet!

Houston: *(hiccups)*

Ruby: Mr. Euclid, I read that if you breathe into a paper bag, it will cure hiccups.

Houston: I . . . have . . . a . . . bag . . . in . . . my . . . locker.

Mr. Euclid: You're not going anywhere!

Alonso: I have a bag right here, Mr. Euclid.

Mr. Euclid: Thanks, Alonso.

Houston: *(sarcastic)* Yeah, thanks, Alonso.

Jake: What about your hiccups?

Houston: Oh, yeah. *(hiccups)*

Mr. Euclid: Hold the bag over your mouth and nose and breathe.

Houston: *(does it)* Hey, I think it worked. Thanks, Mr. Euclid. (belches)

Students: *(laugh)*

Mr. Euclid: Silence! Everyone settle down and get to work, or I'll double your assignment.

Houston: Gee, Mr. Euclid. You don't have to yell at us.

Mr. Euclid: *(yelling)* I'm not yelling! *(quieter)* I mean, I'm not yelling. Now get to work, Houston.

Houston: Yes, sir. You don't have to tell me twice!

Scene Five

Narrator: The next morning—you guessed it—Mr. Euclid was back!

Houston: Good!

David: You're glad to see him?

Houston: Yep! He was just beginning to crack. Maybe I can push him over the edge today.

Ruby: But what about the rest of us?

Houston: You can help if you want.

Ruby: No, I mean what about the rest of us who are being pushed over the edge?

Jake: Yeah. If he increases our homework any more, I'll have to give up eating and sleeping.

Houston: Don't worry. After today, he'll never come back again.

Mr. Euclid: Take your seats!

Houston: Where do you want us to take them, Mr. Euclid?

Students: *(laugh)*

Mr. Euclid: Really, Houston. That has to be the oldest joke in the history of public education. I expected something better from you.

Houston: Whatever.

Mr. Euclid: Before we start our work today, I have some news for you.

Bonni: Oh, no! Mr. Franklin is never coming back, is he?

Ming: Did he die?

Ruby: Not Mr. Franklin! We love Mr. Franklin!

Alonso: That would be "loved," not "love."

Mr. Euclid: Please, everyone! Settle down. Mr. Franklin will be fine.

Students: *(cheer)*

Mr. Euclid: However, he is quite ill. There was a note on my desk this morning saying that he probably won't be back for another week or so.

Students: *(moan)*

Mr. Euclid: You know I don't allow moaning in my classroom. Get busy!

Students: *(get to work, but watch Houston)*

Houston: *(holds up math book and five fingers)*

Students: *(pick up math books)*

Houston: *(mouths)* Five . . . four . . . three . . . two . . . one!

Students: *(slam books down)*

Mr. Euclid: How very unoriginal! You can now add pages 65 and 66 to your assignment. I suggest you get cracking. Unless you'd like to serve detention after school.

Students: *(get busy)*

Houston: *(when Mr. Euclid isn't looking, blows a raspberry on his arm)*

Students: *(laugh)*

Mr. Euclid: I have plenty of detention forms here in my desk.

Students: *(get back to work)*

Houston: It's not your desk.

Mr. Euclid: It is for the time being. I *am* the teacher here. The teacher with the detention forms.

Houston: *(waits, then blows another raspberry)* Mr. Euclid, Mr. Euclid, can I go to the bathroom?

Mr. Euclid: No.

Houston: But I really, really, really need to go.

Mr. Euclid: No, you don't. Now stop playing around or I'll send you to the office.

Houston: You mean, Mr. Abner's office?

Mr. Euclid: If you keep acting up, I will be forced to send you to Mr. Abner.

Houston: But why?

Mr. Euclid: Because this is an institution of learning, not your personal playground!

Houston: No, I meant why would you send me to the custodian?

Mr. Euclid: I wouldn't!

Houston: But you just said that you would send me to Mr. Abner.

Mr. Euclid: I said that I would send you to the principal.

Houston: But Mr. Abner is the custodian. See? That's the problem with substitute teachers. They don't really know anything.

Mr. Euclid: Listen here, you little—

Mrs. Pembroke: *(entering)* Excuse me. Is this—

Mr. Euclid: No! No, it's not! Just go away, and leave us alone.

Mrs. Pembroke: Very well. *(leaves)*

Houston: Gee, Mr. Euclid, she seemed like a nice lady. Why were you yelling at her?

Mr. Euclid: I've had just about enough of you, Houston. If you don't straighten up, you're going to get it!

Houston: Has anyone ever talked to you about your anger management problem?

Mr. Euclid: Get out! Get out right now!

Houston: Well, okay, but I thought you didn't want me to go to the bathroom.

Mr. Euclid: I didn't say anything about the bathroom. You're going to the office. Right now!

Houston: Oh. Okay. *(rises and starts to walk out)*

Mr. Euclid: *(nervously)* Wait! Don't go!

Houston: Why?

Mr. Euclid: I have a better idea. Sit down.

Houston: Okay, but I was really looking forward to a good chat with Mr. Abner.

Students: *(laugh)*

Mr. Euclid: Stop that!

Students: *(cut off laughter)*

Mr. Euclid: I know how to handle troublemakers like you. Today's assignment will include pages 67 through 70, too. For everybody.

Houston: But that's not fair! They didn't do anything.

Mr. Euclid: Let's add page 71 to that.

Houston: But—

Mr. Euclid: 72.

Alonso: Shut up, Houston!

Mr. Euclid: I believe you have plenty of work to do. Get to it!

Scene Six

Narrator: The next morning, Houston walked into first period class, eager to tell all his friends his latest idea for cracking Mr. Euclid.

Houston: I saw Mr. Piehole in the copy room. It looked like he had a hundred worksheets to run off. But don't worry. I have a plan.

Alonso: What kind of plan is that, Houston? Are you going to see if you can get Mr. Euclid to give us all one hundred papers to do today?

Houston: Of course not!

David: Why don't you just keep your big mouth shut for once?

Houston: But—

Ming: Just look at how cramped up my hand is!

Houston: Aaah! It's the Creature from the Math Lagoon!

Ming: Real funny.

Jake: We don't want any more work, okay, Houston?

Houston: But I have a fantastic idea—

Alonso: No!

David: Behave yourself.

Mr. Euclid: Why are you all standing around, chattering like a flock of chickens? Sit down and get to work on the problems on the board.

Houston: Do chickens chatter?

Jake: Shut up, Houston!

Bonni: Yeah. Do us all a favor.

Houston: Okay, okay.

Mr. Euclid: Once you've finished with those problems, then you can come up here and pick up one of each of these worksheets. That would be Worksheets 38 through 88.

Houston: We can't possibly do all of those!

Mr. Euclid: Not if you keep talking.

Houston: But that is so unfair!

Mr. Euclid: You know, I also have copies of Worksheet 89 ready.

Students: *(moan)*

Mr. Euclid: And Worksheet 90, too.

Narrator: Quickly, everybody got to work, while Mr. Euclid graded papers. When Mr. Euclid wasn't looking, Houston wrote a note and passed it around the room. Each person read the note, nodded to Houston, then passed the note on. When everyone had seen the note, Houston folded his arms. So did everyone else.

Mr. Euclid: What's going on here? Get to work!

Houston: We're on strike.

Mr. Euclid: On strike?

Houston: Because of unfair working conditions.

Mr. Euclid: I must say, at least you've finally come up with something original, Houston. Now everybody get busy before I give all of you detention.

Houston: Nobody move!

Mr. Euclid: Get to work! Now! I mean it! I am the teacher here, and what I say goes!

Houston: There's that anger management problem again.

Mr. Euclid: You're not funny. Not the—

Mr. Stephano: *(offstage)* Squawk! Sorry for the interruption, Mrs. Pembroke.

Mr. Euclid: Who said that?

Houston: Substitutes! It's the principal, Mr. Stephano, calling on the intercom.

Mr. Euclid: Th-th-the principal?

Mr. Stephano: Mrs. Pembroke? Are you there?

Mr. Euclid: *(in a high-pitched voice)* Yes, sir?

Mr. Stephano: I'm sorry to bother you, Mrs. Pembroke, but there's a problem with your attendance reports.

Mr. Euclid: Oh, really? I'm so sorry.

Houston: What's the matter with this guy?

Alonso: And who's Mrs. Pembroke?

Mr. Stephano: That's all right. It's hard to be a substitute teacher, I know. I'm just wondering why you don't have Trevor Riley marked as absent. According to his other teachers, he hasn't been in class all week.

Mr. Euclid: T-t-t-t-trevor?

Mr. Stephano: He's a new student who was supposed to start this week, but so far no one's seen hide nor hair of him.

Mr. Euclid: Haven't seen him! No sir, Mr. Stephano!

Mr. Stephano: Well, please mark that on your attendance sheet.

Mr. Euclid: Of course! Thanks ever so much for your help!

Mr. Stephano: You're welcome. Click!

Mr. Euclid: *(starting in high voice, then changing to normal)* Well, then . . . I mean well, then. Get busy, people.

Scene Seven

Narrator: Everybody looked at Houston. For a moment, he just sat there, thinking. Then he smiled and slowly stood up.

Houston: Why didn't you report us to the principal while you had the chance, Mr. Whoever?

Mr. Euclid: I prefer to handle my own discipline.

Houston: Sure you do. Why was the principal calling you Mrs. Pembroke?

Mr. Euclid: Heh, heh. Just a little joke, you know. We always kid around like that.

Houston: But yesterday you didn't even know who the principal was!

Mr. Euclid: I've gotten to know him since then, okay?

Houston: Look, buddy—

Mrs. Pembroke: *(enters)* Oh, no! Haven't I been here before?

Mr. Euclid: Yes, you have. Several times!

Mrs. Pembroke: I'm so sorry! I'll be on my way.

Houston: Wait! Are you Mrs. Pembroke?

Mrs. Pembroke: Why, yes, I am.

Houston: Are you supposed to be Mr. Franklin's sub?

Mrs. Pembroke: Yes! Yes! Every morning they call me to substitute and every day I hurry over here and I simply cannot find my room.

Houston: This is it!

Mrs. Pembroke: Finally! *(to Mr. Euclid)* And who are you?

Other Students: Yeah! Who are you? What's the deal? etc.

Mr. Euclid: I . . . uh . . . see . . . it was just . . .

Houston: I'll tell you who he is! He's that new kid, Trevor Riley.

Alonso: What?

David: You're joking!

Mr. Euclid: No, he's right. I am Trevor.

Ming: What in the world is going on?

Houston: He fooled us! For days! He pretended to be Mr. Franklin's sub.

Mr. Euclid: I'm sorry, you guys. It's just that when I walked in and heard Houston bragging about making subs cry and all that, I just had to give it a try. It was like a personal challenge! I didn't think I'd have to keep it up for so long.

Mrs. Pembroke: I don't understand. Are you the substitute or am I the substitute?

Ruby: You're the sub, Mrs. Pembroke. He's just playing around.

Mrs. Pembroke: Oh. Well, then. Shall we all be seated? Now where's the seating chart?

Mr. Euclid: Here it is.

Mrs. Pembroke: Just let me take a look at this . . . *(keeps turning it around, confused, finally tosses it aside with a shrug)*

Mr. Euclid: Listen, you guys. I'm really, really sorry about all this.

Bonni: I worked my fingers to the bone.

Alonso: I had to stay up to midnight to get everything done.

Mr. Euclid: That's terrible, really terrible. *(breaks into a big grin)* I gotcha! Every one of you! And I gotcha bad!

Houston: I have to admit he's right. You were masterful, man.

Mr. Euclid: Thanks!

Houston: But *you* have to admit that I cracked you.

Mr. Euclid: Yeah, okay, I'll admit it. *(they shake hands)*

Mrs. Pembroke: Is everything okay now? You're friends, right?

Houston: Right!

Mr. Euclid: The best of friends!

Houston: The perfect team!

Mrs. Pembroke: Isn't that nice? Now who can tell me what page you're on?

Houston: That would be page 11, right . . . Houston?

Mr. Euclid: That's right . . . Trevor.

5

Dr. Evil Will See You Now!

Summary

In "Dr. Evil Will See You Now!" Gabriel knows that he shouldn't tease his little brother, Trent, but it's just too much fun! Trent is so gullible he even believes Gabriel's stories that their new dentist is evil. Then Gabriel learns a lesson when he comes face-to-face with an angry Dr. Evil.

Costumes/Props/Sets

For the most part, characters can wear ordinary clothing. To give Trent the appearance of being a little kid—and also to add some humor!—he can wear a hugely oversized T-shirt and a baseball cap with a tipped-up bill. He could also black out his front teeth. Dr. Vicki and her receptionist could wear large white shirts or actual lab coats, if available. Dr. Vicki could wear a frightening mask in the scenes where she is Dr. Evil. In the final scene, she can wear a dentist's mask and vampire teeth.

A row of stools can be set up across the back of the stage where characters can sit when not performing. Dr. Evil should face away from the audience. Three stools should be set to one side to serve as the reception area. Two stools on the other side can serve as the boys' bedroom and the examination area.

Trent can use a torn-up and duct-taped science poster for Scene Three.

Presentation

Gabriel is not a terrible person—he's just a big brother! He should appear quite sincere when he finally begins to regret his treatment of his little brother.

Trent should go for the laughs by playing up his gullibility and his childlike behavior.

Dr. Evil, as imagined by Trent, should behave in an exaggerated, maniacal way.

Supplemental Reading

Blume, Judy. *Double Fudge*. New York: Dutton Children's Books, 2002.

Coffin, M. T. *My Dentist Is a Vampire*. New York: Avon, 1998.

Weston, Carol. *The Diary of Melanie Martin, or, How I Survived Matt the Brat, Michelangelo, and the Leaning Tower of Pizza*. New York: Knopf, 2000.

Cast of Characters

Gabriel

Dad

Mom

Trent, Gabriel's little brother

Dr. Evil/Dr. Vicki

Child and two parents, victims of Dr. Evil

Receptionist

Dr. Evil Will See You Now

Scene One

Gabriel: *(to audience)* I know I shouldn't tease my little brother. I mean, haven't I been told that a million times?

Dad: Gabriel! Don't tease your brother.

Mom: Don't tease your brother.

Dad: Don't tease your brother.

Mom: Don't tease your brother, Gabe.

Gabriel: And so on and so on and so on for . . . let's see . . . 999,996 more times! Anyway, even though I shouldn't tease my brother, I always end up doing it somehow. It's like this powerful, irresistible force just compels me! Like this! Hey, Trent, what's that spot on your arm?

Trent: Where?

Gabriel: Right there!

Trent: I don't know.

Gabriel: It looks like . . . nah, it couldn't be . . . that's so rare, really . . . but I guess it could . . . Oh, no! Oh, please, no!

Trent: Wh-wh-what is it?

Gabriel: I'm so sorry, kid.

Trent: Why? What's wrong?

Gabriel: Nothing, buddy. Nothing at all.

Trent: I can tell it's not nothing! Tell me! Tell me the truth!

Gabriel: It's . . . it's . . . it's armafalloffus!

Trent: Is that bad?

Gabriel: Not really. It's actually a fairly peaceful and painless way to go. Well, the part where your arm rots and falls off isn't so great, but after that . . .

Trent: *(starts wailing and continues until Dad tells him to stop)* Waaaaaaaaaaaaaaaaaaaaaah!

Dad: What's going on here? As if I have to ask!

Gabriel: I don't know what's the matter with him.

Dad: Trent. Trent! *Trent!* Stop that noise!

Trent: I have armafalloffus, Dad! I'm going to die! *(wails until Dad stops him)* Waaaaaaaaaaaaaaah!

Dad: And where did he get an idea like that?

Gabriel: I don't know. Maybe you let him watch too much television, Dad.

Dad: Trent! Stop that noise!

Trent: I don't want to die.

Dad: You're not going to die, Trent.

Trent: But look! *(points to arm)*

Dad: That's a freckle, Trent. You don't have armoffus.

Trent: Are you sure?

Dad: Yes, I'm sure. There isn't any such thing as armoffus.

Gabriel: That's "armafalloffus," Dad.

Dad: You're grounded for a week, young man! Don't tease your brother!

Gabriel: *(to audience)* Something like that was always happening! Like I'd be sitting there, thinking how I really should not pretend that I could hear something moving around under Trent's bed, and then suddenly I'd be pretending that something *was* under there and Trent would be crying and then . . . well!

Mom: No television for a week, Gabe! Don't tease your brother!

Gabriel: Or maybe I'd get Trent believing that I spit in his milk. Or I'd convince him that snakes could disguise themselves as sticks. Or I'd swear I saw a spider land in his hair. I was always getting into trouble, but I just couldn't stop myself. My brain would think of something, and then my mouth would say it! I might have gone on teasing Trent forever if it hadn't been for Dr. Evil.

Dr. Evil: *(laughs maniacally)*

Scene Two

Gabriel: See, our dentist retired so we had to start going to a new dentist, Dr. Vicki. I was the first person in the family to visit Dr. Vicki.

Dad: Well, Gabe, how did you like Dr. Vicki?

Gabriel: She was really nice. And I think she did a good job. *(shoves face towards Dad, showing teeth)*

Dad: Yeah, uh-huh, great.

Gabriel: Dr. Vicki *was* great. But that's not what I said when Trent and I were alone in our room. Oh, man! That Dr. Vicki! It was awful!

Trent: It . . . it was?

Gabriel: Yes! Horribly, terribly, awful! Dr. Vicki looks nice, but that's all an act.

Trent: What do you mean?

Gabriel: Well, for one thing, I never saw her smile the whole time I was there! Not once!

Trent: That's strange.

Gabriel: *(to audience)* Of course, she had one of those doctor masks covering her face, but why mention that?

Trent: Maybe she had a good reason for not smiling.

Gabriel: Like what?

Trent: Well, maybe she felt sick or something. Maybe she had a toothache and didn't feel like smiling.

Gabriel: Think, Trent! *Think!* She's a dentist! If she got a toothache, couldn't she fix it herself?

Trent: Oh. Yeah.

Gabriel: Anyway . . . she made me sit in this creepy chair that she tilted way, way, way back so I couldn't escape! *(to audience)* Not that I tried.

Trent: She d-d-did?

Dr. Evil: *(creeps up behind Gabriel, Trent "sees" her, Gabriel does not)*

Gabriel: And then . . . and then . . . maybe I shouldn't tell you!

Trent: *(looking towards Dr. Evil with a terrified expression)* Maybe you shouldn't!

Gabriel: No, you have to know! She had all these metal, pointy things that she stuck in my mouth!

Dr. Evil: *(laughs maniacally)*

Trent: *(starting to run off)* Waaaaaaaaah!

Gabriel: Hey, where are you going?

Trent: I'm going to tell Mom and Dad.

Gabriel: No, please no! She'll be really mad if she finds out that I told. Who knows what she might do?

Trent: Something bad?

Gabriel: Something te-e-e-e-e-errible!

Trent: To both of us? Or just to you?

Gabriel: To all of us! So don't tell, okay?

Trent: Well, okay.

Gabriel: Promise?

Trent: I promise.

Gabriel: Thanks, buddy. Now leave me alone, will you? *(casually reads script)*

Trent: *(copies Gabriel)*

Gabriel: *(without looking up)* Hey, don't you have a dentist's appointment next week?

Dr. Evil: *(laughs maniacally)*

Trent: *(hides behind script)*

Scene Three

Gabriel: I knew I was just being mean. I told myself that the whole Dr. Evil thing was awfully scary for Trent and I should just drop it. And I really was going to do that. Really! But then Trent reminded me why I'm always wishing that I were an only child!

Trent: *(fooling around with poster)*

Gabriel: Hey, what is that?

Trent: *(hiding poster behind his back)*

Gabriel: What. Is. It.

Trent: I'm sorry, Gabe! Really, really, really, really, really, really sorry!

Gabriel: Really?

Trent: Really!

Gabriel: For what?

Trent: I accidentally knocked your science poster on the floor by accident and then I tried to pick it up but I accidentally had my foot on top of it and then when I pulled on it I accidentally ripped it just by accident! *(shows poster)*

Gabriel: What?! Oh, man! I spent hours on this thing! And now it's ruined! Totally ruined!

Trent: Well, Gabe, it *was* an accident, you know.

Gabriel: *(to audience)* I was ready to clobber Trent, but then I got a better idea. A much better idea! Hey, Trent, when is your dentist's appointment?

Trent: T-t-t-tuesday.

Gabriel: Listen, buddy, it's okay about the poster. Don't you worry about it.

Trent: *(surprised)* Okay.

Gabriel: You have bigger things to worry about than some old poster.

Dr. Evil: *(laughs maniacally)*

Trent: *(covers face and cowers)*

Scene Four

Gabriel: It was just too easy! Whenever Trent acted like he might be forgetting about his appointment, I ever-so-casually reminded him. Hey, Trent! You know, her real name is Dr. Evil. She has to call herself Dr. Vicki or she'll never get any victims . . . I mean, patients.

Dr. Evil: *(chuckles)*

Trent: *(acts scared)*

Gabriel: *(wiggles "scary" fingers at Trent)* That light she shines on you is so weird. I think it hypnotizes you.

Dr. Evil: *(chuckles a little louder)*

Trent: *(acts scared)*

Gabriel: You've been a good little brother, Trent.

Dr. Evil: *(laughs maniacally)*

Trent: Waaaaaaaaaaaaaah!

Gabriel: *(clamping hand over Trent's mouth)* Shhh! Remember! Mom and Dad can't know about Dr. Evil. Okay?

Trent: *(nods)*

Gabriel: *(releases Trent, turns to audience)* You're probably thinking that I'm totally heartless. Go on! Admit it! *(if no response, says)* Chicken, huh? *(if someone responds, says)* Aah, who asked you? Well, I'm not totally heartless! When Trent started having nightmares about Dr. Evil, I felt terrible. Really!

Dr. Evil: *(laughs maniacally)*

Trent: No! No! Go away! Please don't hurt me!

Mom: It's okay, Trent! Wake up!

Trent: Don't let Dr. Evil get me!

Mom: No one's going to get you. You're safe here.

Dr. Evil: *(laughs from behind Gabriel)*

Trent: Aaaah! It's Dr. Evil!

Mom: That's Gabriel! You just had a bad dream, Trent. Now go back to sleep.

Gabriel: *(to audience)* I felt so guilty when that happened! He was just a little kid, you know, and I was scaring the living daylights out of him.

Dr. Evil: *(laughs maniacally)*

Gabriel: Hey, beat it!

Dr. Evil: *(exits and changes for next scene while offstage)*

Gabriel: *(to audience)* So I decided that I had to stop the Dr. Evil routine. I was planning to sit down with Trent the next day and explain everything. At least, that was the plan until Trent took my scooter out without permission and wrecked it!

Scene Five

Trent: I'm really, really, really, really, really, really, really sorry, Gabe!

Gabriel: *(glares at Trent)*

Trent: Really!

Gabriel: *(glares)*

Trent: It was an accident!

Gabriel: *(glares)*

Trent: I can't watch television for a week! A whole week!

Gabriel: Oh, okay then! As long as you're getting a really big punishment!

Trent: I am, I am, I really am!

Gabriel: Hey, did I ever tell you about that one little kid who went to Dr. Evil's office?

Trent: Which kid?

Gabriel: Oh, just an ordinary, nice little kid.

Child: *(skips around stage)*

Trent: What about him (her)?

Gabriel: He went into Dr. Evil's office and never . . . came . . . out!

Dr. Evil: *(laughs offstage)*

Child: *(jerked offstage)* Aaaaaaah!

Trent: But didn't his parents go after him?

Gabriel: Of course!

Parents: *(enter and walk around searching for child)*

Trent: And they found him, right? And took him home, right? And they all lived happily ever after, right?

Gabriel: Not exactly. *(parents are snatched offstage, too)*

Parents: Aaaaaaah!

Dr. Evil: *(laughs offstage)*

Gabriel: And *they* . . . never . . . came . . . back!

Trent: But . . . but . . . but . . . *you* came back!

Gabriel: *(shakily)* But I've never been the same, have I?

Trent: N-n-not really.

Scene Six

Gabriel: Finally, the day of doom arrived. Mom had an errand to do, so she had me take Trent into the office for his dentist's appointment. I had to drag Trent from the door to the receptionist's desk.

Receptionist: Can I help you?

Gabriel: This is my brother, Trent. He has an appointment with Dr. Vicki.

Trent: Let me go!

Receptionist: Is he okay?

Gabriel: He's just a teeny bit scared of dentists.

Trent: I don't want to go in there! Dr. Evil will get me! Dr. Evil! Dr. Evil! Dr. Evil!

Gabriel: See what I mean?

Receptionist: Please have a seat.

(Boys sit. Trent makes several attempts to escape, but Gabriel snatches him back each time.)

Receptionist: Dr. Ev—I mean, Dr. Vicki will see you now, Trent.

Gabriel: Be brave.

Trent: *(follows receptionist, trudging off like a man who has accepted his fate)*

Gabriel: *(hums while he waits)*

(Dr. Vicki, wearing a dental mask, Trent, and the receptionist mime talking to each other in examination area. Then Dr. Vicki "hides" to one side.)

Receptionist: Gabriel, would you come with me please?

Gabriel: Huh?

Receptionist: Just follow me.

Gabriel: *(puzzled, follows receptionist to where Trent is sitting, receptionist leaves)* Hey, what's going on?

Dr. Vicki: *(tiptoes up behind Gabriel)*

Trent: *(points)* Look out! It's Dr. Evil!

Gabriel: Oh, uh, hi, Dr. Vicki! That is you under that mask, isn't it? Heh, heh.

Dr. Vicki: I am not pleased with you, Gabriel. I don't like it when people talk about me.

Gabriel: Gee, I'm sorry about all that. I was just joking, you know. Heh, heh.

Dr. Vicki: *(stepping closer and closer)* The things you told your brother weren't funny at all. I don't know how you found out about me, Gabriel. But you shouldn't have talked. I can't let you get away with this.

Gabriel: I-I-I'm really sorry! Really, really, really, really—

Dr. Vicki: *(whips off mask, revealing a mouthful of sharp teeth)*

Gabriel: *(screams and blubbers in terror)*

Trent: *(laughs)*

Dr. Vicki: *(takes teeth out and laughs)*

Gabriel: Wha-wha-what? Oh, I get it! That was a good one. Ha, ha. Yeah, really funny.

Dr. Vicki: Now we need to talk.

Gabriel: *(to audience)* Dr. Vicki made me repeat all the stuff that I'd told Trent about Dr. Evil. Then she explained everything. Like how her light was bright so she could see to do a good job. And the tools were sharp, but she knew how to use them without hurting anyone.

Dr. Vicki: And the chair tips back to make it easier to work in my patients' mouths—not to keep them from escaping!

Trent: O-oh!

Gabriel: I really am sorry, Dr. Vicki.

Dr. Vicki: I appreciate that, Gabriel, but shouldn't you be apologizing to someone else?

Gabriel: Listen, Trent. I'm sorry, buddy, okay? That was mean, really mean. I'm not going to tease you like that anymore. I promise.

Trent: We-e-ell, okay!

Gabriel: Of course, Dr. Vicki made me tell Mom everything when we got to the waiting room. And now *I'm* grounded without television until I turn thirty!

Mom: Forty!

Dad: Fifty!

Gabriel: I *am* trying to be nicer to Trent. If he was half as scared by my stories as I was by Dr. Vicki and her teeth, then I really do feel sorry for him! To tell you the truth, I'm a little worried about my next appointment with Dr. Evil.

Dr. Vicki: *(laughs maniacally)*

Trent: *(wiggles "scary" fingers at Gabriel)*

Gabriel: *(runs offstage)*

6

I'll Give You a Nickel

Summary

When Grace comes up with the "I'll-Give-You-a-Nickel" challenge, it seems like such a fun idea. But the game causes problems between Grace and her best friend, Joni, when the challenges go too far. Can Grace and Joni save their friendship?

Costumes/Props/Sets

All characters can wear contemporary clothing. Michelle should dress a little more formally than the other students.

A semicircle of stools or other seats should be provided for the actors. No special settings or props are needed. If desired, the actors could use lunch trays in the cafeteria scene.

Presentation

Grace and Joni have been friends for a long time so their interchanges are quick and sharp. Michelle has a superior attitude. She often speaks in a bored, sarcastic voice.

Supplemental Reading

Cleary, Brigid, et al., eds. *A Girl's World Presents: Talking About Friends, Real-Life Advice From Girls Like You*. Roseville, California: Prima Publishing, 2001.

Pfeffer, Susan Beth. *Truth or Dare*. New York: Four Winds Press, 1984.

Cast of Characters

Grace

Joni, her best friend

Frank

Rosa

Michelle

Old Man Diablo, voiced offstage
Devin, the boy Grace likes
Clay, Devin's friend
Zachary, Devin's friend

I'll Give You a Nickel

Scene One

Grace: It started so innocently. All I did was turn to Joni like this and say, "Hey, I'll give you a nickel if you go up to that lady and pretend she's your aunt." *(points to woman in audience)*

Joni: Of course, I didn't know then what I know now. So I did it! Hi, Aunt Ellen! I didn't know you were in town. Listen, I'd love to talk, but I have to be going. See you next time!

Grace: I can't believe you did that!

Joni: You *told* me to do it. So where's my nickel?

Grace: I'll have to pay you later, okay? *(to audience)* But I didn't have to pay Joni because the next day she came up to me and—

Joni: Hey, Grace, I'll give you a nickel if you stand under that lamppost and sing "I'm a Little Teapot."

Grace: Gee, you're really going to give me a whole nickel?

Joni: Well, no, not really. Since you owe me a nickel already, we'll be even. That is, if you have the guts to do it!

Grace: Are you calling me chicken?

Joni: Yep.

Grace: Well, I'll show you. *(sings song without hand motions as other friends come along)*

Frank: What in the world is she doing?

Rosa: Has she lost her mind?

Michelle: Come on, Rosa. Do you really have to ask?

Grace: There! I did it!

Joni: That doesn't count because you didn't do the handle and the spout.

Grace: You didn't say anything about motions. You just said I had to sing the song.

Joni: Why should I have to *tell* you to do the motions? We all learned that in kindergarten!

Frank: What's going on with you two?

Grace: Joni said that she would give me a nickel if I sang "I'm a Little Teapot," and I did exactly what she said.

Joni: But—

Grace: So now we're even, right, Joni?

Joni: *(mutters)*

Grace: Right?

Joni: Oh, I guess.

Michelle: You did that for a nickel? Really, Grace! I could have lent you the money if you were that desperate.

Grace: We're just having some fun! I challenged Joni to do something for a nickel and she challenged me. We're goofing around with each other. Get it?

Michelle: No.

Rosa: Hey, can we do it, too?

Joni: Actually I think this is something that should stay between me and the teapot.

Frank: You know, I have a whole jar full of nickels at home.

Grace: The nickels aren't the point, Frank.

Michelle: Then what is?

Joni: It's the spirit of competition! The challenge! The struggle! The victory!

Michelle: Whatever.

Grace: *(to audience)* Anyway, we went back-and-forth like that for a few weeks. *(to Joni)* I'll give you a nickel if you scream when they turn off the lights in the theater.

Joni: Okay. *(screams)* Hey, Grace, I'll give you a nickel if you wear your shirt backwards.

Grace: Okay.

Joni: Ha! It looks like you don't know how to dress yourself!

Grace: Like I care! Hey, Joni, I'll give you a nickel if you run through that sprinkler.

Joni: But that's Old Man Diablo's yard!

Grace: Chicken!

Joni: He doesn't scare me. Watch this!

Old Man Diablo: *(offstage)* You kids stay out of my yard or I'll call the police on you!

Joni, Grace: *(laugh)*

Grace: *(to audience)* See? It was fun to start out. Who knew how unfun it would turn out to be?

Scene Two

Grace: One day we were out in the hall waiting for the first bell to ring.

Joni: Hey, Grace, look who just walked in.

Grace: There are a hundred people out here, Joni.

Joni: You know who I mean.

Grace: I'm afraid I don't.

Joni: Yeah, right! Like you don't notice Devin Maguire.

Grace: Oh, him! Is he looking this way?

Joni: Yes . . . no . . . yes . . . kind of.

Grace: He doesn't even know I'm alive.

Joni: Hey, Grace, I'll give you a nickel if you go say hi to him.

Grace: No way!

Joni: Yes, a nickel. I promise.

Grace: Oh, funny.

Joni: So?

Grace: I'm not going to embarrass myself like that.

Joni: You told the principal he'd look good with a moustache. You ate broccoli with catsup and mustard. You sang "I'm a Little Teapot" right out in public. How is saying hi to Devin embarrassing?

Grace: It just is!

Joni: I think that you're chicken.

Grace: Oh, really?

Joni: Buck-buck-buckaw!

Grace: I believe you've made your point.

Joni: So you're not going to do it?

Grace: Let me think . . . hmmm . . . no!

Joni: But we've never not done whatever we were supposed to do for the nickel.

Grace: Well, we've never asked the other person to do something so . . . embarrassing.

Joni: But what's so embarrassing about—

Grace: Drop it, will you?

Joni: Okay, okay, already.

Grace: *(to audience)* That's what she *said,* but the truth was that she had no intention whatsoever of letting it go. *(to Joni)* Did you?

Joni: Not exactly.

Scene Three

Grace: At lunch that day, Joni started tormenting me about Devin and the nickel.

Joni: "Tormenting"? Isn't that a bit harsh?

Grace: Not really.

Frank: Hey, Grace, I'll give you a nickel for the rest of your fries.

Grace: Sorry, no.

Rosa: I'll give you a nickel if you—

Grace: Look, we've told you guys before. This is just something between Joni and me.

Michelle: We know, we know!

Grace: It's nothing personal, you know. We just can't go around doing all this crazy stuff all of the—

Michelle: I'll tell you what: I'll give you a nickel if you just stop talking about it.

Joni: There's no point in talking about it anyway because it's over.

Frank: Over?

Rosa: Why?

Joni: Why don't you ask Grace?

Frank: Over?

Rosa: Why?

Grace: I never said it was over.

Joni: Well, it is. You're refusing to accept the challenge of the nickel, so that ends everything.

Grace: Don't be ridiculous! If I don't do it, then you just don't pay me.

Rosa: What's the challenge?

Grace: It doesn't matter what it is because I'm not going to do it.

Joni: But it's so easy!

Grace: No, it's embarrassing. I don't know how you could even ask me to do it.

Frank: *(to Rosa)* Ooh, it must be really good.

Michelle: Please! Can't we talk about something else for once besides these stupid challenges?

Grace: Good idea!

Joni: Fine.

Frank: *(sighing)* Okay.

Rosa: I guess.

(Everyone is silent a moment.)

Joni: You know, that Devin seems like a really nice person, doesn't he?

Frank, Rosa, Michelle: Sure, uh-huh, etc.

(Silence.)

Joni: Yeah, really nice, that Devin. I bet you could walk up to him and say hi and he'd—

Grace: Joni! Stop it!

Joni: I was only saying that—

Grace: Aargh! I'm leaving!

Joni: Sheesh! What's her problem?

Scene Four

Grace: Of course, Joni just couldn't let it go. When was I going to talk to Devin? Didn't the nickel challenge mean anything to me? What about our friendship?

Joni: Hey, when are you going to talk to Devin? Doesn't the nickel challenge mean anything to you? What about our friendship?

Grace: See? *(to Joni)* Leave me alone!

Frank: Are you two still fighting?

Rosa: It's just a nickel.

Joni: *(exasperated)* It's not about the nickel!

Michelle: Yeah, yeah. It's about the spirit of competition. The challenge. Yadda, yadda, yadda.

Joni: It's not even about that anymore. Now it's about friendship! The special bond between two special friends who share a special—

Rosa: Maybe you could just think of something else that Grace could do for the nickel.

Frank: Hey, that's a great idea. Don't you guys think so?

Joni: We-ell . . .

Grace: It's a fantastic idea. Think of something else, Joni.

Joni: But that wouldn't be right. I mean, once we allow a challenge to be changed like that, then what's to keep us from doing that all the time? It'll ruin the game!

Grace: Look, Joni, either change the challenge or the game is totally over.

Joni: Okay, okay! Let me think . . . *(sees Devin and his friends approaching)* I'll give you a nickel if you sing the teapot song right now—*with* the motions!

Grace: Okay. *(starts singing with motions)*

Frank: Uh, Grace—

Joni: Shut up, Frank.

Rosa: But—

Michelle: Shh! I want to hear Grace's lovely voice.

Clay: *(when Grace finishes)* Now do "Itsy-Bitsy Spider."

Zachary: Ooh! I love that one.

Clay: The best part is the rain coming down.

Zachary: Oh, no! The best part is the sun coming out. Don't you think so, Devin?

Devin: Personally, I think the best part is when the spider comes right back and tries again. It's very inspirational.

Grace: *(to Joni)* I hate you! *(stomps off)*

Scene Five

Joni: It was just a game. A game that Grace invented herself. That's right! She started the whole thing.

Frank: Oh, come on, Joni.

Joni: What?

Rosa: You embarrassed Grace in front of Devin. You know how she feels about him!

Joni: It was a . . . a joke!

Michelle: It *was* amusing.

Rosa: Michelle!

Michelle: *(quickly)* But you have to admit it was also kind of mean, Joni.

Frank: You're going to have to apologize to Grace.

Joni: Okay, okay!

Rosa: How about right now? Here she comes.

Michelle: This ought to be good.

Frank: Michelle!

Michelle: I mean, gosh, I hope that everything works out for you guys.

Grace: Hi, Frank.

Frank: Hi.

Grace: Hi, Rosa.

Rosa: Hi, Grace.

Grace: Hi, Michelle.

Michelle: Hello.

Grace: So how are things with you guys?

Joni: So you're ignoring me? How mature!

Grace: Is there a mosquito in here? I hear this annoying little buzzing sound.

Joni: I'm wasting my time trying to talk to her!

Grace: What *is* that noise?

Frank: Come on, Grace. Joni is sorry.

Joni: No, I'm not!

Grace: Buzz, buzz, buzz! Someone should slap that mosquito flat.

Joni: I'll give you a nickel to try it!

Grace: I'll do it for free!

Michelle: Ooh, this *is* good!

Frank: Stop it! You've been best friends for years. Are you really going to ruin a great friendship over something so stupid?

Grace: It's her fault!

Joni: You started it!

Michelle: Let's all just calm down, shall we? There's only one way to settle this. Joni's last challenge *was* really embarrassing to Grace. So to make things even, Grace has to give Joni an embarrassing challenge to do.

Grace: Sounds reasonable to me.

Joni: But . . . but . . . but . . .

Michelle: You have to admit, Joni, that it would only be fair.

Joni: But . . . but . . . but . . .

Rosa: It makes sense, really.

Grace: Okay, I'll do it.

Joni: But . . . but . . . but . . .

Michelle: Good, it's settled.

Grace: I'm going to need some time to think. I'll get back to you later, Joni.

Joni: But . . . but . . . but . . .

(Everyone exits or takes seats except Joni.)

Joni: But . . . but . . . but . . . but I don't want to! *(exits or takes seat)*

Scene Six

Grace: *(to audience)* I thought long and hard about what challenge to give Joni. She made me feel so terrible with that teapot thing, and I wanted her to feel just as bad as I had.

Michelle: After what she did to you, she deserves it!

Grace: All this time, I thought she was my friend.

Michelle: I know.

Grace: We've always been there for each other.

Michelle: I *know*! So what's the challenge going to be?

Grace: I'm thinking. *(watches rest of cast enter)* Hmmm . . . I have it!

Michelle: Come here, Joni! Quick!

Frank: What's going on?

Michelle: The challenge is about to begin.

Rosa: What is it?

Michelle: I don't know yet, but I bet it's a good one.

Joni: Great.

Clay: *(to Zachary and Devin)* What's going on with them?

Devin: I don't know.

Zachary: Maybe somebody's going to sing again.

Devin: I hope not! Grace got really upset the last time.

Zachary: Let's hang around and see what happens.

Joni: Okay, Grace, what do I have to do?

Grace: Oh, nothing much really.

Joni: Right. Can we just get this over with?

Grace: Okay, then. I'll give you a nickel if you'll be a Chihuahua.

Frank, Rosa, and Michelle: What?

Joni: There is no way I'm going to do that!

Michelle: Do what? What does that mean?

Grace: When we were little, we liked to pretend to be dogs. We even looked in the encyclopedia and chose different kinds of dogs to be.

Michelle: Cute.

Joni: We were playing, okay? Like little kids do.

Grace: Right. We were pretty creative, too. We even tried to act like the particular breed that we'd chosen. You know, we'd walk slowly and look sad when we were basset hounds. We'd stand proud and bark deeply when we were German shepherds. We'd—

Joni: I am *not* going to be a Chihuahua!

Grace: But you're so good at it! That was always Joni's best dog imitation. You should hear her yap!

Michelle: I can't wait! Go ahead, Joni.

Joni: No!

Michelle: If you don't do it, Grace will never forgive you for the terrible trick you played on her. And neither will the rest of us.

Frank: Hey, you don't speak for me.

Rosa: Me neither! I don't want to have anything else to do with this thing.

Frank: It's way out of hand.

Grace: I'm just getting the revenge I so richly deserve. Do it, Joni. Right now!

Joni: But those guys over there will see me!

Grace: It's only fair, Joni. You made me embarrass myself in front of them. Now it's your turn!

Joni: *(quietly)* Yip. Yip.

Michelle: I can't hear you.

Joni: Yip. Yip.

Michelle: Louder!

Joni: Yip! Yip!

Grace: *(to audience)* I had never seen Joni look so embarrassed. But hadn't she made me feel just as bad?

Michelle: Come on, Joni. *Be* a Chihuahua!

Scene Seven

Grace: I told myself that I didn't care how Joni was feeling. So what if she'd been my best friend forever?

Clay: Hey, what are you guys doing?

Joni: Nothing!

Zachary: Then what was that strange noise you were making?

Michelle: She was barking like a Chihuahua. Do it again, Joni, so they can hear you better.

Devin: Never mind. Let's get going, you guys.

Clay: But I want to hear Joni bark.

Michelle: Go ahead, Joni.

Grace: Leave her alone!

Michelle: Hey, this whole thing was your idea.

Grace: Well, I changed my mind. I'm sorry, Joni. I shouldn't have asked you to do that.

Joni: No, you shouldn't have!

Grace: Can you forgive me?

Joni: Only if you forgive me for what I did to you.

Grace: Okay, but you have to forgive me first.

Joni: No, you forgive *me*!

Grace: No, you—

Frank: Let's just say you both forgive each other, okay?

Grace, Joni: Okay.

Zachary: Does this mean that the dog show is over?

Michelle: Unfortunately, yes.

Devin: Wait a minute. Shouldn't *you* be apologizing, too?

Michelle: Me? Whatever for?

Devin: Well, it looked to me like you were pretty mean to Joni yourself.

Rosa: Yeah, Michelle.

Michelle: But . . . but . . . but . . .

Devin: Come on, Michelle. Do the right thing.

Michelle: But . . . but . . . but . . . oh, all right! I'm sorry, Joni. Really. Okay?

Joni: Okay.

Devin: All right then. Let's go, guys.

Grace: Bye!

Devin: Bye! See you later.

Grace: *(to audience)* So everything worked out in the end. Don't get me wrong. Joni and I both got hurt. That kind of hurt takes a long time to go away. But we kept our friendship, which was great!

Joni: Yeah, I'd hate to lose my best friend.

Grace: Me, too.

Joni: Best friends forever!

Grace: You bet!

Michelle: Puh-lease!

Joni: Hey, Grace, do you know what other really fantastic thing happened?

Grace: What?

Joni: You actually spoke to Devin!

Grace: Hey, that's right. I said good-bye to him.

Joni: You did!

Grace: So doesn't that mean that you owe me a nickel?

Frank: Oh, no!

Joni: I don't owe you anything. You were supposed to say hi to Devin.

Grace: Hi. Bye. It's practically the same thing. Isn't it, Rosa?

Rosa: Not exactly.

Grace: As good as! Come on, Joni, pay up!

Michelle: Wait, wait. Didn't you issue the first nickel challenge, Grace?

Grace: Yep.

Michelle: *(pointing to each girl in turn)* And then you guys went back-and-forth and back-and-forth and back-and-forth and—

Joni: That's right! We're even now, Grace.

Grace: Oh, yeah.

Michelle: And now that you're even, could we just keep it that way? How about if you two stop challenging each other and live a normal life?

Grace: Hmmm . . . I guess we could quit.

Joni: If we do, will you give us a nickel?

Everyone: *(laughs)*

7

I'm Not Funny!

Summary

When Carla discovers the book *Make 'em Laugh*, she turns funny overnight. Her hilarious insults are a big hit with everyone—well, almost everyone. Carla figures that some people just don't have a sense of humor. When you're funny, you can't worry about little things like your friends' feelings!

Costumes/Props/Sets

All characters can wear contemporary clothing.

Stools can be arranged on stage in a semicircle, with Carla and Amy at one end, and Delores and Mrs. Morris at the other. Actors can stand and move around when reading their parts. When "teaching," Mrs. Morris can half-turn to the "students" sitting in their stools.

A bookshelf with books could be set up to one side to serve as Mrs. Morris's "personal collection of fine literature." Books can be covered and retitled to serve as Carla's book report book and her book of insults. Mrs. Morris could have a grade book and red pen handy. All the students could use pencils and notebooks.

Presentation

Carla and Amy are both aware of the audience and even address them directly, but they must also blend into the scenes with everyone else. They are both witty and somewhat sarcastic.

Mrs. Morris speaks slowly, clearly, and heavily. When she "blahs" on about Cissy's book report, she should vary her voice as if actually forming sentences.

Supplemental Reading

Hopper, Nancy J. *The Queen of Put-Down*. New York: Four Winds Press, 1991.
Perret, Gene. *Great Book of Zany Insults*. New York: Sterling Publishing, 1996.
Rovin, Jeff. *500 Hilarious Jokes for Kids*. New York: New American Library, 1990.
Sachar, Louis. *Dogs Don't Tell Jokes*. New York: Dell Yearling, 2000.
Weitzman, Ilana, et al. *Jokelopedia*. New York: Workman Publishing Company, 2000.

Cast of Characters

Carla, who becomes funny overnight

Amy, her best friend

Mrs. Morris, their teacher

Cissy, the smartest girl in school

Frank, another student

Eddie, another student

Delores, a student who has trouble in school

Danielle, another student

Pablo, another student

Harlin, another student

I'm Not Funny!

Scene One

Carla: *(to audience)* Don't say I'm funny.

Amy: Don't worry, Carla! I'd never say that.

Carla: *(ignoring Amy)* You can say I'm short.

Amy: You're short.

Carla: You can say I'm a lousy catcher.

Amy: You're a lousy catcher.

Carla: *(becoming annoyed)* You can say I need a haircut.

Amy: You need a haircut.

Carla: *(through gritted teeth)* Amy! Let me talk!

Amy: *(huffy)* Talk all you want!

Carla: *(to audience)* You . . . *(turns to Amy and points to audience)* they . . . *(back to audience)* can say anything at all about me. Just don't say I'm funny. I'm giving that up. I started being funny in a snap, and I'm giving it up the same way.

Amy: About time!

Carla: You wouldn't think a person could become funny all of a sudden, but that's what happened to me. One minute: boring as oatmeal. Next minute: a laugh riot!

Amy: You weren't *that* funny!

Carla: *(gesturing towards audience)* We'll let them decide that, okay?

Amy: Whatever!

Carla: It started at the very beginning of the school year. Right off, our English teacher assigned a book report.

Scene Two

Mrs. Morris: It will be an oral book report, class, which you will present one week from today.

Carla: *(to audience)* One week! Immediately, this slight feeling of panic started to wash over me. Then I realized that I could just do a book that I'd read the year before.

Mrs. Morris: Do not think that you can simply report on a book you've previously read. You must read a new book, class.

Carla: *(to audience)* Of course, teachers always said that! *(to Amy)* Teachers always say that.

Mrs. Morris: To ensure that you follow my directions, I am requiring you to choose a book from my own personal collection of fine literature. Please go to the bookshelf and select your book now.

Carla: I hurried to the shelf so that I could pick out the shortest book in Mrs. Morris's personal collection of fine literature.

Mrs. Morris: Class! Remember, don't judge a book by its cover—or by its size. In other words, class, examine these books thoroughly and make a careful decision.

Carla: I snatched up the skinniest book on the shelf.

Mrs. Morris: Carla, do you have an interest in that topic?

Carla: I sure do!

Amy: Yeah, right!

Carla: I do! I'm really interested in . . . *(looks down at book)* . . . *Famous Bridges and the Men Who Built Them.*

Mrs. Morris: Very well then. You may go to your desk and start reading.

Carla: *(to audience)* You're thinking that bridges aren't a very interesting topic. You're wrong about that. Bridges aren't just *un*interesting. They are *the* most boring topic a person could ever read about! But at least my book was short, and I got it read by the day of the book reports.

Mrs. Morris: Cissy Andrews! Could we have your report please?

Carla: *(to audience)* Everybody knows that Cissy is the smartest girl in school. Everybody, I guess, except Mrs. Morris. Because when Cissy finished her report, Mrs. Morris attacked!

Mrs. Morris: It is so important, Cissy, that you tell a book in order. Otherwise, it is simply too confusing to blah blah blah *(continues blah-ing over Carla's next speech).*

Carla: *(to audience)* She picked Cissy's report to pieces! She went on and on and on and on about what Cissy did wrong and how she should have done things. Finally, she made one last criticism.

Mrs. Morris: You didn't even tell the class the name of the author of your book!

Cissy: *(crushed)* I'm so sorry, Mrs. Morris.

Carla: *(to audience)* I started wondering: hey, who's the author of *my* book?

Mrs. Morris: I'm sure you will do better next time, dear. Now let's have Carla Baldwin's report!

Carla: Oh, no! She's going in alphabetical order! I hate alphabetical order!

Scene Three

Mrs. Morris: Carla?

Carla: Yes, ma'am! *(quietly to audience)* Quickly I flipped my book open, trying to find the author's name.

Mrs. Morris: Carla!

Carla: Ha! Got it! My book is *Famous Bridges and the Men Who Built Them*. And the author is Margaret E. Morris.

Amy: Oh, brother!

Mrs. Morris: Carla, *I* am Margaret E. Morris.

Class (except Delores): *(laughs)*

Carla: Oh. Oo-o-oh! Wow, Mrs. Morris. You wrote this book?

Class (except Delores): *(cracks up)*

Carla: *(to Amy)* What's so funny?

Amy: *(laughing too hard to answer)*

Carla: *(to Frank)* What's so funny?

Frank: It's Mrs. Morris's book!

Carla: Yeah?

Mrs. Morris: Carla, I have stamped my name in each of my books.

Carla: Oh. Oo-o-oh. So you didn't write this book then.

Class (except Delores): *(cracks up)*

Eddie: Good one, Carla!

Delores: I don't get it.

Carla: *(to audience)* That's when I realized that everybody thought I was being funny on purpose. Including Mrs. Morris.

Mrs. Morris: You may take your seat, Carla.

Carla: *(to audience)* Mrs. Morris marked something in her grade book—probably a big, fat F! I didn't really care though because everybody was acting like I was hilarious. And for days, people were talking about me! It was great to be noticed for once in my life.

Danielle: That was so funny, Carla!

Pablo: *(mimicking Carla)* "Wow, Mrs. Morris, you wrote this book?"

Frank: I about fell out of my chair!

Harlin: Me, too!

Amy: It wasn't *that* funny!

Carla: *(to Amy)* It was, too! *(to audience)* The problem was that my new popularity didn't last. Oh, for a while, people watched me like I might break out with something funny at any moment, but soon things went back to normal. Luckily, I found this great book at the secondhand bookstore.

Scene Four

Amy: *Make 'em Laugh*? What kind of book is that?

Carla: Just the kind of book I need! It tells you all about how to be funny.

Amy: I don't think you can learn that from a book.

Carla: Sure you can!

Amy: Whatever.

Carla: *(to audience)* I rushed home and read the whole book in one night. There were chapters about puns, slapstick, and stand-up comedy, but the chapter I liked best was called "Put-Downs, Insults, and Comebacks." It was divided into different insults for different situations. Being funny couldn't get much easier!

Amy: You were never really all that funny.

Carla: *(pointing to audience)* Their decision! *(to audience)* Anyway, I started being funny the next morning before school.

Frank: Why do people go into school before they have to?

Carla: I don't know.

Frank: I mean, school hasn't even started yet. Why go in?

Carla: I don't know.

Frank: Here comes Cissy. You know what she's going to do?

Carla: I don't know.

Frank: She's going to walk right past us and go in even though the bell hasn't rung yet. Why do people do that?

Carla: I don't know. *(to audience)* So I wasn't funny right off! Just wait a second.

Frank: Here she is! *(loudly as Cissy passes by)* Hi, Cissy!

Carla: *(to audience)* Of course, Cissy didn't say anything. She walked right by with her nose in the air. Frank tried to look like he didn't care, but we all know he likes her. *(loudly)* Forget her, Frank. She's a snob. Her nose is stuck so far up in the air that she has to blow it on clouds instead of tissues.

Cissy: *(looks shocked)*

Carla: *(to audience)* I got that insult from the "Snob" section in my book.

Danielle: Yeah, Frank.

Carla: And she's skinny, too! When she grows up she's going to be a bookmark!

Cissy: *(looking more upset)*

Carla: *(to audience)* From the "Thin" section.

Eddie: Now *that's* skinny!

Delores: I don't get it.

Carla: And how about those teeth?

Pablo: What about them?

Carla: Her parents won't let her go into the woods. They're afraid she'll be adopted by beavers!

Class (minus Cissy and Delores): *(laughs)*

Cissy: *(runs off to seat)*

Carla: *(to audience)* Just then, the bell rang, and I walked into school with everyone laughing around me. I felt like the most popular person on earth!

Amy: You wish!

Scene Five

Carla: *(to audience)* You know, once people start thinking of you as a funny person, then just about anything you do is funny. Whenever anybody looked my way that morning, all I had to do was buck my teeth out and move them up and down like a beaver. *(demonstrates as class snorts and chuckles)* Mrs. Morris knew that people were snickering about something, but she couldn't figure out what. She was really irritated with the big burst of laughter she got when she started passing out fire safety bookmarks!

Mrs. Morris: There is nothing humorous about fire safety, class.

Class (except Cissy and Delores): *(snorts and chuckles)*

Carla: *(to audience)* With my book, it was so easy to be funny. Every night I memorized a few good insults. Then the next day, I entertained my many friends by casually dropping some real zingers, like . . . .

Pablo: I can't believe that Delores flunked the spelling test—again!

Carla: I can! She's so dumb that once I saw her trying to write with the wrong end of her pen!

Class (except Cissy, Delores, and Amy): *(laughs)*

Carla: And when I tried to tell her about her mistake, she said she was writing with invisible ink!

Class (except Cissy, Delores, and Amy): *(laughs)*

Danielle: *(clutching stomach)* Stop it, Carla! I can't laugh any more!

Amy: Puh-lease!

Carla: *(to audience)* I had a million funny lines! Like . . . *(turns to kids)* You know, Harlin eats so much, I hear they're naming a vacuum cleaner after him!

Class (except Cissy, Amy, Delores, and now Harlin): *(laughs)*

Carla: Now I'm not saying that Mrs. Morris is old, but she graduated from high school a year before Christopher Columbus did!

Class (as before): (laughs)

Carla: You know, I think Amy has more freckles than a Dalmation has spots!

Class (as before): (laughs)

Carla: (to audience) I sort of spaced the insults out—no use wasting them all in just a couple of days. In between the insults, I filled in with a few ideas of my own, (demonstrates) like crossing my eyes, making beaver teeth, hanging a pencil out of my nose, and other hilarious stuff.

Mrs. Morris: (catching her with pencil) Carla, really! Pencils are writing utensils.

Carla: (snatching pencil out) Sorry, Mrs. Morris.

Amy: Oh, brother!

Scene Six

Carla: (to audience) After a while, I started to notice something strange. Amy didn't hang around me much anymore. One day I went up to her before class, just to talk. She was in this big conversation with Harlin of all people!

Carla: Hi, Amy.

Amy: (flatly) Hi.

Carla: Hi, Harlin.

Harlin: Whatever.

Carla: So, Amy, do you want to come over to my house after school?

Amy: I can't.

Carla: Well, how about tomorrow?

Amy: I don't think so.

Harlin: Hey, we were having a private conversation, you know.

Carla: (sarcastically to Harlin) Right! (to Amy) So how about the next day?

Amy: I'm busy.

Carla: Be that way then! (to audience) What was her problem? Was she mad about that remark about her freckles? Sheesh, it was just a joke! I mean, everyone laughed!

Cissy: (walks by)

Frank: Hey, it's Bucky the Beaver!

Eddie: How's it going, Bookmark?

Cissy: Shut up! (runs to seat)

Danielle: Ooh, somebody's in a bad mood!

Carla: (looking at Amy) I guess some people just have no sense of humor!

Pablo: You said it!

Carla: *(to audience)* And talking about no sense of humor! Every time we read about some famous person, Mrs. Morris always said how very *long* ago the person lived and how he had been dead a *long* time and how everyone who ever knew him had died a *long* time ago.

Mrs. Morris: Long, long, long, long ago! *(looking directly at Carla)* Before Columbus sailed the seas, you might say.

Scene Seven

Carla: *(to audience)* One day when things were really dull, I entertained people by pretending to write with the wrong end of my pencil. When Mrs. Morris wasn't looking, of course! I stuck my tongue out the way Delores does when she's working really hard, which I guess is most of the time for her. *(demonstrates)*

Amy: But she never really wrote with the wrong end of the pencil.

Carla: No, I just got that out of my book. So anyway, I had Frank about ready to explode into laughter when I noticed Delores looking right at me! I sucked in my tongue and flipped my pencil real fast, but it was too late.

Frank: *(whispers)* Hey, Delores! *(imitates her as Carla was doing)*

Pablo: *(whispers and imitates)* Delores!

Danielle: *(whispers and imitates)* Delores!

Mrs. Morris: Now, class, let's take a look at these sentences. Delores, please come to the board and diagram the first sentence for us.

Carla: *(as Delores stands and faces audience as if board is in front of her)* I guess we had Delores pretty upset, because she walked to the board with a pencil, lifted up her hand, and almost wrote on the board! *With* the pencil!

Class (minus the usual exceptions, and this time, Carla): *(cracks up)*

Delores: *(runs off, upset)*

Mrs. Morris: That's quite enough! *(follows Delores)*

Class: *(continues to laugh, mimic Delores, etc.)*

Carla: *(to audience)* All around, people were laughing, but somehow things didn't seem so funny to me anymore. I noticed that Cissy wasn't laughing. Neither was Harlin. Or Amy.

Amy: Are you happy now?

Carla: I was only joking! There's nothing wrong with making people laugh!

Amy: Yeah, right.

Carla: Hey, I'm funny, okay?

Harlin: Yeah, you're hilarious.

Cissy: I can't stop laughing. Ha. Ha.

Carla: *(to audience)* I kept trying to convince myself that I hadn't done anything wrong, but I knew better. When Delores came back to class *(Delores and Mrs. Morris return)* and I saw her face, I knew I had to do something to make things right. So I wrote an apology note and passed it to Amy when Mrs. Morris wasn't looking.

Amy: What's this? *(opens note, reads it, looks at Carla)*

Carla: Pass it to Delores! *(to audience)* The note passed on until it reached Delores. She read it and gave me a dirty look. Then she viciously crumpled up the note into a teeny, little ball. That made me feel terrible!

Amy: Hey, don't worry. You'll work it out.

Carla: Are *we* still friends, Amy?

Amy: Are you through with the whole funny guy thing?

Carla: You bet!

Amy: Okay then!

Mrs. Morris: No talking please!

Carla: *(to audience)* So—I'm not funny anymore. I'm giving that up. I hope that Delores and the other people I hurt will get over the things I said. Maybe they'll forgive me after I apologize. Or maybe they'll be friends with me again when they see I'm not acting like that anymore. And if that doesn't work, maybe I'll cheer them up by hanging *two* pencils out my nose!

Amy: *(warning)* Carla!

Carla: *(grinning)* Well, maybe not!

8

The Magic Touch

Summary

Raj wishes he had some kind of magic control over other people, especially the school bully, Amos. When a mystical visitor grants his wish, Raj finds out that having magic powers isn't all it's cracked up to be!

Costumes/Props/Sets

All characters can wear contemporary clothing. Harry Godfather needs a wand to cast his spell.

Eight stools can be placed in a semicircle for all the student characters. Raj and Bradley should be seated at one end, followed by Amos, Melissa, and Peyton, then the other students. The adult characters can enter and exit as needed.

Presentation

If desired, actors could stand and gather together for their scenes, then sit again when their parts are finished. When speaking to the audience, Raj should step forward a bit then step back when he's finished.

Once Peyton is under Raj's power, he sticks out his tongue and leaves it out as he tries to speak. Once Mrs. Smedvig is under Raj's power, she shouts all her lines. As Melissa's belching goes on, she should act as if it is becoming more and more painful. Amos bawls like a baby.

Raj "honks" his nose by pressing on it with a finger.

Harry does not have his wand in Scene Eight.

Though Bradley's words are brave in the last scene, he sounds uncertain.

Supplemental Reading

Catling, Patrick. *The Chocolate Touch.* New York: Laureleaf, 1996.

Craft, Charlotte. *King Midas and the Golden Touch.* New York: Morrow, 1999.

Etchemendy, Nancy. *The Power of UN.* New York: Scholastic Paperbacks, 2002.

Manes, Stephen. *An Almost Perfect Game.* New York: Scholastic Paperbacks, 1995.

Peterson, P. J. *Liars.* New York: Simon and Schuster Books for Young Readers, 1992.

Cast of Characters

Raj, who wishes he could control other people

Bradley, his best friend

Dad (Mom) Raj's parent

Harry Godfather, a magical visitor

Amos, a bully

Melissa

Mrs. (Mr.) Smedvig, the English and Literature teacher

Peyton

Dawn

Tamara

Noah

The Magic Touch

Scene One

Raj: *(to audience)* Maybe you don't believe in magic. Not many people do, I guess. I'm a believer myself. Just listen to what happened to me, and maybe you'll be a believer, too. It all started when Bradley came to spend the night at my house.

Bradley: This is great—a sleepover on a school night! I'm kind of glad that my roof leaked.

Raj: Lucky things like that are always happening to you.

Bradley: Lucky? I don't know that I'd call a leaky roof "lucky"! My parents sure don't think—

Raj: You know what I mean, Bradley. Things always work out for you. Your roof leaks and you get a sleepover. If my roof leaked, everything I own would be ruined and I'd catch a cold!

Bradley: Well, the leak did drip on some of my games.

Raj: Ooh, I feel so sorry for you.

Bradley: What's the matter, Raj? You're not usually so negative.

Raj: I'm negative because there's a big, black cloud of doom hanging over my head.

Bradley: What are you talking about?

Raj: I don't know! It's just that I feel like a powerless little speck. A helpless atom of . . . of . . . helplessness.

Bradley: Is this about Amos?

Raj: I guess. I'm so tired of his bullying.

Bradley: Did you ever get all the mashed potatoes out of your ears?

Raj: What?

Bradley: Did you ever . . . oh, ha ha.

Raj: I wish I had some kind of magic power over people. Then I could make Amos do whatever I wanted. Like poof! Put mashed potatoes in your own ears, Amos.

Bradley: Yeah, or poof! Eat that caterpillar, Amos.

Raj: Right!

Bradley: How did that taste anyway?

Raj: You don't want to know. *(sighs)* Nothing like that is ever going to happen. Magic! Ha!

Dad: Time to turn off the lights, guys.

Raj: Okay, Dad.

Dad: And no more talking! Go to sleep.

Bradley: Yes, sir.

Raj: I don't know, Dad, I'm not really very . . . Z-z-z-z . . . *(dozes off)*

Dad: Good night, Bradley.

Bradley: Good night. Z-z-z-z . . . *(dozes off)*

Scene Two

Raj: *(to audience)* I don't know how long we'd been asleep when this glowing light woke me. I sat up in bed and got a huge surprise.

Harry: Hi there, Raj!

Raj: Who are you?

Harry: I'm Harry Godfather.

Raj: You don't look that hairy to me.

Harry: I always get the wise guys. Listen, Raj, I'm here to help you.

Raj: Oh, boy! Do I get three wishes? I already know what my first wish is going to be. I'm going to wish for a million more wishes. Why doesn't anybody ever think of that?

Harry: No, I'm not giving you three wishes. But I am going to change your life.

Raj: How?

Harry: With magic, of course! Alakazam! Presto-change-o! Abracadabra! Kalamazoo, Michigan!

Raj: Nothing happened.

Harry: Oh, yes, it did. Just wait until tomorrow. Now you'll have to excuse me. I have to go wake up this beautiful girl who's been asleep for a hundred years.

Raj: Isn't a handsome prince supposed to do that?

Harry: Funny. Hey, is that a troll behind you?

Raj: I don't see any . . . where did he go? He just disappeared! Oh, man, I must have been dreaming. Like anything can change my stinky life.

Bradley: Are you talking to yourself?

Raj: Hey, how long have you been awake?

Bradley: Not long.

Raj: Did you see my hairy godfather?

Bradley: You're nuts, Raj!

Raj: Thanks for the support, Bradley.

Bradley: Just go back to sleep.

Raj: I'll try, but I'm so wound up I don't think I'll be able . . . Z-z-z-z . . . *(dozes off)*

Scene Three

Raj: *(to audience)* The next morning, we headed off to school completely unaware that my life had changed. At first, it seemed like any other day. Amos was standing right out in front of the school when we got there. Just like always!

Amos: Where do you think you're going, worm-eater?

Raj: To school.

Amos: Ha! You answered me! How did you know I wasn't talking to your buddy?

Raj: He's a vegetarian.

Amos: You're a riot. Give me your lunch money and I won't hurt you.

Raj: Here.

Amos: Where's your money, veggie boy?

Bradley: I carried my lunch today. You want it?

Amos: I don't eat that vegetarian garbage. You can pay me double tomorrow.

Bradley: Gee, thanks.

Amos: Okay, you guys can go on in.

Raj: *(muttering)* Wow, my life has really changed.

Bradley: What was that?

Raj: Never mind. Let's just go to our lockers.

Melissa: Hi, you guys.

Bradley: Hi, Melissa.

Raj: Hi.

Melissa: *(belches)* Maybe it wasn't a good idea to have those leftover tamales for breakfast.

Raj: Maybe not.

Melissa: *(belches)* Sorry!

Raj: Do you have to keep doing that?

Melissa: No, but maybe I just feel like it. *(belches)*

Raj: *(to audience)* That's when it happened. Melissa was getting on my last nerve, so I reached out and gave her a little shove. *(to Melissa)* Hey, cut it out, will you?

Melissa: *(belches)*

Raj: Funny.

Mrs. Smedvig: Good morning, everyone!

Bradley: Good morning, Mrs. Smedvig.

Raj: Good morning.

Melissa: *(belches)*

Mrs. Smedvig: Melissa!

Melissa: Sorry, Mrs. Smedvig. *(belches)*

Mrs. Smedvig: That is very rude, Melissa.

Melissa: I'm sorry. *(belches)* But I can't help it!

Mrs. Smedvig: Well, get rid of that problem before you come into my classroom.

Melissa: Yes, ma'am. *(belches)*

Raj: See you later, Mrs. Smedvig!

Mrs. Smedvig: Good. Bye.

Melissa: *(belches)*

Bradley: You'd better stop, Melissa.

Melissa: *(belches)*

Raj: Hey, don't listen to us. We don't care if you get in trouble.

Melissa: I can't stop myself. *(belches)*

Raj: *(to audience)* Of course, we didn't believe her. Not yet, anyway.

Scene Four

Raj: *(to audience)* The warning bell hadn't rung yet, so Bradley and I walked down the hall. Soon we ran into Peyton. He always acts like he's about three years old.

Bradley: Hey, Peyton. What's that on your face?

Peyton: What? What?

Raj: Oh, never mind. It's just your nose.

Peyton: Quit teasing me! I'm going to tell on you guys and you'll be sorry. *(sticking out tongue)* Nyah!

Raj: Aah! Put that disgusting thing back in your mouth.

Peyton: *(repeatedly sticking out tongue)* Nyah! Nyah! Nyah!

Raj: *(to audience as Peyton continues on)* His tongue really was disgusting. I mean, I could tell what he had for breakfast! So I pushed him back a bit to get away from his oatmeal breath.

Peyton: Hey! Nyah!

Raj: Quit it, man.

Peyton: Nyah!

Raj: Stop!

Peyton: *(leaving tongue out)* Nyah! I can't stop!

Bradley: What?

Peyton: Nyah! I can't stop!

Raj: Weird.

Peyton: Nyah! Somebody help me!

Bradley: Maybe you should go see the nurse, Peyton.

Peyton: Nyah! Okay.

Raj: What's the matter with people today? First it was Melissa and the belching. Now it's Peyton and his automatic tongue. One minute they're normal and the next . . . Hey . . . You know, Bradley, that nurse isn't going to be able to help Peyton.

Bradley: Nobody can help Peyton.

Raj: What I mean is, nobody can help Peyton.

Bradley: Is there an echo in here?

Raj: Wait! What I really mean is: nobody can help Peyton because he doesn't have some ordinary, normal sickness. He's under the influence of magic!

Bradley: What are you talking about?

Raj: I know this will be hard to believe, but last night I was visited by my magic godfather.

Bradley: The hairy guy you were babbling about?

Raj: He's not hairy. He's Harry.

Bradley: Okay.

Raj: Anyway, he did this spell and now when I touch somebody it does something.

Bradley: "Something"?

Raj: Yeah, something magic. Like Melissa was belching, and when I touched her, she couldn't stop. And I touched Peyton while he was sticking out his tongue and voila! *He* couldn't stop. I have some kind of magic power!

Bradley: Sure you do.

Raj: I'll prove it to you. I'll touch somebody else.

Bradley: Like who?

Raj: Hmmm . . . maybe I should touch Frank. But who wants to listen to him humming like that forever? I could touch Joanne.

Bradley: Go ahead.

Raj: Nah, she's blowing her nose. If she keeps doing that, she could blow her brains out.

(Bell rings.)

Bradley: I guess we'd better get to class. Lucky for you!

Raj: Hey, don't worry. I'll prove my powers later.

Bradley: I can't wait.

Scene Five

Raj: *(to audience)* So we went to English. I barely sat down before Mrs. Smedvig made me come to the overhead and do the daily grammar exercise.

Mrs. Smedvig: Now, Raj, explain the corrections as you make them.

Raj: Yes, ma'am. Well, "the boys is" is not correct because the subject and verb don't agree.

Melissa: *(belches)*

Mrs. Smedvig: Melissa! Stop that!

Melissa: Believe me, Mrs. Smedvig, *(belches)* I've tried!

Mrs. Smedvig: Go on, Raj.

Raj: So this should be changed to "the boys are."

Peyton: *(tongue out)* Nyah! Sorry I'm late, Mrs. Smedvig. I was in the nurse's office.

Mrs. Smedvig: What did he say?

Dawn: He said that he's sorry he's late, but he was in the nurse's office.

Mrs. Smedvig: Oh. Take your seat, Peyton.

Melissa: *(belches)*

Peyton: Nyah!

Mrs. Smedvig: Behave yourselves!

Peyton: Nyah! I'm sorry. I can't stop myself. And the nurse couldn't help me either.

Mrs. Smedvig: What did he say?

Tamara: He said that he can't stop himself and the nurse couldn't fix it.

Amos: *(threatening)* I can fix it if you want, Mrs. Smedvig.

Mrs. Smedvig: No, thank you, Amos. Go on, Raj.

Raj: Okay. This part where it says "there" should really say "they're" with an apostrophe.

Melissa: *(belches)*

Peyton: Nyah!

Mrs. Smedvig: Oh, good heavens!

Peyton: Nyah! I'm really, really sorry, Mrs. Smedvig. I don't know what the problem is. I've tried and tried to stop, but I just can't! I'm really sorry!

Noah: He said—

Mrs. Smedvig: Never mind. Continue, Raj.

Raj: Okay. The next mistake is—

Melissa: *(belches)*

Peyton: Nyah!

Mrs. Smedvig: *(shouting)* Stop it! Stop it right this minute or I'll send you both to the office! And you'll have detention until you're thirty years old!

Raj: *(to audience)* Mrs. Smedvig seemed to be getting a bit hysterical so I just reached out and patted her on the arm, forgetting about my magic powers. *(to Mrs. Smedvig)* Relax, Mrs. Smedvig.

Mrs. Smedvig: *(shouting)* GO ON WITH THE EXERCISE, RAJ!

Raj: Yes, ma'am. Finally, a period has to go right here.

Mrs. Smedvig: GREAT JOB, RAJ! YOU MAY GO BACK TO YOUR SEAT! EVERY-BODY TAKE OUT YOUR BOOKS!

Dawn: Why is she yelling?

Melissa: *(belches)* I don't know.

Amos: Maybe because she's sick of you.

Mrs. Smedvig: *(shouting)* CLASS! YOU DO NOT HAVE PERMISSION TO SPEAK! QUIET!

Raj: *(to audience)* I looked at Bradley. He was staring at Mrs. Smedvig with his mouth hanging open. Then he turned to me with this stunned expression. Finally, he recognized my power!

Scene Six

Raj: *(to audience)* When the bell rang at the end of class, everybody rushed out of the room.

Noah: Man! Mrs. Smedvig was driving me crazy with all that yelling.

Tamara: I can take the yelling. Why doesn't she make that stupid Melissa shut up?

Dawn: Who cares about Melissa? If I have to look at Peyton's disgusting, drooly, yucky tongue one more time, I'm going to be sick!

Raj: So, Bradley, do you believe me now?

Bradley: I . . . I don't know. Magic isn't real. I mean, I know it's not real.

Raj: But you saw what happened with your own eyes. I touched those people, and now they can't stop what they were doing. I'm magic!

Bradley: So now what?

Raj: Remember how I was wishing that I could control Amos? And get him back for everything?

Bradley: Yeah. What are you going to do?

Raj: I guess I'll have to watch Amos and when he's doing something really embarrassing, I'll touch him. Then he'll be stuck, just like the other people.

Bradley: Hey, what about the other people?

Raj: Look! There's Amos now. Let's try to get close without him seeing us.

Bradley: Okay, but you need to—

Raj: *(to audience)* We moved closer until we could see what Amos was doing. He was standing near Peyton who looked scared to death.

Amos: If you don't stop that, I'm going to rip your tongue right out of your head.

Peyton: Nyah! I can't stop! Really!

Amos: Okay, here goes.

Raj: *(to audience)* Amos grabbed Peyton's tongue in his big, meaty fist.

Bradley: Stop him, Raj!

Raj: I'm not going to touch him while he's got a hold on Peyton's tongue. He'll never let go.

Amos: Oops! That thing is slippery. Let me have it back again.

Peyton: Nyah!

Amos: Got it!

Melissa: Stop it! *(belches)*

Amos: You're next, Betty Burp.

Melissa: Let go of him! *(belches)* Please, Amos!

Amos: *(mocking)* Please, Amos. Please!

Mrs. Smedvig: *(still shouting)* WHAT'S GOING ON OUT HERE?

Amos: Nothing.

Mrs. Smedvig: ARE YOU OKAY, PEYTON?

Peyton: Nyah! Yes, ma'am.

Mrs. Smedvig: AMOS, I'VE HAD JUST ABOUT ENOUGH OF YOUR BULLYING!

Amos: I didn't hurt him. He's just a big baby.

Mrs. Smedvig: GO TO THE OFFICE, AMOS! I'LL MEET YOU THERE IN A FEW MIN-UTES AFTER I HAVE THE NURSE CHECK OUT PEYTON! LET'S GO, PEYTON!

Peyton: Nyah! Yes, ma'am.

Amos: What a baby! Wah, wah, wah! Poor widdle thing! Boo-hoo-hoo!

Scene Seven

Raj: *(to audience)* I saw my chance, and I took it! While Amos was still acting like a baby, I reached out and touched him on the shoulder.

Amos: Ow! That hurt! Wa-a-ah!

Bradley: You did it, Raj!

Melissa: *(belches)* Are you okay, Amos?

Amos: No! Boo-hoo-hoo! Wah!

Noah: Sheesh! What's the matter with you?

Amos: Don't yell at me! Boo-hoo!

Melissa: *(belches)* Man! My throat is getting so sore.

Amos: Wa-a-ah!

Dawn: I thought you were supposed to be a tough guy, Amos. You're nothing but a big baby.

Amos: Don't make fun of me! Boo-hoo!

Tamara: What a loser!

Amos: Wah!

Melissa: *(belches)* Ouch!

Raj: Man, this is great, Bradley. Finally Amos is getting what he deserves.

Bradley: I guess. But what about the other people, Raj?

Raj: What other people?

Melissa: *(belches)* O-o-ow!

Raj: Oh.

Bradley: You have to do something to take the spell off the innocent people.

Raj: But I don't know how to do that.

Bradley: Well, you'd better figure something out. Mrs. Smedvig is going to lose her voice soon. And Melissa is in pain. And Peyton . . . well, no one should have to live like that.

Raj: Maybe they'll be cured if I touch them while they're not doing their thing.

Bradley: Good idea!

Raj: Hey, Melissa.

Melissa: *(belches)* Ouch! What?

Raj: *(to audience)* I reached out and quickly touched her while she wasn't belching.

Melissa: What do you want, Raj?

Raj: Uh . . . how are you feeling?

Melissa: *(sarcastically)* Great, just great.

Raj: Good!

Bradley: It worked!

Melissa: What worked?

Raj: Never mind, Melissa. Everything's okay now.

Melissa: Okay? I don't think so! I have a serious problem here. *(lets out a huge belch)*

Bradley: Oh, no!

Amos: Aagh! That big noise scared me! Waaah!

Scene Eight

Raj: *(to audience)* The bell rang then, and we all had to go on to class. I was very careful not to touch anybody during Math or Social Studies. I did try to cure Peyton during P.E. by touching him while his tongue was in his mouth. It didn't work! When everyone else left the locker room after class, I stayed behind and tried to think how I could fix things. Of course, Bradley stayed, too. You know . . . to give me his support.

Bradley: This is terrible, Raj.

Raj: Don't you think I know that?

Bradley: Really, really terrible.

Raj: I know.

Bradley: This is the worst thing I've ever seen.

Raj: Okay, Bradley! Lay off, before I clobber you.

Bradley: Don't touch me!

Raj: Okay, okay! Sorry. Why did I ever make that stupid wish? I'm ruining people's lives with my magic powers. I feel just awful, Bradley.

Bradley: I bet you do. Would you mind standing a little farther away?

Raj: I think I'd better stay far away from everybody. You go on to Lit class without me. I'm going to hide out here in the locker room until school gets out.

Bradley: See you later.

Raj: I just had to wish for magic powers. What an idiot! I wish I could take it back.

Harry: Problems, Raj?

Raj: Harry! You have to help me! Everything's a big mess.

Harry: Having magic powers isn't so wonderful, is it?

Raj: No, it's not.

Harry: Perhaps you've learned a lesson from this little experience?

Raj: I really have! I don't want to control other people. Please take my powers away.

Harry: Why, Raj, you don't need me for that. You've always had the ability to get rid of your powers. Just honk your nose three times.

Raj: Shouldn't I click my heels together?

Harry: Wrong story, kid.

Raj: Okay. Honk! Honk! Honk!

Harry: There! Now everything's back to normal.

Raj: Are you sure?

Harry: Of course! Go to class. You'll see.

Raj: Thanks!

Scene Nine

Raj: *(to audience)* I hurried off to Literature, which Mrs. Smedvig also teaches. Of course, I was late.

Mrs. Smedvig: *(in normal voice)* You're tardy, Raj. I'm afraid you'll have to serve a detention.

Raj: You're okay, Mrs. Smedvig!

Mrs. Smedvig: Uh . . . thank you, Raj. You still have to serve the detention.

Raj: No problem. Hey, Melissa! How are you?

Melissa: I'm okay now. I finally finished belching those tamales.

Raj: Great! What about you, Peyton?

Peyton: Fine, except my shirt is kind of wet.

Dawn: Ew!

Bradley: Amos is okay, too.

Noah: Yeah, he finally quit bawling like a baby.

Amos: I was funning. That's all. It was a joke. I swear.

Noah: Right.

Tamara: Sure.

Raj: Thank goodness everyone is all right.

Bradley: How did you do it?

Raj: I'll tell you later. Honk! Honk! Honk!

Mrs. Smedvig: Take your seat, Raj.

Raj: Honk! Honk! Honk!

Bradley: Oh, no!

Mrs. Smedvig: Please, Raj, we've had enough trouble today.

Raj: Honk! Honk! Honk!

Mrs. Smedvig: Don't make me send you to the office.

Raj: Honk! Honk! Honk! Sorry!

Bradley: Stop it, Raj. Stop!

Raj: Honk! Honk! Honk! I can't stop!

Bradley: Raj! Raj! Wake up!

Raj: What?

Bradley: Wake up. We have to get ready for school.

Raj: (*to audience*) Suddenly I was in my bed with Bradley standing over me. That's when I realized that I had been dreaming. What a relief! When my heart slowed down to normal, I told Bradley the whole weird thing.

Bradley: That is so strange.

Raj: You know what? Even though it was a dream, it seemed so real. Maybe something like that really could happen, Bradley.

Bradley: You actually believe that wishes can come true?

Raj: Yep, I do!

Bradley: Come on. You think that a person could really make a wish and a fairy godfather could really come along and make the wish come true?

Raj: Yes, I believe it. I believe in magic.

Bradley: Whatever floats your boat, man.

Raj: I tell you what, Bradley. If something like that ever happens to me for real, I'm going to be smart about it. I mean, what was I thinking, asking for the power to control people? Next time I'm wishing for something really good. Like how about if everything I touched turned to gold? Now that would be great!

Bradley: We need to get you to the library, man. There's this story you just have to read.

Raj: Okay. Hey, what's that on the floor? It looks like . . . No! It can't be! (*snatches up wand*)

Bradley: What is that thing?

Raj: It's . . . it's . . . it's a wand.

Bradley: Real funny, Raj.

Raj: I didn't put it there! It's Harry's wand.

Bradley: Yeah, right.

Raj: He was really here, Bradley. And he really said those magic words, and he really—

Bradley: Come on, Raj. There's no such thing as magic!

Raj: Are you sure about that, Bradley? Really sure?

Bradley: Sure, I'm sure!

Raj: Then you won't mind if I touch you.

Bradley: Aaah! Get away from me! *(exits)*

Raj: *(waving wand around)* I wonder what this thing can do. *("remembers" audience)* Oh. Well, I guess you can see why I believe in magic. I hope you're believers, too. And now you'll have to excuse me. I have to get a move on. It's going to be a very interesting day at school! *(exits, waving wand)*

9

Mandi-for-a-Day

Summary

Mandi was expecting Job Shadow Day to be fun. She can't understand why she was chosen to shadow the school custodian. No one could care less about cleaning! To her surprise, Mandi learns a lot about the custodian's job—and herself.

Costumes/Props/Sets

Actors can wear contemporary clothing. Mr. Weber could wear a shirt and pants of the same color to resemble a uniform. Brandon could have a whistle and a cap.

If props are desired, Mr. Weber could have cleaning supplies like rags, a bucket, a mop, and a broom. A janitor's cart would be useful. The students could have trays, lunch bags, etc. in the cafeteria scene.

Nine stools should be arranged in a semicircle for the actors. Three stools should be separated to one side for the narrator, Mandi, and Mr. Weber. Actors can stand and move around as desired during their scenes.

Presentation

The narrator starts out disgustingly cheerful, but becomes annoyed with Mandi as the play progresses. Mandi thinks only of herself throughout most of the play. She is annoyed that *she* has to do all these disgusting jobs, not even thinking about how Mr. Weber has to do them every day. Mr. Weber could enter and exit for his parts. He and Mandi can act out their cleaning tasks. Mandi should face the audience when cleaning the mirror and the water fountain.

Mandi's friends could start out on stage, exit during the middle scenes, return during the cafeteria scene, and exit afterwards.

Supplemental Reading

Clements, Andrew. *The Janitor's Boy.* New York: Aladdin Paperbacks, 2001.

Mazer, Anne, ed. *Working Days: Short Stories About Teenagers at Work.* New York: Persea Books, 1997.

McKenna, Colleen O'Shaughnessy. *Live from Fifth Grade.* New York: Scholastic, 1994.

Schwager, Tina, and Michele Shuerger. *Cool Women, Hot Jobs: How You Can Go for It, Too!* Minneapolis, Minnesota: Free Spirit Publishing, 2002.

Cast of Characters

Narrator

Mandi

Lyle

Summer

Brandon

Jamail

Tasha

Amy

Mr. Weber, the school custodian

Mandi-for-a-Day

Scene One

Narrator: Once upon a time, in a middle school not so far away, a group of happy students eagerly awaited a special, special day. Yes, it was "Job Shadow Day," that one time a year when the happy students got to follow a real live working person all through the day. How the happy students looked forward to this special, special learning experience!

Mandi: This stinks!

Lyle: What's wrong?

Mandi: Job Shadow Day is supposed to be fun, right?

Lyle: Right. And it will be!

Mandi: Oh, really, Lyle? And what job did you get?

Lyle: Cafeteria-Chef-for-a-Day! Which is perfect for me. I love cooking.

Mandi: Lucky you! And what job did you get, Summer?

Summer: Librarian-for-a-Day. I can't wait!

Mandi: Hmph! What'd you get, Brandon?

Brandon: Coach-for-a-Day. I even get my own whistle. Wanna hear it?

Mandi: No! And I suppose you got Principal-for-a-Day, didn't you, Jamail?

Jamail: Of course! A position for which I am well qualified, I'm sure you'll agree.

Mandi: I guess.

Tasha: And I got Bus-Mechanic-for-a-Day. I hope we get to take apart the engine on one of those bad boys!

Amy: I'm Receptionist-for-a-Day. Listen to this: Good morning! Welcome to our school! How may I help you?

Mandi: Aaaaugh! This whole thing is so unfair! I knew I wouldn't get Principal-for-a-Day—

Jamail: Well, of course not!

Mandi: But I would have been happy with Coach-for-a-Day. Or Librarian-for-a-Day. Or just Anybody-Else-for-a-Day besides who I got!

Lyle: So what job *did* you get, Mandi?

Mandi: Custodian-for-a-Day!

Everyone: *(laughs)*

Mandi: I know! I know! They couldn't have picked a worse person for Custodian-for-a-Day. No one could care less about cleaning than I do!

Summer: No one!

Lyle: On the face of the earth!

Brandon: Or any other planet!

Jamail: Anywhere in the universe!

Tasha: You know, a hurricane could go through her room, and it would be an improvement.

Amy: I know!

Mandi: I just don't get it! You each got a job that you like—something that you're actually interested in. Why didn't I get a job that fits me?

Lyle: And what job would that be, Mandi?

Mandi: I don't know! But it sure wouldn't be Custodian-for-a-Day!

Lyle: Well, Mr. Weber is really nice. I'm sure you'll have a good time.

Mandi: Ooh, I can't wait!

Narrator: And so the eager, happy students eagerly set out to begin their special, special day!

Scene Two

Mandi: This stinks so bad! Like I care about how clean the school is. How can they make me do this? I don't have to put up with this kind of abuse. I'm an American, and I . . . oh, hi, Mr. Weber.

Mr. Weber: Are you Mandi?

Mandi: Ye-es.

Mr. Weber: Nice to have you along!

Mandi: Uh . . . thanks.

Mr. Weber: Well, we'd better get started. This school won't clean itself. Ha! Ha!

Mandi: Yeah, no such luck.

Narrator: Mr. Weber took Mandi to one of the most important and popular places in the whole entire school!

Mandi: The bathroom? We're going to clean the bathroom?

Mr. Weber: Well, bathrooms don't clean themselves, you know!

Mandi: I know, but couldn't we start with something . . . cleaner?

Mr. Weber: Ha! Ha! If something's already clean, then why would we need to clean it?

Mandi: Right. Silly me.

Narrator: Mr. Weber had Mandi clean the long mirror while he picked up all the paper towels thrown on the floor.

Mandi: It's really hard to get this lipstick off!

Mr. Weber: I know. Every day the girls write on the mirror like that. I don't know why, do you?

Narrator: What an opportunity for personal growth! Mandi herself had written messages on the mirror, and now she could admit her mistake and form a bond of honesty and trust with Mr. Weber.

Mandi: *(nervously)* No! Of course not! Why would I know? I mean, I guess they just do it for fun.

Mr. Weber: Well, it's not much fun to get off, is it?

Mandi: No, it's not.

Mr. Weber: You know what else I don't understand? Why do the kids throw all these paper towels on the floor when there's this nice big trashcan sitting right here?

Narrator: Mandi didn't always dispose of paper towels in the proper manner herself, so here was another chance to tell the truth. How lucky!

Mandi: Well, I don't do that kind of thing myself, but maybe the kids who do do that kind of thing actually mean to hit the trashcan, but maybe they don't have very good aim and they accidentally miss the can. Not on purpose or anything.

Mr. Weber: Or maybe they could just be a little more careful.

Mandi: Maybe they could.

Narrator: *(scolding)* Mandi!

Mandi: *(to Narrator)* I won't do it anymore, okay?

Mr. Weber: Now how about you take this broom and I'll take this mop and we'll clean the ceiling?

Mandi: Clean the ceiling? Is that really necessary, Mr. Weber? I hate to say it, but that seems a bit . . . well . . . ridiculous!

Mr. Weber: It's not as ridiculous as throwing wads of wet paper towels and seeing if they'll stick up there.

Narrator: Mandi looked up and saw what Mr. Weber was talking about.

Mandi: Ew! That is so disgusting! And something that I have *never* done! Ever! *(looks at Narrator)*

Mr. Weber: You can pry them off with the handle of your broom. Just watch out when they fall!

Mandi: This stinks! Why should someone who didn't make a mess have to clean it up?

Mr. Weber: I know just what you mean! But it's part of my job so I have to do it.

Narrator: Which meant that Mandi had to do it, too. She was, after all, Custodian-for-a-Day!

Mandi: Lucky me.

Scene Three

Narrator: After the ceiling was free of debris, Mandi helped Mr. Weber clean the rest of the bathroom. Then they moved on and tackled all the other bathrooms in the school.

Mandi: Yecch! They're all so messy!

Mr. Weber: And they're like this every single day.

Mandi: What a pain! Why are people so sloppy?

Narrator: After the bathrooms, they turned to the water fountains. The first step in cleaning a fountain was to remove all foreign matter.

Mandi: You mean, I have to pick up that wad of gum?

Mr. Weber: I'm afraid so.

Mandi: But it's been in someone's mouth!

Mr. Weber: It sure has.

Mandi: I mean, you can see their actual tooth marks! Right there on the gum!

Mr. Weber: M-hm, you sure can.

Mandi: That gum has been smushing around in someone's mouth on someone's slimy tongue, just sloshing around in someone's slobber!

Mr. Weber: It certainly has. Here! Use this paper towel to pick it up.

Narrator: Of course, Mandi had never spit out *her* gum into a water fountain.

Mandi: *(to Narrator)* That's right, I haven't!

Narrator: Oh, really?

Mandi: *(muttering)* Well, it might have accidentally fallen out a time or two.

Narrator: Uh-huh! After the fountains were all clean, it was time for lunch.

Mandi: Like I have any appetite left!

Scene Four

Narrator: At the lunch table, all Mandi's friends were talking about their jobs. Which they actually appreciated! Unlike *some* people.

Jamail: There's a lot more to the principal's job than just joking around with the kids and talking to the teachers. You wouldn't believe the paperwork! A principal has to be so organized in order to get everything accomplished.

Mandi: Sounds like your dream job, Jamail.

Jamail: You may be right, Mandi. I am quite organized and efficient. I might make a good principal. That paperwork is awfully boring though.

Mandi: Gee, that's too bad.

Lyle: How do you guys like this pizza?

Brandon: It's good!

Summer: Did you make it, Lyle?

Lyle: Yep! It's a lot of fun working in the kitchen.

Mandi: Of course it is! That's an easy job!

Lyle: Oh, I wouldn't say that! It's hard work to stand there and chop vegetables and knead dough and all that for hour after hour. And it's way too hot in there! But I like the job anyway.

Brandon: Me, too. There's a lot of work to being a coach, but it's a great job.

Amy: I like my job, too, but I don't think I'd want to do it every day. I never knew how busy a receptionist can be! Things are always happening and you don't have a moment to think!

Mandi: And you have to sit at that nice, clean desk all the time.

Amy: Right!

Tasha: At least your hands don't look like this! I like working on the buses, but I wish I could get all the grease off. My fingernails look disgusting.

Mandi: Oh, like you know what disgusting is! You should try prying mushy gobbets of paper towels off the ceiling! Or picking up trash all over the place! Or pulling already-chewed gum out of the water fountains! The kids here are such pigs!

Others: *(laugh)*

Mandi: What's so funny?

Lyle: You always spit your gum into the fountains, Mandi.

Narrator: I thought so!

Mandi: *(muttering)* Well, I can't drink and chew at the same time.

Summer: And you throw trash on the floor all the time.

Narrator: Aha!

Mandi: So I miss the trashcan every once in a while.

Brandon: Yeah, right!

Tasha: Sure you do!

Amy: What about your orange peels?

Mandi: What about them?

Lyle: Whenever you have an orange at lunch, you drop half the peeling on the floor.

Mandi: I do not! I put all my trash in my sack and throw the whole thing away.

Summer: No, you don't!

Lyle: You leave a mess everywhere you go!

Jamail: Think about it, Mandi. Is this the kind of mature behavior we expect to see in our students?

Mandi: Oh, put a lid on it, Jamail!

Jamail: I could give you a detention for that, you know.

Mandi: Ooh, I'm scared.

Lyle: Look at the mess you have right now. I bet not even half of those wrappers and cartons and stuff will make it into the trashcan.

Mandi: So? Like I care!

Narrator: And that's when Mandi swept all her trash off the table and onto the floor!

Scene Five

Narrator: Mandi's friends shook their heads at her and started talking about other things. *(to Mandi)* See? You didn't impress them at all.

Mandi: Whatever.

Narrator: As the conversation went on, Mandi looked away and noticed that Mr. Weber was standing near the door.

Mandi: Oh, no! Did he see me knock my trash onto the floor?

Narrator: I don't know.

Mandi: I . . . I don't think he did! He's not even looking this way. I bet he's just waiting to clean the lunchroom.

Narrator: Which would include your little mess, wouldn't it?

Mandi: I guess.

Narrator: It doesn't seem fair that someone who didn't make a mess should have to clean up the mess, does it?

Mandi: No, but I can't pick that stuff up. Not in front of everybody! I mean, I made such a big deal about not caring and all that. But I don't want Mr. Weber to know what I did either. Maybe if I could slide the trash under the table . . .

Narrator: Mandi tried to reach the trash with her foot so she could hide the evidence of her wrongdoing, but she reached out so far that she tipped her chair over and fell to the floor with a crash!

Other Kids: *(laugh)*

Mandi: *(from floor)* You know, I think I'll just stay down here until I graduate. Yep, they can call my name and I'll just hold up this arm and—

Mr. Weber: Mandi, are you all right?

Mandi: I'm okay.

Mr. Weber: Let me help you up.

Mandi: Thanks. I'm fine now.

Mr. Weber: Sure?

Mandi: Yeah, I'm great, really. Never better! Feeling fantastic!

Mr. Weber: What's all this trash here?

Mandi: Don't touch that!

Narrator: Mr. Weber dropped Mandi's sandwich bag like it was a poisonous snake.

Mr. Weber: Why not?

Narrator: And so . . . another opportunity presents itself! Once again, Mandi has the chance to do the right thing. Will she do it?

Mandi: Just watch me!

Scene Six

Mandi: That's my trash, Mr. Weber. I should pick it up.

Mr. Weber: Oh, that's all right. You must have knocked it onto the floor when you fell. You just take it easy, Mandi. I'll get it.

Narrator: So Mandi sat there and watched Mr. Weber pick up *her* mess and take it to the trashcan. All of her friends watched, too.

Lyle: Sheesh, Mandi!

Brandon: I can't believe you.

Summer: How can you do that?

Mandi: Because I'm a worm, okay? A low-down, good-for-nothing, lousy worm!

Narrator: Well, at least she's honest about that.

Jamail: True, true.

Lyle: You're not a worm, Mandi. You just have to get yourself together and do the right thing!

Narrator: Gee, what a great idea!

Mandi: I know, I know.

Narrator: The bell rang, and everyone went back to work. While Mandi helped Mr. Weber pick up the mess around the trashcan, she tried to get up the courage to do what she had to do.

Mr. Weber: There! That's done. Now it's time to sweep the floor.

Mandi: Mr. Weber, I have to tell you something. Sometimes I don't get my trash into the can. I don't even try, really.

Mr. Weber: Is that so?

Mandi: Yes, it is. And sometimes I spit my gum into the fountain. And . . . and other stuff, too.

Mr. Weber: You do?

Mandi: And I've marked on the mirrors in the bathrooms. And I've dropped orange peels on the floor. And that trash that you threw away for me . . . it didn't fall on the floor. I threw it down there. I'm sorry.

Mr. Weber: Are you going to do any of those things again?

Mandi: Oh, no, Mr. Weber! I wish I had never done any of that stuff. I just didn't realize how I was making work for somebody else. For you. And I'm never going to act like that again. Never!

Mr. Weber: Well, then, you learned something today, didn't you?

Mandi: I sure did! I guess it's lucky that I got picked to be Custodian-for-a-Day.

Mr. Weber: *(laughs)* I don't know that "lucky" is the word for it. Don't you have the third locker in the north hall?

Mandi: How did you know?

Mr. Weber: I didn't exactly know. When your teacher asked me about Job Shadow Day, I told her that I wanted the student with the Volcano Locker. That's what I call it!

Mandi: Volcano?

Mr. Weber: Mandi, if I just *breathe* on that locker, it pops open and something erupts out onto the floor!

Mandi: *(laughs)* It's like a small version of my room! I'm sorry, Mr. Weber. I'll work on that.

Mr. Weber: Okay! Now let's get this floor swept.

Narrator: And so! It was another successful Job Shadow Day for the happy students of a not-so-far-away middle school! Another exciting learning experience in the lessons of life and—

Mandi: Hey, maybe next year I'll get to be Principal-for-a-Day.

Narrator: *(so shocked he/she drops script)* Principal?!

Mandi: It could happen!

Narrator: *(stares)*

Mandi: Hey, aren't you going to pick that up?

10

My Friend, Mr. Inventor

Summary

Damon and his friends think that Freddie's inventions are a big joke. Who needs junk like the Frederick Quincy Rogers Mouse-o-lator? Damon gets into an argument with smart aleck Maggie and somehow finds himself bragging that Freddie will beat Maggie in the Science Fair. Now Damon's going to look like a total idiot if Freddie doesn't come through with a fantastic invention!

Costumes/Props/Sets

All actors can wear contemporary clothing.

Actors can sit on stools or chairs in a semicircle. Damon should be seated at one end where he can easily stand and move forward to address the audience.

Props can be mimed, but mockups of Freddie's inventions would add to the play. A blue ribbon with fishing line attached will be needed for the last scene.

Presentation

Actors can enter and exit as needed, or all may remain seated throughout the play. When not involved in a scene, actors could turn away from the audience.

In the first scene, Damon and his friends should face the audience as if they are watching television. Mrs. Faraday should stand to address the class. Maggie and Damon should act as if they already dislike each other.

Freddie is enthusiastic and open. While Maggie does try to brownnose the teacher, Freddie is genuinely interested in reading ahead in his text.

Supplemental Reading

Bochinski, Julianne Blair. *The Complete Handbook of Science Fair Projects.* New York: John Wiley and Sons, 1996.

Dolan, Ellen M. *Thomas Alva Edison, Inventor.* Springfield, New Jersey: Enslow Publishers, Inc., 1998.

Erlbach, Arlene. *The Kids' Invention Book.* Minneapolis, Minnesota: Lerner Publications Company, 1997.

Sullivan, Otha Richard. *African American Inventors.* New York: John Wiley and Sons, 1998.

Thimmesh, Catherine. *Girls Think of Everything: Stories of Ingenious Inventions by Women.* Boston: Houghton Mifflin, 2000.

Todd, Pamela. *Pig and the Shrink.* New York: Delacorte Press, 1999.

Weiss, Harvey. *How to Be an Inventor.* New York: Thomas Y. Crowell, 1980.

Cast of Characters

Damon

Freddie, the inventor

Alberto, Kip, and Mike—Damon's friends

Mrs. Faraday

Maggie, the smartest kid in school

Shawnta, Inez, and Ashley—Maggie's friends

My Friend, Mr. Inventor

Scene One

Damon: The whole thing started when my friends and I were at my house, watching the big game, and Freddie started acting weird. Well, weirder than usual.

Alberto: Go! Go! Go!

Damon: You can do it!

Everybody: *(cheers)*

Mike: Man, they're playing great today.

Kip: What did that announcer just say?

Alberto: Turn it up, Damon.

Damon: Okay. Hey, where's the remote?

Freddie: You don't need the remote. Not when you have the Frederick Quincy Rogers Channel Changer!

Damon: *(to audience)* Freddie reached under the sofa and whipped out this short metal . . . thing . . . with this round . . . doojie . . . stuck on the end of it. He stretched it out between his two hands until it was a long metal . . . whatzit. It looked a lot like a radio antenna with a ball stuck on the end.

Freddie: Gentlemen, I want you to be the first to experience my new and amazing invention!

Alberto: Damon, go and turn up the TV, will you?

Freddie: Stay where you are, Damon. And watch the Frederick Quincy Rogers Channel Changer in action!

Damon: *(to audience)* Freddie slowly moved the antenna towards the TV, lined up the ball over a button, and pushed. Unfortunately, it wasn't the volume control.

Kip: Hey, you changed the channel!

Mike: Turn it back!

Freddie: Just a minute . . . hold on . . . There! It's back on the right channel.

Kip: But it still needs to be turned up.

Freddie: Luckily, the Frederick Quincy Rogers Channel Changer can adjust the volume, too.

Damon: *(to audience)* Slowly, slowly, slo-o-owly Freddie moved the antenna towards another button, then pressed.

Alberto: You turned it off!

Freddie: Oh. I thought that was the volume.

Kip: Give me that! *(grabs device)* Now get up, Freddie, and fix the TV.

Freddie: I don't have to get up. Here's the old remote.

Mike: Give it to me! There! It's on.

Alberto: Frederick Stupid Rogers Channel Changer!

Freddie: I guess my invention needs some work.

Damon: Yathink?

Freddie: But one day, I'm going to make a million dollars off that baby.

Other Guys: Yeah, right! Sure! etc.

Damon: *(to audience)* We all went back to watching the game, never imagining that we hadn't seen the end of Freddie's million-dollar inventions.

Scene Two

Damon: In Science the next day, Mrs. Faraday started the chapter on famous inventors.

Mrs. Faraday: This is a very interesting chapter, class. We'll be reading about Gabriel Fahrenheit, the inventor of the first mercury thermometer. And Garrett Morgan. He invented the gas mask and the first traffic signal. And, of course, we'll spend a lot of time studying the greatest inventor of all time, Thomas Alva Edison.

Freddie: *(waving hand)* Mrs. Faraday! Mrs. Faraday!

Mrs. Faraday: Yes, Freddie?

Freddie: I've already read the whole chapter. So I can verify what you said. This *is* a very, very, very interesting chapter!

Mrs. Faraday: Thank you, Freddie. I appreciate your vote of confidence.

Maggie: *(mutters)* Suck-up! *(to teacher)* *I've* read the chapter, too, Mrs. Faraday. Twice!

Mrs. Faraday: How nice, Maggie. *(to all)* Perhaps this chapter will give you some ideas for the Science Fair. Maybe you'll even come up with some inventions of your own.

Damon: *(to audience)* I get it! Freddie read ahead like he always does. That's where he got the idea to invent that ridiculous channel changer thing. I hope he doesn't mention—

Freddie: I already invented something, Mrs. Faraday.

Damon: Oh, brother!

Mrs. Faraday: That's wonderful, Freddie. Maybe you can enter your invention in the fair.

Maggie: What is it, Freddie?

Freddie: It's the—

Damon: Shh, Freddie. Don't reveal your secrets.

Freddie: What? Oh, okay.

Maggie: Well, I invented something, too, Mrs. Faraday.

Mrs. Faraday: That's lovely, dear.

Maggie: And I'm planning to win first prize with my invention!

Damon: *(to audience)* She always acts like that. If her head got any bigger, the rest of us wouldn't fit in this room with her. *(to Maggie)* So what's this great invention?

Maggie: I don't reveal my secrets either.

Damon: You'll never beat Freddie anyway.

Maggie: I will, too!

Damon: No, you won't!

Mrs. Faraday: Let's settle down. Everyone turn to page 37, please, and we'll get started.

Damon: *(to audience)* What was I thinking—defending Freddie? Maggie's the smartest kid in school—maybe in the whole United States! Freddie's no dope, but there's no way his piece-of-junk invention is going to be better than Maggie's Science Fair project. No way!

Freddie: Hey, Damon. Thanks for your support.

Damon: Sure. No problem.

Scene Three

Damon: After school, my friends and I went over to Mike's house. We got some snacks and plopped down in Mike's family room. Everybody was talking and joking around, but I just sat there thinking about the Science Fair. I guess I should have been worrying about what *my* project was going to be, but all I could think about was Freddie's lame invention. When Maggie saw that pathetic channel changer, I was going to look like a fool.

Mike: So, Freddie, are you really going to enter that channel changer in the Science Fair?

Freddie: Of course not!

Damon: What?

Freddie: That invention didn't work very well. I need to put more research into it. I'm going to enter a better invention.

Damon: Great! That'll show Maggie—bragging on herself all the time.

Kip: So what's your new invention, Freddie?

Freddie: Gentlemen, let me present the Frederick Quincy Rogers Mouse-o-lator!

Damon: As Freddie reached into his backpack, I had high hopes that the Mouse-o-lator would be something amazing, something that would put Maggie's project to shame.

Alberto: What *is* that?

Freddie: It's a combination computer mouse and calculator. What could be handier?

Damon: We all leaned in for a good look. Basically, Freddie had used little strips of duct tape to attach a small calculator to the back of a mouse. It looked totally ridiculous.

Mike: And I thought the channel changer was weird!

Alberto: Where are you supposed to put your hand while you're using the mouse?

Freddie: You just rest your hand on top like usual.

Damon: But won't that be uncomfortable with all those calculator buttons?

Freddie: Oh, I'm sure you'll adjust after a while. Isn't it great?

Damon: You're not going to enter that in the fair, are you?

Freddie: Why not?

Damon: You know Maggie's going to have something way better than that.

Freddie: I'm going to make a million dollars off of this invention. It's certainly good enough for the school Science Fair.

Kip: *(fake-serious)* Hey, Freddie, maybe some important guy with his own company will come to the fair and see your invention.

Mike: Yeah, and he'll be so impressed that he'll write you a million-dollar check right there.

Alberto: And then he'll put you on an infomercial and you'll be famous.

Freddie: See? They have faith in me.

Scene Four

Damon: One day Mrs. Faraday took our class to the library to do research for our projects. I looked through a lot of science project books, but I just couldn't decide on an idea for the fair. I was too worried about how stupid Freddie's stupid Mouse-o-lator was going to make me look stupid in front of stupid Maggie. After I tried every book on one shelf, I wandered around to the other side and found Maggie and her friends clustered around the rest of the science project books.

Shawnta: Hi, Damon.

Inez: What are you doing for your project?

Damon: I don't know yet. I can't decide . . . Hey, wait a minute! Why are you looking at these books, Maggie? I thought you already had this amazing invention.

Maggie: Well . . . I . . . uh . . .

Ashley: She does! She has a fantastic project.

Damon: Hmmm . . . again I have to ask: why is she looking at these books? These science project books? These books with ideas for—

Ashley: She's helping me.

Shawnta: Us!

Inez: Yeah, she's helping us find projects.

Damon: Sure she is.

Maggie: You just wait, Damon. When you see my invention, you're going to be . . . so . . . very . . . like . . . speechless!

Damon: Right! You don't even have an invention, do you?

Maggie: I do, too. But Freddie doesn't, does he?

Damon: Yes, he does. And his invention is going to blow you out of the water!

Maggie: What could Freddie invent that would be that great?

Damon: I'm not telling.

Maggie: Because there's nothing to tell!

Mrs. Faraday: Less talk, more work please!

Maggie: You just wait until the fair, Damon. I'm winning!

Damon: No, Freddie's going to leave you in the dust. You'll see.

Mrs. Faraday: Class!

Damon: *(to audience)* That Maggie! She always gets me mad, and before I know it, I'm saying dumb stuff. Why can't she just leave me alone?

Scene Five

Damon: Even if Maggie didn't already have an invention, I knew she could come up with something better than Freddie's messed-up mouse. Luckily, Freddie's parents freaked when they saw what he'd done to their computer mouse. They made him take the thing apart and clean off all the duct-tape glue. So Freddie had to come up with something new for the Science Fair.

Freddie: I don't know if I can think of *another* million-dollar invention.

Damon: Well, give it a try, will you?

Freddie: You know, you can't force genius.

Damon: Come on, Freddie.

Freddie: Okay. I'll see what I can do.

Damon: One Saturday we all met at Kip's house. Freddie was going to show us his latest invention.

Kip: Freddie, if you damage anything, my parents will kill me.

Freddie: Don't worry. Do you have any good, sharp scissors?

Kip: You can use the ones in Mom's sewing basket.

Freddie: Very well. Now, gentlemen, feast your eyes on the Frederick Quincy Rogers Perfect Haircut Cap!

Damon: *(to audience)* The channel changer was strange. The Mouse-o-lator was even stranger. This latest invention was bizarre! Somehow Freddie had fastened pieces of measuring tape all around a baseball cap so that they hung down like weird, yellow hair.

Freddie: Now if I could have a volunteer for a simple demonstration of the device . . .

Mike: I don't think so!

Alberto: Do we look stupid?

Freddie: I assure you it is perfectly safe. See? *(puts cap on)*

Others: *(laugh)*

Mike: Rapunzel! Rapunzel! Let down your hair!

Kip: You need a haircut, Freddie.

Freddie: Precisely! And with the Frederick Quincy Rogers Perfect Haircut Cap, I can have a haircut of scientific accuracy.

Damon: Huh?

Freddie: The person getting a haircut wears this. The person giving the haircut uses the measuring tapes to cut the hair to exactly the same length all around. Voila! A perfectly perfect haircut!

Mike, Kip, and Alberto: What a joke! How dumb! etc.

Damon: Please tell me you're not entering that in the fair.

Freddie: Of course, I'm entering it in the fair. It's my best invention yet. One day every barber in the world will buy one of these, and I'll make a million dollars!

Damon: I'm doomed!

Scene Six

Damon: The Science Fair was fast approaching, and I still hadn't started my own project. One day I was digging around in my closet, looking for the styrofoam planets from last year's Science Fair, when Freddie showed up.

Freddie: Hi, Damon.

Damon: Hi, Freddie.

Freddie: Guess what I did?

Damon: Freddie, I don't have time to fool around with you. Jupiter and Mars are missing.

Freddie: Gee, you'd think something like that would be on the news.

Damon: For my project, Freddie.

Freddie: Oh. Well, anyway, I have a brand-new invention. And it's the best one ever! It'll make a million—

Damon: —dollars, I know. But will it win first prize at the Science Fair?

Freddie: I'm positive it will!

Damon: *(to audience)* I couldn't help but feel hopeful. *(to Freddie)* So show it to me.

Freddie: I have it set up in my room. You'll have to come over to see it. I tried to call you, but your line was busy.

Damon: Maybe you should invent something to keep my sister off the phone! *(to audience)* So I went over to Freddie's house and sat down in his bedroom. I looked around, trying to figure out what the new invention was, but Freddie had so much junk around that I couldn't spot anything.

Freddie: Ready?

Damon: Sure.

Freddie: Gentlemen . . . gentleman . . . Damon, let me present the Frederick Quincy Rogers Never-Move-Again System!

Damon: *(to audience)* He whipped out a fishing rod with a magnet attached to the end of the line instead of a hook. I didn't know what it was supposed to do, but at least it didn't look as freaky as some of the other inventions.

Freddie: So what do you think?

Damon: What does it do?

Freddie: Watch! Let's say I want that comb on the dresser. I just cast over there and pick it up like this! And reel it over to where I'm sitting. I don't even have to get up.

Damon: How did you do that?

Freddie: I glued a magnet to the comb.

Damon: *(to audience)* I took the comb off the fishing rod. Sure enough, there was a small magnet stuck to it. Right over the teeth!

Freddie: Watch me reel in that sock!

Damon: *(to audience)* I couldn't believe it. Maggie was going to win first prize for sure. Even my incomplete solar system could beat this idiotic invention!

Freddie: There! And I never had to move.

Damon: You glued a magnet to your sock?

Freddie: Sure! I glued magnets to everything.

Damon: Could you be any dumber?

Freddie: What do you mean?

Damon: How are you going to wash your socks if they have magnets on them? And this comb is useless with that magnet blocking the teeth!

Freddie: Well, sure, there are a few bugs to work out, but—

Damon: You've had some pretty stupid inventions, Freddie, but this has to be the stupidest one ever!

Freddie: You . . . you think my inventions are stupid?

Damon: *Everybody* does. It's not like we've kept our opinions a secret.

Freddie: But I thought you guys were just joking.

Damon: Well, you thought wrong. Man! There is no way that any of your goofy inventions are ever going to win anything.

Freddie: Oh. I see. You know, I have some homework to do, so maybe you should go now.

Damon: I should be working on my project anyway. I don't know why I wasted my time coming over here. Bye!

Freddie: Bye.

Damon: *(to audience)* As I walked back home, it hit me that I might have hurt Freddie's feelings with all that stuff I said. But then I told myself that all I did was tell the truth. I couldn't help it if the truth made him feel bad. Could I?

Scene Seven

Damon: The next day, Freddie didn't talk about his inventions. In fact, he hardly talked at all.

Alberto: What's the matter with Freddie?

Damon: How should I know?

Mike: Hey, why is Maggie talking to Freddie?

Kip: Probably trying to steal his ideas!

Damon: Let's move closer so we can hear.

Maggie: So, Freddie, I can't wait to see your Science Fair project.

Freddie: Oh, it's nothing special.

Maggie: I thought you had this amazing invention that was going to win first prize.

Freddie: I'm just making a solar system display.

Damon: But that's what I'm doing!

Maggie: Hey, this is a private conversation.

Damon: Not when your big mouth blasts it all over the place.

Freddie: *(walks off as they argue)*

Maggie: My, isn't that mature?

Damon: Hey, I can't help it if you're a loud mouth.

Shawnta: Leave Maggie alone.

Mike: She started it!

Inez: She did not!

Ashley: Yeah, Damon started this whole thing with his big, fat lies!

Damon: What?

Maggie: That's right. You're a liar, Damon.

Alberto: He is not!

Maggie: Okay, then. Why is Freddie doing the solar system for his Science Fair project? Where's that unbelievable invention Damon promised us?

Damon: Freddie had a great invention.

Kip: He did?

Damon: Yes, he did.

Kip: Oh, yeah, I remember now.

Damon: It just had a few bugs, that's all. And he's not going to be able to work them all out in time for the fair.

Alberto: You know, I don't think he even cares about the Science Fair any more.

Mike: Yeah, he seems really down. I don't know why.

Damon: Well, I don't know why either, okay?

Maggie: Maybe he's depressed because he has a big, fat liar for a friend!

Damon: You don't know what you're talking about!

Maggie: Well, I know one thing for sure. I'm winning first prize at the Science Fair.

Scene Eight

Damon: I spent the next couple of days feeling terrible. I hated being called a liar. I was very honest. Totally honest! Just look at how straightforward I was with Freddie. Hey, I was so honest that . . . well, it hurt. I felt bad about that, too.

Mrs. Faraday: I know that some of you still aren't finished with your Science Fair projects, but don't be discouraged. Work hard over the next few days, and you'll make it.

Damon: I doubt it.

Mrs. Faraday: Now, Damon, remember what we learned about Thomas Edison and the light bulb?

Damon: Sure.

Mrs. Faraday: And that would be . . . ?

Damon: Thomas Edison invented a good light bulb.

Mrs. Faraday: And . . . ?

Damon: And we're all really glad so we don't have to do our homework by candlelight.

Mrs. Faraday: What I mean, Damon, is that Edison had to work really hard to find the right filament for his light bulb. Class, do you remember some of the things he tried before he found out that the carbonized thread worked?

Maggie: Cork.

Alberto: Coconut hair.

Inez: And *human* hair.

Shawnta: Fishing line.

Kip: Different kinds of fibers.

Ashley: And woods.

Mrs. Faraday: And lots of other things, too. He really worked hard to find the perfect filament, and he kept on working in the face of continuing failure.

Damon: *(to audience)* This whole discussion was not making me feel any better. I kept thinking that Freddie had worked hard on his inventions, too. Not that I appreciated that before!

Mrs. Faraday: Edison once said that "Genius is one percent inspiration and ninety-nine percent perspiration." What do you think he meant by that, Damon?

Damon: Well . . . it's great to have an idea, but you're going to have to put in a lot of work to make your idea a reality?

Mrs. Faraday: Very good! I hope each of you will work hard and make your idea a reality.

Damon: *(to audience)* I felt lower than a worm after Mrs. Faraday's pep talk. My Science Fair project was still in pieces on my bedroom floor, but Freddie had come up with three ideas *and* he'd worked hard on all of them. Why did I say all that mean stuff about his inventions? If only I could make things right with Freddie! But how?

Scene Nine

Damon: After school, I went over to Freddie's house and found him in his room trying to get the magnets off his sneakers. Hi, Freddie!

Freddie: *(dully)* Hi.

Damon: Listen, Freddie, I . . . uh . . . well, I just wanted to say that I'm sorry. I didn't mean what I said about your inventions.

Freddie: You don't think they're stupid?

Damon: They don't work perfectly, but that doesn't mean that they're stupid. Thomas Edison had a lot of failures before he got his inventions to work. Maybe it'll be the same way for you.

Freddie: You think I'm like Thomas Edison?

Damon: You could be. And anyway, even if you don't invent something that makes you a million dollars, you're using your brain. And you're having fun, too, right?

Freddie: Yeah. I think it's a lot of fun to invent things.

Damon: That's all that really matters. You don't have to win first prize at the Science Fair. I'm sorry I made such a big deal out of that.

Freddie: It's okay.

Damon: Well, I'd better go put my solar system together. I'm sure it won't be as good as yours.

Freddie: I'm not making a solar system. I changed my mind about that.

Damon: You did?

Freddie: Yes, I'm entering my latest invention.

Damon: You have a new invention? That's great, Freddie!

Freddie: Thanks! Hey, I have a present for you, Damon. Here!

Damon: *(to audience)* He handed me this first place blue ribbon. *(to Freddie)* Isn't this your Science Fair award from second grade? I can't take this, Freddie.

Freddie: You bet you can't!

Damon: *(to audience)* Before I knew what was happening, Freddie snapped this line he had attached to the ribbon and I was left holding nothing.

Freddie: Bwoop! Bwoop! Stop, thief! Bwoop! Bwoop!

Damon: So is this your new invention?

Freddie: Yep! It's the Frederick Quincy Rogers Burglar Alarm.

Damon: *(to audience)* I could've said, "What if you're not home when the burglary happens?" But I didn't. *(to Freddie)* Good idea! I bet you'll make a million dollars on that some day!

11

My Roommate— Grandpa!

Summary

Kevin thinks it's great that his grandfather is moving in. Then he discovers that the "funny" things Grandpa does seem embarrassing now that Kevin isn't a little kid anymore. Can he adjust to his new roommate?

Costumes/Props/Sets

All characters can wear contemporary clothing. Grandpa can wear false teeth.

Props can be used if desired, but they are not necessary. Food, dishes, napkins, etc. can be used for scenes at the dinner table and at the restaurant. In Scene Four, Grandpa can use a newspaper, coffee cup, money, and a wallet. In Scene Five, he can have fishing poles and a bucket. Gifts can be used in Scene Six, and groceries can be used in Scene Seven.

Five seats positioned together can serve as Kevin's dinner table and the restaurant. Two seats to one side can be the bedroom he shares with Grandpa. Also the other customers can sit there during the restaurant scene.

Presentation

Kevin's family can sit on stage at all times, but the people in the restaurant, Kevin's friends, and the people in the store should enter and exit as needed.

Grandpa is a fun and friendly person. He is puzzled and hurt by Kevin's behavior. Kevin is impatient with and embarrassed by his grandfather. He can show this by rolling his eyes, sighing, etc.

If space permits, the store employees could stand in the back of the room for most of their scene, "calling" back and forth with Grandpa, then moving to the front to "unlock" the door.

Supplemental Reading

Perkins, Mitali. *The Sunita Experiment.* New York: Hyperion Paperbacks for Children, 1993.

Smith, Robert Kimmel. *The War with Grandpa.* New York: Yearling Books, 1984.

Cast of Characters

Kevin

Mom, Kevin's mother

Taleisha, Kevin's sister

Kim, Kevin's sister

Grandpa, Kevin's grandfather

Blake, Kevin's friend

Luis, Kevin's friend

Woman in restaurant

Man in restaurant

Store owner

Other workers in store

My Roommate—Grandpa!

Scene One

Kevin: *(to audience)* When I heard that Grandpa was moving in, I thought: Good deal! I won't be the only guy in the house anymore. And it'll be fun! I always had so much fun whenever Grandpa used to visit. You know—back when I was little.

Mom: I know everybody's excited about Grandpa moving in, but just remember: it will be an adjustment for all of us. Okay?

Taleisha: Okay, Mom.

Kim: Okay.

Kevin: Okay, Mom. *(to audience)* But I wondered what she was talking about. Like how much of an adjustment could it be? Ha! It didn't take long before I understood exactly what Mom meant!

Grandpa: Well, here I am!

Kim: Grandpa!

Taleisha: Hi, Grandpa!

Kevin: How are you doing, Grandpa?

Mom: We're glad you're here, Dad.

Grandpa: It's great to be here. Now where should I put my stuff?

Mom: First door on the right.

Kevin: First door on the . . . Hey! That's my room!

Mom: Yes, it is. I figured you guys could bunk together.

Grandpa: Sounds like a good idea, eh, Kevin?

Kevin: Uh . . . sure.

Grandpa: Great! I'd better go tell the movers to bring in my bed.

Kevin: *(to audience)* To fit Grandpa's bed in, the movers had to put my dresser out in the hall, right next to Grandpa's dresser! You could hardly get through that hall, but it was better than the bedroom. If I wanted to get something out of the closet, I had to suck in my stomach, squeeze past the head of Grandpa's bed, crack open the closet door, grab whatever I wanted, and escape back out all on one breath! It was ridiculous!

Grandpa: It's great being roommates, eh, Kevin?

Kevin: Oh, sure, Grandpa. Great. Just great. *(to audience)* I figured I would adjust to sharing my room with Grandpa. Sure, it was crowded, but I could get used to that, couldn't I?

And soon we'd be having all kinds of fun together, right? Ha! I didn't know that my problems were just beginning!

Scene Two

Kevin: *(to audience)* Have you ever been in an earthquake? Wait, that's not quite right. Have you ever had a train pass right through the room you're sitting in? No, that's not it. Okay, have you ever had a train pass through your room while an earthquake was shaking your house apart and jets swooped by inches from your ceiling? If you have, then you know what it's like to try to sleep in the same room as my grandpa!

Grandpa: *(snores)*

Kevin: See what I mean? Listen!

Grandpa: *(snores)*

Kevin: He rattles the windows!

Grandpa: *(snores)*

Kevin: I can feel the vibrations in my mattress!

Grandpa: *(snores)*

Kevin: He's going to wake the neighbors!

Grandpa: *(snores)*

Kevin: I didn't sleep one wink the first night Grandpa stayed with us. Could you sleep with all that going on? Obviously, I couldn't function without proper rest. Something would have to be done! Like maybe Grandpa couldn't be my roommate after all. I casually brought up the subject at breakfast. *(turns to family)* Grandpa, you snore.

Grandpa: Kevin! Now why would you tell a tale like that?

Kevin: It's true, Grandpa!

Grandpa: Why, I don't snore! Never have. Never will.

Kevin: But you did snore last night. Didn't you hear it, Mom?

Mom: I didn't hear anything. And I don't think you did either.

Kevin: *(to audience)* I could hear the warning in Mom's voice, but I went on anyway. *(to family)* But I did hear something! Taleisha, did you hear Grandpa snoring?

Taleisha: Well . . .

Kevin: Did you hear something or not?

Taleisha: I'm thinking, I'm thinking!

Mom: You didn't hear anything, did you, Taleisha?

Taleisha: Nope! Not a thing!

Kevin: What about you, Kim? Did you hear anything?

Kim: I did hear this big, loud, noisy—

Mom: *(warning)* Kim . . .

Kim: . . . truck go driving by. Several times. Over and over.

Mom: Kim . . .

Kim: But that was all! Just a truck.

Grandpa: See, Kevin? I told you I don't snore. You must have been dreaming.

Kevin: You have to be asleep to dream, and I was never asleep. Never!

Mom: Kevin . . .

Kevin: *(to audience)* I decided to just shut up about the snoring. I figured that the neighbors would be complaining soon. And anyway, I started to get used to it after a few nights. Or maybe I was just so tired that nothing could keep me awake! And after a while, the snoring was nothing compared to the other problems Grandpa was causing!

Scene Three

Mom: Aah! I'm so glad it's Friday.

Grandpa: I have an idea! How about we celebrate my first week here with dinner out? My treat!

Kevin: Great! Can we go to Hamburger Hutch?

Grandpa: Sure!

Taleisha and Kim: Yay!

Mom: Yay, too! I don't have to cook.

Kevin: Hamburger Hutch is my favorite place, so I thought we would have this really nice family dinner out. And we did have a nice time, driving to the restaurant and ordering our food, but when we sat down, things started going so wrong.

Kim: Mmm, I love Hutchburgers.

Kevin: Me too. You know why?

Kim: Why?

Kevin: Because they are so small, I can fit a whole burger into my mouth! *(to audience)* Which I demonstrated right there and then.

Mom: Kevin! Stop that!

Grandpa: Oh, he's just having some fun.

Kevin: *(chews and swallows)* Thanks, Grandpa! *(to audience)* I was thinking, hey, if Grandpa's going to defend me like that, maybe I can handle having him for a roommate! But then Grandpa stuck a whole burger into his mouth and pushed his dentures out until they looked like they'd fall on the table, Hutchburger and all! It was so embarrassing!

Taleisha and Kim: *(laugh)*

Mom: *(smiling)* Now, Dad . . .

Kevin: *(to audience)* Everybody in the whole restaurant was looking at us—and most of them seemed pretty disgusted.

Woman in restaurant: Oh, my!

Man in restaurant: Just don't look, dear.

Kevin: I figured that Grandpa would take the burger out and apologize to the people. But no! He took out the burger *and* his dentures all together!

Grandpa: Why don't you take a picture? Then this special memory can last forever.

Mom: Oh, Dad!

Woman: Let's go now.

Man: Of course, dear.

Kevin: I was thinking, please, take me with you! But I didn't say anything. I just tried to eat really fast so we could get out of there before Grandpa snorted soda out his nose or something.

Scene Four

Kevin: On Saturday, my friends, Blake and Luis, came over. As soon as they came in, I yelled, "I'm going now!" Then I tried to hurry them out the door before Grandpa saw them. But I wasn't quick enough.

Mom: Kevin, introduce your friends to your grandfather.

Kevin: But we were going . . . oh, all right! *(to audience)* I took the guys to the kitchen where Grandpa was sitting at the table, drinking coffee and reading the paper, like a normal person. What could be embarrassing about that?

Grandpa: Well, hello, boys!

Blake, Luis: Hi!

Kevin: Grandpa, these are my friends, Blake and Luis.

Grandpa: Glad to meet you! What are you boys going to do with this beautiful Saturday?

Blake: We're going to the park.

Luis: Yeah, we're going to play basketball and hike around and stuff.

Grandpa: When I was a kid, I used to love to go to this park near my house. All of us kids would meet there on Saturdays. Boy, we had a grand time! I remember there was this huge hill right in the middle of the park—I must have climbed that hill a thousand times! You boys ever do any sledding?

Luis: Yes, sir.

Grandpa: Oh, that hill was wonderful for sledding! Why I must have sledded down that hill a thousand times! And there was this big lake—

Kevin: Grandpa, we have to get going.

Grandpa: It was just a huge lake! Huge! You boys do much swimming?

Blake: Sometimes.

Grandpa: I must have gone swimming in that lake a thousand times!

Kevin: Grandpa! We have to go!

Grandpa: Oh! Okay. See you . . . Wait a minute! What's that behind your ear, Blake?

Kevin: *(to audience)* No! Please no!

Blake: *(feels ear)* Where?

Kevin: Grandpa reached up to Blake's ear and "found" a quarter behind it. I guess I thought that old trick was great when I was little, but now it seemed so lame!

Grandpa: There you go, Blake. You keep that quarter.

Blake: Thanks!

Luis: Hey, maybe you'd better check my ears, too.

Grandpa: Okay. Well, what do you know? There's a quarter behind your ear, too.

Luis: You don't see any twenty-dollar bills back there, do you?

Grandpa: *(laughing)* Sorry, no, Luis!

Kevin: Let's go already.

Grandpa: Want me to check behind your ears, Kevin?

Kevin: No! I mean, no, thanks. We need to get going.

Grandpa: Oh. See you later then.

Blake, Luis: Bye!

Grandpa: Wait a minute, boys.

Kevin: Grandpa! We want to get to the park sometime today, you know!

Grandpa: I know, but just hold on.

Kevin: *(to audience)* Grandpa got out his wallet and gave us some real money.

Grandpa: You boys get yourself something at the Stop and Shop.

Blake: Thanks!

Luis: Thanks a lot!

Kevin: Yeah . . . uh . . . thanks, Grandpa.

Grandpa: Sure, Kevin. Have a good time.

Kevin: *(to audience)* While we headed down the street to the Stop and Shop, I thought about how to apologize to my friends about Grandpa. Before I could say anything . . .

Blake: Your grandpa sure is funny.

Kevin: He is?

Luis: Yeah. Can he do any more tricks?

Kevin: *(to audience)* I really didn't want to tell the guys about Grandpa's adventures with his dentures so I just shrugged.

Blake: That was funny how he said he did everything a thousand times.

Luis: Yeah. I bet it's fun having him for a grandfather, huh, Kevin?

Kevin: Sure. *(to audience)* They really liked that old stuff! I used to think Grandpa was funny, too, like when I was five years old. *And* when we weren't around other people. Being embarrassed is never funny!

Scene Five

Kevin: *(to audience)* When I was in bed that night, listening to Grandpa snore, I started thinking about the divorce. When Mom and Dad broke up, I didn't think I'd ever smile again. Grandpa was always calling me up and pretending to be the President or Michael Jordan or somebody. He knew how to make me laugh, which made me feel a little better. I told myself, he tries to be so nice. You're just going to have to adjust, that's all! And I was really going to do that. Really! But then I walked out of school Monday afternoon and saw Grandpa waiting for me by the fence. Was he going to embarrass me in front of the whole school?

Luis: Hey, there's your grandfather!

Blake: Let's go talk to him.

Kevin: Listen, guys, we really have to go, and if he gets started talking, we'll be late so . . . you know.

Blake: Well, okay.

Luis: See you tomorrow!

Kevin: Yeah, bye!

Grandpa: Hi, Kevin. How was school?

Kevin: Fine.

Grandpa: What did you learn today?

Kevin: Stuff.

Grandpa: We learned that when I was in school, too.

Kevin: Right.

Grandpa: Say, how about some fishing? We can walk to the river from here.

Kevin: That's when I noticed that he had fishing poles leaning against the fence. Other kids were staring and laughing as they walked by!

Grandpa: I already dug up some bait for us.

Kevin: Grandpa held up this metal bucket that had a rusty lid. It looked like a hillbilly's lunchbox!

Grandpa: I hear the fish are—

Kevin: I have homework, Grandpa. I need to go home and work on it. Right now!

Grandpa: You'd rather do homework than fish?

Kevin: No, but . . . well, I just want to get ahead so I don't have to work on my birthday.

Grandpa: You have a birthday coming up? You don't say!

Kevin: Ha. Ha. Like you didn't already know that. Could we go now?

Grandpa: Oh, sure. Maybe we'll fish another day.

Kevin: *(to audience)* I couldn't have him showing up at school all the time! What if he started finding quarters behind everyone's ears? What if he "pulled off" the principal's nose? Remember that old trick? What if he performed dental stunts right out there in front of school? *(to Grandpa)* Maybe we could fish on the weekends, Grandpa. I'm usually pretty busy right after school.

Grandpa: Oh. Sure. Well, let's head home.

Kevin: *(to audience)* I could tell that his feelings were hurt, but what could I do? I couldn't let him ruin my life.

Scene Six

Kevin: *(to audience)* In our family, you get whatever you want for your birthday dinner. I wanted a feast: turkey, dressing, cranberries, and all that. Mom was going to go shopping and bring home the food the night before my birthday. But things just couldn't go right for me! That night, Mom got home really late because the car had broken down. And she didn't have the groceries for my birthday dinner!

Mom: I'm so sorry, Kevin. I had to pay to have the car fixed. I'm afraid your special dinner will have to wait until next payday.

Kevin: Oh, that's okay. *(to audience)* I was mad, but I could see that Mom really felt bad. I went to what used to be my room and kicked Grandpa's bed for a while, but I still felt mad afterwards. I didn't feel any better the next night either.

Taleisha: Happy birthday, Kevin!

Kim: *(singing badly)* Happy birthday! Happy birthday to Kevin! Oh, happy, happy birthday—

Kevin: Okay, okay! Please stop!

Kim: *(quickly)* Happy, happy, happy birthday!

Kevin: *(to audience)* We had chili for supper. Boring, old, ordinary chili! On a birthday!

I opened my presents afterwards. My sisters got me some art supplies, and Mom and Grandpa got me this leather jacket I've been wanting. I tried to act happy, but it just didn't seem like a real birthday. I told myself: Adjust! But I kept feeling disappointed. I even went to bed early.

Mom: Are you okay, Kevin?

Kevin: I'm just kind of tired, that's all. Thanks for everything, Mom.

Mom: You're welcome. Happy birthday.

Kevin: *(to audience)* I lay there in the dark for a long time, feeling sorry for myself. Then Grandpa came in and flipped on the light.

Grandpa: Get dressed, Kevin.

Kevin: What for? Is this another joke?

Grandpa: It's no joke. We're going out.

Scene Seven

Kevin: *(to audience)* Everyone was waiting in the living room when I came out of the bedroom. Grandpa made us all get in the car.

Mom: So where are we going, Dad?

Grandpa: To the grocery store.

Mom: But it closes in five minutes!

Grandpa: Better get going then.

Kevin: *(to audience)* When we got there, Grandpa marched up to the store, and we followed slowly. The door was already locked, but Grandpa jerked on the handle a few times.

Mom: Let's go home, Dad.

Grandpa: The lights are still on.

Kevin: *(to audience)* Then he started pounding on the door! I couldn't believe it.

Taleisha: They're closed, Grandpa.

Grandpa: I bet somebody's still in there.

Kevin: So what? They're still closed. What do you want anyway?

Grandpa: Something important.

Kevin: *(to audience)* So Grandpa kept pounding and pounding on that door. Finally, this man (woman)—the owner of the store, I guess—came out of door at the back to see what all the noise was about.

Store Owner: We're closed!

Kevin: See, Grandpa? Can we go now?

Grandpa: I just need one thing!

Store Owner: We're closed!

Kevin: *(to audience)* Some other people came out of back room, too. They all stared as Grandpa pounded on the door some more.

Store Owner and Workers: We are closed!

Kevin: This is so embarrassing. Let's go!

Grandpa: No, not until we get what we came for.

Kevin: Which would be what?

Mom: What do you need, Dad?

Grandpa: It's not for me. Let me in! I'll only take a minute.

Store Owner and Workers: We're closed!

Kevin: *(to audience)* Then Grandpa did the strangest thing I ever saw him to do, which is saying a lot. He stuck his thumbs in his armpits and flapped his arms up and down and bellowed out—

Grandpa: Gobble, gobble, gobble! Gobble! Gobble! etc.

Store Owner and Workers: *(laugh)*

Store Owner: Okay, okay, let me get my keys.

Grandpa: Kevin, you're going to get your birthday dinner. I can't buy it all, but I can get your turkey.

Kevin: *(to audience)* Suddenly my throat was so tight that I couldn't talk.

Mom: It's too late to fix a turkey tonight.

Grandpa: Is tomorrow okay, Kevin?

Kevin: *(in a choked voice)* Yes, sir.

Grandpa: Happy birthday, Kevin!

Kevin: *(to audience)* Would you believe that the store owner gave us some cranberry sauce for free? And a cake, too?

Store Owner: Your grandpa's a funny guy, huh?

Kevin: Yeah.

Store Owner: And a pretty nice fellow, too, I bet.

Kevin: Yes, sir.

Grandpa: Thanks, everybody! Gobble, gobble, gobble!

Store Owner and Workers: Gobble, gobble!

Grandpa: Well, I'd love to talk turkey all night, but we have to be going.

Store Owner and Workers: Bye!

Mom and Girls: Bye! Thanks!

Kevin: *(to audience)* As we headed out to the car, I kept thinking that I wanted to tell Grandpa something. Thanks, of course, but that didn't seem like enough. Mom and my sisters got into the car while Grandpa and I loaded the food into the trunk—and still I hadn't thought what to say. Finally, I just said, *(turning to Grandpa)* Thanks, Grandpa.

Grandpa: Oh, you're welcome, Kevin. I'm happy to do it.

Kevin: And, Grandpa . . .

Grandpa: Yes?

Kevin: I'm glad you're living with us.

Grandpa: *(quietly)* Thank you, Kevin.

Kevin: *(to audience)* I have to say: we're still adjusting to having Grandpa with us. But the way that he cares about us . . . well, I know that things are going to work out. Now if I can just borrow Blake's tape recorder, I'm going to prove a thing or two to the Snore-meister!

12

The Nose Uses His Head

Summary

When "The Nose" and the rest of his gang set out to climb Roundtop Mountain, they don't appreciate some guy they hardly know inviting himself along. Who does he think he is—King Robert of Hot Stuff? Then Robert disappears! Can "The Nose" sniff him out?

Costumes/Props/Sets

Actors can wear normal, contemporary clothing. If desired, "The Nose" can wear a large, fake nose. Jessica can be given freckles.

The use of props can be mimed, but if props are desired, the gang can carry packs with water bottles and food. Arf can use a leash stiffened with wire to pretend that he is leading Puddles around.

To start the play, the Narrator, Nose, and the rest of the gang can sit on stools placed in a semi-circle with an extra stool for Robert to use later. Mr. and Mrs. Kazarinski can walk onstage for their parts, then exit.

Presentation

"The Nose" should be quite sensitive about his nickname. Mouth talks quickly and runs his sentences together. His friends should act annoyed with him. Robert seems a bit superior.

If desired, actors can stand and move about for their parts. The gang can "hike" around the perimeter of the room, up and down aisles, across the stage, etc. Or they can hike in place, which can add humor to the hiking scenes.

When the friends joke about the phrase *climb the mountain,* they cup a hand to their mouths and make their voices sound echo-y.

When Puddles escapes, Arf could "chase" him offstage and call for him now and then during the following scene.

Robert can "hike" right offstage when the friends refuse to follow him. He can call for help from offstage, and the friends could carry him in and put him on a stool when they rescue him.

Supplemental Reading

Brimmer, Larry Dane. *Rock Climbing*. New York: Franklin Watts, Inc., 1997.
Hooks, Kristine. *Essential Hiking for Teens*. San Francisco: Children's Book Press, 2000.
Korman, Gordon. *The Sixth Grade Nickname Game*. New York: Hyperion Press, 2000.

Cast of Characters

Narrator

Nose, whose nose isn't *all* that big

Arf, his friend who loves dogs

Mouth, his friend who talks a lot

Pit, his friend who eats constantly

Tiny, his tall friend

Jessica, his friend who's a girl

Mr. and Mrs. Kazarinski, Arf's parents

Robert, a guy they don't know

The Nose Uses His Head

Scene One

Narrator: They call him . . . "The Nose." I know what you're thinking. You figure this guy must have one *big* nose. You're imagining this monstrously huge honker, this gigantically enormous schnozzola like the snout that ate Tokyo or something, this—

Nose: Hey, it's not *that* big!

Narrator: Whatever.

Nose: *(muttering)* Well, it's not.

Narrator: Nose has been hanging out with the same group of friends since he was in kindergarten. There's Arf.

Arf: *(waves to audience)*

Nose: We nicknamed him that because he loves dogs.

Narrator: And there's Pit.

Pit: *(waves)*

Nose: As in "bottomless"!

Pit: Which reminds me, I'm hungry!

Mouth: Me, too. You know isn't it funny how—

Pit: Shhh!

Narrator: And Mouth.

Mouth: *(waves)*

Nose: *(hides hand from Mouth as he moves it like a talking mouth)*

Narrator: And Tiny.

Tiny: *(waves)*

Narrator: *(to Nose)* Isn't he kind of tall to be nicknamed "Tiny"?

Nose: It's a joke.

Narrator: Oh. Funny.

Nose: And don't forget Jessica.

Jessica: *(waves)*

Narrator: Wait a minute. What kind of name is "Jessica"?

Nose: That's her real name.

Narrator: So you just call her . . . "Jessica"?

Nose: Yeah. So?

Narrator: Well, why does everybody else have a nickname, but she's just "Jessica"?

Jessica: That's been my question for years! Personally, I think it's some kind of discrimination!

Nose: No, it's not! We just can't think of a clever nickname for you.

Narrator: *(rolling eyes)* "Clever"? You mean like "The Nose"?

Nose: Hey, we thought of all those nicknames when we were little kids, okay?

Jessica: So why didn't you think of one for me?

Nose: Like what?

Jessica: How about something that shows who I am? A nickname that reflects my . . . my spirit!

Pit: You want us to call you "Spirit"?

Jessica: No, no, just something that communicates that part of my personality.

Nose: How about "Spunky"?

Jessica: No, that sounds like a dog's name.

Nose: "Sparky"?

Jessica: No, that sounds like a dog's name, too.

Nose: "Spitfire"?

Jessica: Doggy.

Nose: "Spot"?

Jessica: Funny, Nose, real funny.

Nose: Well, why can't you just let it go?

Jessica: I guess I'm just such a spunky, sparky, spitfire that I can't do that.

Nose: You left out spotted.

Jessica: Hey, listen here, Nose—

Narrator: Okay, people. Let's move on. As our story begins, the whole "Nickname Gang" is sitting around doing absolutely nothing. But that won't last for long!

Scene Two

Nose: What do you want to do?

Arf: I don't know.

Tiny: Whatever

Pit: Something.

Nose: Doesn't anybody have any ideas?

Mouth: Nope, not one idea, not one single idea, I don't have the least idea of anything to do, not one single, solitary idea, nosirree, not one good idea, not—

Jessica: Zip it, Mouth!

Mouth: *(snaps his mouth shut)*

Nose: Hey, why don't we *climb the mountain*? *(to audience)* Okay, don't ask me why, but we always say it that way. We started it when we were munchkins, and now it's like one of our in-jokes, I guess.

Tiny: Yeah, let's *climb the mountain*.

Mouth: That sounds like so much fun to go *climb the mountain*, I mean we always have so much fun when we *climb the mountain*, I don't know why we don't go *climb*—*(Pit interrupts him by reaching over and folding Mouth's cupped hand over his mouth)*

Arf: Hey, my parents were talking about going to the lake. Let's see if they'll leave us off at the trailhead so we can *climb the mountain*!

Narrator: *(shaking head)* Okay. These people have spent way too much time with each other.

Scene Three

Narrator: So soon it was all arranged, and everyone was standing at the base of Roundtop Mountain.

Arf: *(pretends to have dog on leash)*

Mrs. Kazarinski: Now, do you have plenty of food?

Guys (even Arf!) and Jessica: Yes, Mrs. Kazarinski.

Mouth: We have all kinds of food in our packs, and water, too, you can't go hiking without a supply of water because that just isn't—

Nose: Mouth!

Mouth: Huh?

Nose: *("zips" his own mouth as a hint)*

Mouth: Oh! Yes, Mrs. Kazarinski.

Mr. Kazarinski: I know that you're all experienced hikers, but just let me say this anyway: respect the environment.

Guys and Jessica: Yes, Mr. Kazarinski.

Mr. Kazarinski: Leave only footprints behind.

Guys and Jessica: Yes, Mr. Kazarinski.

Mr. Kazarinski: And always remember—

Mrs. Kazarinski: We'll pick you up at two o'clock, okay?

Guys and Jessica: Yes, Mrs. Kazarinski.

Mr. Kazarinski: *(to Arf)* Zachariah, you take good care of Puddles. *("pets" dog)*

Arf: Yes, Mr. Kazarinski . . . I mean, Dad.

Mr. and Mrs. Kazarinski: Well, good-bye!

Guys and Jessica: Bye!

Narrator: *("pets" Puddles)* What a cute dog! I bet I know why he's called "Puddles!"

Nose: I bet you don't.

Narrator: Okay, then. Why *is* he—eeewww! I have never in my life seen a dog drool like that!

Nose: Okay, so now you know.

Narrator: Yeah, great. Anyway, they were all ready to start their hike when something happened that would change their lives forever.

Scene Four

Nose: Okay, let's hit the trail.

Narrator: At that moment, Puddles jerked his leash and ran off.

Arf: Puddles! Puddles! Come back here!

Nose: Not again!

Tiny: What an ijit!

Narrator: Ijit?

Nose: "Ijit." It's our word for "idiot."

Narrator: *(to audience)* Now they have their own language? *(to Nose)* Do you people ever interact with the rest of society?

Nose: Of course! *(coughing)* Ijit!

Pit: I'm hungry! I'm going to get out my lunch.

Tiny: Not now, Pit! You'll be sorry after we've been hiking for a while and you don't have anything to eat.

Pit: But who knows when we'll get to start? It always takes Arf forever to catch Puddles!

Mouth: Personally, I think that Arf's nickname should be "Butterfingers" because he is always letting that dog get away and we're stuck waiting, waiting, waiting, waiting, waiting, see? We're still waiting and it's just not—

Jessica: Okay, Mouth! We get it! And speaking of nicknames . . . I want one!

Nose: Come on, Jessica.

Jessica: I'll never feel like I'm really accepted by you guys as long as I don't have a nickname.

Pit: But you've been hanging around with us for years!

Tiny: There just isn't a name that fits you, Jessica.

Jessica: Hey, I'm not totally devoid of personality, am I?

Guys: *(look at each other and say nothing)*

Jessica: *(threatening)* Am I?

Guys: Oh, no! Of course not! Heck, no! etc.

Jessica: So why is it so hard to come up with a nickname for me?

Nose: Just drop it, Jessica!

Narrator: You people are in such a rut! You need somebody to shake things up, break your old routines, jazz up your relationships.

Jessica: Like that's ever going to happen!

Scene Five

Narrator: Just then this guy came walking out of the woods, holding on to Puddles.

Robert: Is this your dog?

Guys and Jessica: Puddles!

Arf: Hey, what are you doing with my dog?

Robert: I found him in the woods.

Arf: What a bad puppy! Running off like that! Daddy was berry, berry worried about Puddles.

Robert: *(sticking hand out towards Nose)* I'm Robert Evans.

Nose: Sorry, man. We don't have any money for a tip.

Robert: A tip? Oh, I didn't mean that. I was just introducing myself. Robert Evans.

Nose: *(shakes hand awkwardly and mumbles)*

Robert: Pardon me? I didn't quite catch your name.

Tiny: He's Nose. I'm Tiny. This is Pit, Mouth, Arf, and Jessica.

Robert: Hi! Nice to meet you.

Guys and Jessica: Hi. Nice to meet you. etc.

Robert: So are you guys climbing Roundtop?

Nose: Yeah.

Robert: Great! Just let me get my pack. *(walks over to one side and fools with pack)*

Guys and Jessica: *(look at each other, stunned)*

Tiny: *(to Nose)* Aren't you going to do anything?

Nose: Me? Why me?

Mouth: Well, it was your idea to *climb the mountain*, though of course you're not the first person who (*notices everyone glaring at him*) so I think I'll shut up now.

Nose: Good idea!

Jessica: Well?

Nose: I'm not going to say anything!

Jessica: Somebody needs to say something or we're going to be stuck with . . . Here he is right now!

Robert: Let's go, gang!

Narrator: Robert led the way down the trail. Nose looked at his friends, shrugged, and followed. Then everybody else followed Nose. What a bunch of chickens!

Scene Six

Narrator: Right away, Nose started to smell something disgusting. Of course, he *would* be the one to notice it first.

Nose: Hey, look, buster! It has been scientifically proven that there is absolutely no relationship whatsoever between the size of your nose and your ability to smell!

Narrator: If you say so.

Nose: (*gets into Narrator's face*) And furthermore—

Narrator: The Nose that Ate Tokyo! Aaaah!

Nose: Funny. (*to others*) Hey, did something die around here?

Arf: It smells like skunk.

Tiny: No, it doesn't smell *that* good!

Mouth: You think this smells bad! You should have been at my Aunt Frieda's last Thanksgiving when she got so hot what with all the cooking that she took off her wig and—

Jessica: Please, Mouth! I don't want to know!

Narrator: Robert set a pretty quick pace.

Nose: Too quick!

Tiny: We can't even enjoy the scenery!

Arf: Was that a blue spruce?

Nose: Who knows? All I saw was a blur!

Robert: Onward and upward, guys!

Everybody: Sure! Yeah! Let's go! etc.

Jessica: (*hissing to Nose*) Do something!

Nose: Maybe your nickname should be "Bossy!"

Jessica: Hmmm . . . Nah, that sounds like a cow's name.

Robert: Let's pick up the pace, shall we?

Everybody: Okay! Sure! etc.

Nose: *(after Robert turns away)* Hey, I have an idea.

Narrator: Nose slowed down and so did everybody behind him. Soon Robert pulled ahead and hiked right out of sight!

Arf: Good idea, Nose!

Pit: Can we eat now?

Nose: Yeah, let's give Mr. Hot Stuff a chance to get way ahead of us.

Narrator: They all got their food out of their packs, but before anyone could take a bite, Robert suddenly reappeared.

Robert: Hey, guys, what's going on?

Scene Seven

Nose: Well, uh, yeah, uh, see we, uh, always stop here, for, uh, lunch.

Robert: Okay. Well, let's eat, shall we?

Everyone: Yeah. Sure. Okay. Etc.

Nose: There's that putrid smell again! What *is* that? I can't eat with that stink hanging over me!

Tiny: Me neither!

Nose: You know, I think that smell is coming from right here near Robert. Ew! What in the world are you eating?

Robert: Limburger.

Pit: What kind of burger?

Nose: Limburger. It's a kind of cheese.

Robert: It has a rather ripe odor, but it's delicious. I have several sandwiches. Would anybody like one?

Pit: Let me see one of those! *(sniffs sandwich and gives it back)* Maybe we should finish eating when we get to the top of the mountain.

Tiny: Yeah, where there's that nice breeze.

Arf: Sounds good to me.

Jessica: Really!

Robert: Okay, then. Off we go!

Narrator: Robert shoved everything into his pack and set off down the path. No one bothered to follow.

Nose: Who made him king?

Mouth: Yeah, like he's in charge of us! I don't think so, I mean we don't need that—

Nose: We don't need King Robert.

Tiny: Yeah, King Robert of Hot Stuff!

Jessica: Wait a minute! You've known the guy for fifteen minutes and *he* gets a nickname? Give me a break!

Nose: Well, I guess we'd better get going.

Tiny: Yeah, let's hit the road.

Arf: Onward and upward!

Pit: Let's go! That mountain won't wait around forever!

Jessica: *(muttering to herself)* Mumble, mumble, ijits, mumble mumble, mumble, nickname, mumble, mumble . . .

Scene Eight

Narrator: Without "King Robert" around—

Jessica: Hey!

Narrator: I mean, without that Robert guy around, they were able to take their time and enjoy the scenery. It was a tough hike, but well worth it. When they reached the summit of Roundtop Mountain, the view was fantastic.

Pit: Let's eat!

Tiny: This food is so much tastier without that repulsive cheese stinking up the air.

Jessica: How can anybody eat that stuff?

Mouth: Oh, you think that was bad, you should have been at my house the time that I forgot about this tuna sandwich that I was saving—

Nose: Wait a minute! Robert isn't up here.

Jessica: And we're so sad about that.

Nose: But the thing is, we didn't pass him on the trail either. So where is he?

Arf: Yeah, he should have been here a long time ago.

Tiny: That ijit! He must have gone off the trail!

Jessica: Oh, no!

Pit: He could be lost.

Tiny: Hey, do you smell anything around here, Nose? Like that Limburger cheese?

Nose: Look! I've told you a million times—

Pit: Yeah, we know, but what if something happened to the guy?

Arf: Hey, Puddles smells something over there!

Narrator: Everyone hurried over to that spot—which was right next to a big cliff.

Mouth: Man, that is a long, long, long, long, long way down there, like way long, like so long that a person could—*(snaps mouth shut, looking worried)*

Tiny: What an ijit! Everybody knows you shouldn't go hiking alone!

Jessica: Actually, he thought he wasn't alone.

Pit: What are we going to do?

Narrator: Luckily, the Nose knowed . . . uh, knows . . . knew what to do.

Scene Nine

Nose: *(sniffs)* He *was* here! I can smell that gross cheese.

Jessica: Oh, no! You don't think he fell, do you?

Nose: Let's holler for him. On the count of three . . . one . . . two . . . three . . .

Everybody: Robert!

Nose: Let's try it again. One . . . two . . . three . . .

Everybody: Robert!

Robert: Help!

Everyone: *(cheers)*

Nose: Robert! Where are you?

Robert: *(more weakly)* Help!

Nose: Robert!

Narrator: No matter how many times they called after that, Robert didn't answer.

Jessica: He must be hurt somewhere down below.

Nose: But he didn't fall off this cliff. It's too high for anybody to survive a fall like that.

Pit: Then where is he?

Nose: As fast as he was moving, I bet he got up here pretty quickly. Then he ate some more sandwiches and waited around for us.

Tiny: Yeah, and he got tired of waiting.

Nose: And headed back down. Somewhere along the way back, he wandered off the trail. Or maybe he lost his footing and slid down the slope. That's why we didn't pass each other.

Arf: He could be anywhere!

Nose: We'll just have to backtrack until we find him. We'll keep calling to him from the path. And we'll have to look off into the woods a bit, too. Let's go!

Scene Ten

Narrator: They searched and searched for Robert. Finally, Nose found him.

Nose: And no, I didn't sniff him out! I used my head—and my eyes. I remembered this badly eroded spot on the trail, the kind of place where someone going too fast might slip. Looking down the slope below, I spotted Robert in some bushes.

Narrator: Robert's ankle was broken, but the guys managed to get him back to the trail and down the mountain. Arf's parents were waiting in the parking lot, so they were able to get Robert to the hospital right away.

Nose: We must have hiked right by him while he was passed out.

Jessica: I bet he felt terrible when he woke up all alone and injured like that.

Tiny: We shouldn't have let him hike alone.

Arf: No, we shouldn't have.

Pit: We were such ijits!

Jessica: We were more than ijits! We were . . . well, mean, really. You know, we always do that to other people. We just shut them out.

Nose: Yeah, like we're the only people who matter.

Arf: So what do we do now?

Nose: I think we all know what we need to do.

Pit: Right! They have a great cafeteria in this hospital.

(Everyone glares at him.)

Pit: I mean, for later, you know.

Nose: We have to go see Robert and apologize.

Others: *(reluctantly)* Okay.

Nose: Hey, Robert, how are you doing?

Robert: The doctor says I'll be fine. Thanks so much for getting me out of there, you guys.

Everybody: *(mumbles)*

Nose: Listen, Robert. We wanted to say that we're sorry. We never should have let you go off by yourself like that.

Robert: Oh, that's okay. I guess I was moving a little faster than the rest of you wanted to go, wasn't I?

Everybody: *(mumbles)*

Robert: Look, I know that I can be a little . . . well, pushy. If I go too far, all you have to do is tell me. Okay?

Everybody: Okay!

Jessica: Okay, *King Robert.*

Robert: King Robert?

Tiny: Yeah, that's your nickname. We give all our friends nicknames like that.

Robert: Thanks, guys!

Nose: We'll see you later!

Everybody: Bye! See you! etc.

Nose: *(to audience)* So things worked out in the end. We all learned that you have to be open to people. That's how you make new friends. And life can hold some unpleasant surprises, but also—

Narrator: *(nudges Nose, nods towards Jessica)* Aren't you forgetting something?

Nose: But I don't know what . . . look, Jessica, if you don't know where you stand by now, no nickname is going to make you feel . . . He-e-ey, I just got an idea! You've always been a good friend to all of us—like our best buddy, you know—so how about if we call you "Buddy"?

Jessica: Buddy . . . Buddy . . . hmmm . . . okay!

Narrator: *(quietly to Nose)* Sounds like a dog name to me.

Nose: Shh . . . keep it to yourself.

Narrator: Hey, I'm just saying that—

Nose: *(getting into Narrator's face)* Put a lid on it!

Narrator: Aaah! The Nose That Ate Tokyo! Aah!

13

Not for Weak Stomachs

Summary

Diego can't believe it when his pen pal, Marcellus, comes to visit over spring vacation. Marcellus is just as strange in person as he seems to be in his letters. Diego and his friends have to get rid of Marcellus somehow, before he ruins their whole vacation!

Costumes/Props/Sets

All characters can wear normal, contemporary attire, but Marcellus should wear mismatched clothing. He might also wear something unusual such as an ascot, a suit coat, or other item that makes him look strange.

Stools can be arranged in a semicircle for the actors. Actors can sit in their places the whole time, or they can move about as fits the play. Bonita, Mom, Marcellus, Dad, and the Visitor should exit and enter at the appropriate times instead of sitting on stage continuously.

A table at one side can be used for the kitchen. Props can be used for Marcellus' possessions, the food, dishes, etc., or characters can mime using the props.

Presentation

Frank should enjoy some of Marcellus's antics, but hide his pleasure from his friends.

The confusion over Ish's name comes from the running together of the last consonant of the word before his name and the short "i" sound at the beginning of "Ish."

Supplemental Reading

Cleary, Beverly. *Dear Mr. Henshaw*. New York: Harper Trophy.
Marriott, Janice. *Letters to Lesley*. New York: Random House, 1991.
Skolsky, Mindy Warshaw. *Love from Your Friend, Hannah*. New York: Harper Trophy, 1999.

Cast of Characters

Narrator One
Narrator Two

Diego
Frank, Diego's best friend
Ryan, Diego's friend
Ish, Diego's friend
Bonita, Diego's sister
Marcellus, Diego's special visitor
Mom, Diego's mother
Dad, Diego's father
Another Visitor

Not for Weak Stomachs

Scene One

Narrator One: Today we bring you a story the likes of which you have never heard before!

Narrator Two: A fable of friendship and betrayal!

Narrator One: The tale of a mysterious visitor!

Narrator Two: A saga of annoying behavior!

Narrator One: And disgusting personal habits!

Narrator Two: A yarn not meant for the faint of heart!

Narrator One: Or the weak of stomach!

Narrator Two: A narrative of—

Diego: Oh, come on! Let's get started already.

Narrator One: *(holding up thesaurus)* But there are still a lot of words left in this thesaurus.

Diego: *(exasperated)* Please! Just start the play!

Narrator Two: Well, all right.

Narrator One: This is the adventure . . . uh . . . story of Diego *(Diego bows)* and his encounter with a strange visitor.

Narrator Two: The whole thing began on the first day of spring break.

Narrator One: At Diego's domicile.

Diego: My what?

Narrator One: House, okay? At your house.

Frank: He's coming here?

Diego: Yep.

Ryan: Here?

Diego: Yep.

Ish: Today?

Diego: Yes!

Ish: Here?

Diego: *Yes*! He's coming here! Today!

Frank: Why? Did you invite him?

Diego: You must be joking! You've seen his letters. Does he seem like the kind of guy I would invite to my house?

Frank: Not really.

Ryan: What's it say in his letters?

Ish: Can we read them, too?

Diego: Hey, I didn't save them!

Frank: *(in a singsong voice)* But he's your pen pal!

Diego: It's a class project, okay? If you had Mrs. Mooney for English, you'd have to write to a pen pal, too. Only you'd probably be lucky and get a *normal* person for your pen pal!

Ryan: So what's so abnormal about this . . . what's his name?

Frank: *(singsong)* Marcellus!

Diego: Well, for one thing, he types all his letters on an actual old-fashioned typewriter. You can tell because the "a" is always jumping up and the "o's" are filled in with ink.

Ish: Wow! What a weirdo! I mean, lock the guy up!

Ryan: Yeah, he shouldn't be loose in society.

Diego: Okay, okay! That's not all that's strange about him. He also collects milk bottles like they used back in the day when a milkman came to your door. And he is *way* into his collection, let me tell you.

Frank: Tell them about his lessons.

Diego: Yeah, he takes all kinds of lessons.

Ish: So? I take piano lessons.

Ryan: *(muttering)* What a waste of money!

Frank: But this guy takes lessons in ballroom dancing, yoga, basket making, and . . . what else?

Diego: Glass blowing, needlework, and gourmet cooking. Plus lessons in playing the accordion.

Frank: Oh, and the tuba, too.

Diego: And he's reading the encyclopedia volume by volume. For the third time!

Frank: I couldn't believe that letter he wrote about Volume C.

Diego: Don't remind me!

Frank: Castanets . . . cement . . . Chattanooga . . . civil defense—

Diego: I *said,* don't remind me!

Ryan: Gee, he sounds like a real fun guy.

Ish: Why is he coming here?

Diego: I don't know! I didn't ask him to come! *(pulls out letter and flaps it around)* I just got this letter from him that says he's coming to visit over spring break. And he's arriving today!

Ish: Hey, that letter isn't typed.

Diego: Well, it's the only one that he's written by hand.

Frank: Gee, he has lovely penmanship!

Diego: Who cares? He's coming *here*!

Ryan and Ish: Today?

Scene Two

Narrator One: Diego's friends wanted to leave before Marcellus arrived, but Diego implored them to stay.

Diego: I what?

Narrator Two: Begged them to stay.

Diego: Oh. *(in a stilted manner)* Yeah. Don't leave, guys. Okay?

Frank: *(to Ryan and Ish)* That didn't sound like begging to me.

Ryan: No, it didn't.

Ish: Not at all.

Narrator One: Anyway, the guys all waited in Diego's room.

Narrator Two: When they heard the doorbell, they thought about making a run for it.

Diego: It's too late for that!

Bonita: Hey, Diego, your friend is here.

Diego: He's not my friend.

Bonita: Then who is he?

Frank: Who knows, Bonita? Can one person ever truly know who another person is?

Bonita: Of course! Just ask their name. Then you know them. *(to Diego)* Aren't you coming downstairs?

Diego: Maybe.

Bonita: What do you mean by that? You *have* to come downstairs. He's *your* friend.

Diego: No, he's not.

Bonita: *(exasperated)* Well, then who *is* he?

Frank: Who knows? Can one person ever truly—

Bonita: I'm leaving while I'm still sane.

Diego: Too late!

Bonita: *(pouting)* I'm telling Mom and Dad. *(leaves)*

Narrator One: At that point, Diego could still hope that Marcellus wouldn't be as repugnant as he sounded in his letters.

Diego: Repugnant?

Narrator Two: You know . . . disgusting, repulsive, that kind of thing.

Diego: Oh.

Narrator One: But soon all hope vanished!

Scene Three

Mom: *(enters with Marcellus)* Diego, here's your friend, Marcellus, come to visit.

Marcellus: Greetings, gentlemen!

Diego, Frank, Ryan, and Ish: *(flatly)* Hi.

Mom: Diego, aren't you going to introduce everybody?

Diego: *(speaks quickly, running words together)* This is Frank, Ryan, and Ish.

Marcellus: I am pleased to make your acquaintances. *(shakes hand with each one)* Frank . . . Ryan . . . Dish . . .

Ish: That's Ish.

Marcellus: I do beg your pardon, Zish.

Ish: Ish! Ish!

Marcellus: Thanks ever so much for correcting me, Ish Ish.

Ish: *(to Diego)* I need to go home.

Diego: *(to Ish)* No, you don't!

Ish: *(to Diego)* But I feel sick.

Diego: *(to Ish)* Join the club!

Marcellus: It's a privilege to finally meet you, Diego, and shake your hand.

Mom: *(simpering)* Isn't he such a gentleman?

Diego: *(reluctantly takes and shakes Marcellus's hand)* Nice to meet you.

Mom: Well, I'll leave you boys now. Have fun!

Diego: Thanks, Mom.

Frank: We certainly will!

Ryan: Sure thing!

Ish: Right!

Narrator One: But every person in that room *knew* that a cloud of doom and despair hung over their little gathering.

Narrator Two: Every person but one.

Marcellus: Guess what, guys? I brought my accordion!

Scene Four

Narrator One: When Marcellus asked for help bringing his luggage upstairs, all the guys volunteered.

Narrator Two: Probably hoping to slip away into the darkness.

Diego: It was morning!

Narrator Two: It's a figure of speech, okay?

Narrator One: But no one could get away because Marcellus had something for each one to carry. Besides his accordion, he had two large suitcases, a briefcase, a telescope, and a brown paper sack full of books.

Frank: *(picks ups sack)* Man, this sack is heavy! What's in here?

Marcellus: Only the essentials: a dictionary, a thesaurus, an almanac, and Volumes D through G of the encyclopedia. *(Narrator One sneaks up and slips thesaurus into sack)*

Frank: *(sarcastic)* Oh, okay. Just as long as it's something necessary for your survival. *(sets sack out of the way)*

Narrator Two: For quite some time—

Diego: Hours and hours!

Ryan: No, day after day!

Ish: It seemed like years!

Narrator Two: Marcellus entertained everyone with his accordion.

Ryan: *(to audience) His* music lessons were a waste of money, too.

Marcellus: Would you like to hear my rendition of "The Flight of the Bumblebee"?

Others: No!

Marcellus: Well, then. Shall we peruse my album?

Ish: What's "perusing"?

Marcellus: Ha ha ha! I see you are quite a wit, Ish Ish.

Ish: I'm Ish, not Ish Ish!

Marcellus: Oh, do forgive my error, Mish!

Ish: *(to Diego)* I'm sick. Really. *(coughs weakly)* Please. Ple-e-ease let me go.

Diego: No way! *(to Marcellus)* What's in your album, Marcellus?

Marcellus: Something that you've been dying to see, Diego.

Diego: What's that?

Marcellus: Photographs of my milk bottle collection! All 317 of them!

Diego: Hey, wait a minute! Isn't it time for lunch?

Ish: Why, you're right!

Ryan: It's actually *past* time for lunch.

Marcellus: You eat lunch at 10:30?

Diego: It's like the . . . uh . . . custom around here.

Frank: Maybe you read about it in Volume C of your encyclopedia.

Marcellus: Hmmm . . . no, I don't believe I did, but let me think . . . Cuba . . . cucumber . . . cuneiform . . .

Ryan: Man, I'm starving!

Ish: Me, too!

Diego: I guess your album will just have to wait, Marcellus.

Marcellus: That's quite all right! I'm always glad to set aside my other activities for a foray into the culinary arts.

Diego, Frank, Ryan, and Ish: Huh?

Narrator One: He's going to cook for you.

Diego, Frank, Ryan, and Ish: *(worried)* Cook?

Marcellus: Indeed! I am an excellent cook! Follow me to the kitchen, fellows!

Diego: I feel sick.

Ish: Hey, that's my line.

Scene Five

Narrator One: It turned out that Marcellus had also brought along a box of food that he left in the kitchen.

Narrator Two: Food? I don't know that I'd call it food!

Marcellus: You guys just relax while I prepare my secret recipe!

Diego: You know, I think we have some peanut butter and jelly.

Ryan: My favorite!

Ish: Love that p.b. and j.!

Frank: Now, guys, let's give Marcellus a chance. It'll be nice to have something different to eat.

Diego: That depends on how different it is!

Marcellus: Oh, don't worry—it's quite unusual. And nutritious, too!

Narrator One: The guys watched as Marcellus took things out of his box.

Narrator Two: Brussels sprouts, a can of peas, various spices, a bag of rice, a foil-wrapped . . . something, and a jar of . . . red, slimy, who knew what?

Diego: *(nervously)* Hey, Marcellus, what's in this secret recipe of yours?

Marcellus: *(shaking his head sadly)* Diego, Diego, Diego! If I *told* you then it wouldn't be a secret anymore, would it?

Diego: Well, I guess not.

Marcellus: Diego, Diego, Diego! You *(making finger quotation marks)* "guess" it wouldn't be a secret?

Diego: Yeah, I guess.

Marcellus: But it wouldn't really be a *(finger quotations)* "guess" now would it?

Diego: I guess not.

Narrator One: *(to Narrator Two)* What's that thing he's doing with his fingers? *(copies Marcellus)*

Narrator Two: Those are quotation marks.

Narrator One: Oh, really? I don't think I've ever seen that before.

Narrator Two: By putting quotation marks around the word "guess," *(makes finger quotations himself)* he's showing that the word doesn't really mean what it usually means. In fact—

Diego: Excuse me! Performing a play here!

Narrator One: Go ahead.

Narrator Two: Don't let us stop you.

Diego: Now where were we?

Marcellus: I was saying that if I told you my recipe then it wouldn't be a secret, would it?

Diego: I guess not.

Marcellus: *(shaking head)* Diego, Diego, Diego! Your choice of—

Diego: *(grabbing Marcellus by the collar)* Marcellus, Marcellus, Marcellus!

Frank: Come on, Diego. Don't kill the cook!

Diego: *(letting go)* Sorry, Marcellus!

Marcellus: I quite understand. It's almost 10:45. You must all be starving!

Frank: Yeah, we sure are.

Ryan: I'm not! I'm not hungry at all!

Ish: Me neither!

Marcellus: *(disappointed)* Really? I do hope you'll at least taste my special dish!

Ryan: That depends. Is the slimy stuff in that jar going into it?

Marcellus: Why, yes! That's a very important ingredient.

Ish: What is it? Some kind of hot sauce?

Marcellus: Heck, no! I mean . . . certainly not! A good recipe need not be drowned in unnecessary sauces. And anyway, I have a rather sensitive stomach. I can't even put ketchup on my food.

Ish: So what *is* that slimy stuff?

Marcellus: *(shaking head sadly)* Mish, Mish, Mish!

Ish: *(grabbing Marcellus by the collar)* Call me Ish!

Marcellus: Is that some sort of nickname?

Frank: *(pulling Ish away)* Hey, maybe we should all wait in the living room while you fix lunch, Marcellus. So we don't see your cooking secrets.

Marcellus: I think that is an excellent idea, Frank.

Narrator One: So the guys cleared out of the kitchen and gathered in the living room. Immediately, Diego's *(making finger quotation marks and smiling proudly at Narrator Two)* "friends" started talking about leaving!

Narrator Two: Like rats deserting the sinking ship!

Scene Six

Ish: I think maybe I'll just go home for lunch.

Ryan: Yeah, me, too.

Diego: You can't go and leave me with that . . . that . . . Marcellus! Please, please, please don't go!

Frank: Now *that* sounded like begging.

Ryan: Yes, it did.

Ish: Indubitably! *(everyone looks at Ish, shocked)* Hey, I know how to use a thesaurus, too.

Diego: I know what's going to happen. Even if you guys stay here today, you'll never come back, will you? I'll be stuck with the pen pal from the Planet of the Freaks for the whole vacation!

Frank: Maybe.

Diego: What do you mean "maybe"?

Frank: We-e-ell . . . I have an idea for how to get rid of Marcellus.

Diego: You do?

Frank: In fact, I have a great idea.

Diego, Ryan, and Ish: You do?

Diego: So what is it?

Frank: What's it worth to you?

Diego: You're going to charge me?

Frank: I'm not asking for money.

Diego: Then what?

Frank: We-e-ell . . .

Diego: Oh, no! No, no, no. Not that! No! No way, man. Uh-uhn! Nosireebob! N-O, no!

Frank: *(to Ryan and Ish)* Did you see that one long package Marcellus had? You know, the one that was wrapped in foil?

Ish: Yeah, what *was* that?

Frank: I don't know, but I think I saw it move!

Diego: Okay, take it! It's just a stinking baseball! Nolan Ryan probably didn't really sign it anyway, you know! I bet my dad signed it himself right before he gave it to me.

Frank: Diego, you *saw* Nolan Ryan autograph it!

Diego: Well, the guy *did* look a lot like Nolan Ryan, but who knows?

Ryan: Yeah, right!

Diego: So anyway, what's your idea, Frank?

Frank: Okay, everybody, listen up because you all have a part to play.

Scene Seven

Narrator One: After everyone heard Frank's plan, they had to admit it was brilliant!

Narrator Two: As soon as Marcellus called that lunch was ready, they put "Operation Lose-the-Geek" into motion.

Marcellus: Voila! May I present: Stir-fry Marcellus!

Diego: Hey, that smells good!

Ryan: It sure does!

Frank: It looks great!

Ish: Let's dig in!

Narrator One: They all started eating right out of the dish! Marcellus just sat there, looking disgusted.

Diego: Wait! Everybody stop!

Frank: What's the matter, Diego?

Diego: We forgot something!

Frank, Ryan, and Ish: *(laughing)* Oh, man! Can you believe it? etc.

Marcellus: Ha ha. I thought something was missing.

Diego: It sure is! The Volcano-on-the-Sun hot sauce!

Frank: We put it on everything.

Marcellus: Everything?

Diego: I'll just pour some on your stir-fry.

Ryan: That wasn't enough.

Diego: Okay, I'll add some more. Mmm . . . that looks good.

Ryan: This stuff is great on ice cream.

Marcellus: It is?

Ish: And in chocolate milk!

Diego: There's nothing like a volcano sandwich!

Frank: I love to dip donuts into it!

Marcellus: I'm sure it's quite delicious, but I don't believe I care for any so maybe I'll just have that peanut butter and jelly you mentioned.

Diego: *(angry)* What's the matter? Volcano-on-the-Sun isn't good enough for you?

Marcellus: No, I didn't mean—

Frank: Oh, so you think you're better than us?

Marcellus: I didn't say—

Ryan: And here I thought you were so nice! You're nothing but a snob!

Marcellus: I told you that I can't—

Ish: Don't call me "Ish!" Don't call me anything! I don't ever want to speak to you again!

Marcellus: Listen!

Diego: I think you've said quite enough, Marcellus. Maybe you should go.

Marcellus: But . . . but . . . but . . .

Frank: Look, are you going to sit here and eat this lunch with us?

Marcellus: No! I can't stand—

Diego: Stop right there, Marcellus! There is no need to get personal. Please just get your things and go.

Narrator One: So Marcellus called home for a ride and gathered his things while the guys disposed of his eponymous stir-fry. Down the garbage disposal!

Ryan: It sure was eponymous! Man, it stank to high heaven!

Ish: It was even more eponymous with all that hot sauce on it. Talk about disgusting!

Frank: Totally eponymous! That stuff was not meant for weak stomachs, I'll tell you that!

Narrator One: *(disgusted)* The dish is eponymous because it's named after somebody. That's what "eponymous" means. Get it? "Stir-fry Marcellus" is named after Marcellus so it's eponymous.

Diego: It sure is! And so is his name. I hate that name!

Ryan: Marcellus! How eponymous is that?

Narrator Two: Anyway, the guys stayed in the kitchen until they heard Marcellus leave. Then Diego went and got his Nolan Ryan baseball and paid his debt to Frank.

Narrator One: Then they made themselves a *real* lunch.

Scene Eight

Ish: Love that p.b. and j.!

Diego: You know, guys, I feel kind of bad about getting rid of Marcellus like that.

Frank: He was annoying!

Ryan: And strange!

Ish: And he couldn't say my name right! I mean, how hard can it be? Three little letters!

Diego: But he didn't mean to be like that. I'm sure he's really a nice person. Look at how friendly he was—playing his accordion and all.

Frank: Yeah, right.

Diego: And he wanted to make lunch for us. That was nice.

Ryan: If you like eating food that looks regurgitated!

Diego: Well, he tried. He tried to be nice. We shouldn't have treated him like that!

Frank: We? What do you mean "we"? *You're* the one who wanted to get rid of him. You wanted it so badly that you were willing to give up your most prized possession! *(holds up ball)*

Diego: *(muttering)* I don't think that guy was the real Nolan Ryan.

Bonita: Hey, Diego, there's somebody here to see you.

Ish: Oh, no! Do you think he came back?

Ryan: We can escape out the back door.

Frank: Who is it, Bonita?

Bonita: Oh, I don't know, Frank. Can we ever truly know another person?

Frank: Funny.

Dad: Diego, you have a visitor!

Visitor: Hi!

Diego, Frank, Ryan, and Ish: *(flatly)* Hi.

Dad: Well, Diego, introduce everyone.

Diego: Okay. *(starts out quickly)* This is Bonita, Frank, Ryan, and . . . uh . . . *(slo-owly over-enunciating)* This is Bonita, Frank, Ryan, and Ish.

Visitor: Hi, everybody! *(to Diego)* It's a pleasure to finally make your acquaintance, Diego. We were just passing through, and I asked my parents to stop here a minute. I hope that I'm not disturbing you and your comrades.

Diego: Oh, no problem . . . uh . . . what was your name?

Ish: Yeah, who are you?

Visitor: I beg your pardon! How rude of me! I'm your pen pal, Marcellus.

Frank: Uh-oh!

Diego: *You're* Marcellus?

Frank: Dang! I just remembered that I have this really big dentist's appointment. I have to go right now.

Dad: But you didn't finish your sandwich, Frank.

Frank: I don't have enough time! The dentist is waiting!

Dad: Maybe you'll want that sandwich later. Do you want me to wrap it up for you?

Frank: No, thanks! I won't be able to eat anyway! Dental work, you know! Well, bye!

Diego: *(with power and threat in his voice)* Hold it right there! If *this* is Marcellus, then who was that other guy?

Frank: Heh, heh. You're going to die laughing when I tell you.

Diego: Try me.

Frank: *(mutters something)*

Diego: *(shakes head sadly)* Frank, Frank, Frank! It's no use trying to hide the truth.

Frank: It was my cousin, okay? It was just supposed to be a joke, okay? He was going to pretend to be your pen pal and freak you out, okay?

Diego: Oh, is that all? What about the part where I gave you my Nolan Ryan baseball?

Dad: What? You gave him your Nolan Ryan baseball? Are you nuts?

Frank: I'm not keeping it. Here, Diego. You can have it back. It wasn't part of the plan anyway. I just got the idea to try that when Josh talked about the hot sauce. He reminded me about how much he hates the stuff, and I figured . . . well . . . you know.

Diego: You figured you might as well cheat your best friend out of his most prized possession?

Frank: *(quietly)* Something like that.

Dad: Will somebody please tell me what's going on?

Visitor: I haven't the foggiest idea, but my parents are waiting in the car for me, so I'll have to go without unraveling this fascinating mystery. It was a pleasure to meet you all.

Dad: I'll walk you out, Marcellus.

Visitor: Ta ta!

Diego, Frank, Ryan, and Ish: *(flatly)* Bye.

Bonita: I don't understand. Who *are* all these people? *(looks at Frank expectantly, shakes head and leaves when he doesn't take the bait)*

Frank: Listen, Diego, I only meant it as a joke. Those letters were so strange that I started thinking about what this Marcellus guy might be like—in person! I talked Josh into impersonating him, just for fun, you know! You have to admit he did a good job. If you think about it, this is like the best joke ever! It was funny! Really funny!

Diego: Ha. Ha.

Ryan: It *was* funny how he brought all that ridiculous stuff with him.

Frank: And that wasn't easy! It took us forever to make that album with the pictures of the milk bottles. We had to spend hours in the Milk Bottle Museum.

Narrator One: *(to Narrator Two)* There's a milk bottle museum?

Narrator Two: *(shrugs)*

Ish: Hey, does Josh really know anything about playing an accordion?

Frank: No! That's the great thing! He borrowed that from his grandfather and practiced on it for hours!

Diego: *(grudgingly)* I guess it was kind of funny the way he kept messing up Ish's name.

Frank: That was my idea!

Diego: Oh, yeah, right! Sure it was!

Ish: Hey, if the joke was on Diego, then why pick on me?

Ryan: Yeah, why did we have to suffer?

Frank: It was just funnier that way!

Diego: Wait a minute! I just realized something. *(to Frank)* You wrote that last letter, didn't you?

Frank: *(pretending modesty)* Okay, I admit it. That perfect penmanship was mine!

Diego: You really put a lot into this thing, didn't you?

Frank: *(fake-serious)* Yes, I did. I wanted it to be the biggest, bestest, funniest prank ever! For you, man. For you.

Diego, Ryan, and Ish: *(stare at Frank a moment, then burst out laughing)*

Frank: *(to Diego)* So we're okay?

Diego: Yeah, we're okay.

Narrator One: So the guys ended up having a great spring vacation.

Narrator Two: One day, they even got together with Marcellus and Marcellus.

Narrator One: That's Josh and Marcellus.

Narrator Two: The real Marcellus *was* a bit offbeat, but he turned out to be a pretty fun guy.

Diego: And I probably wouldn't have given him a chance before. But Frank's prank made me realize something.

Frank: Like what?

Diego: We-e-ell. Someone can be different and still make a good friend. *If* you get to know the person.

Frank: That was my plan all along—to teach you an important life lesson!

Diego, Ryan, and Ish: Yeah, right! Sure! etc.

Diego: Anyway . . . people can surprise you. Like Marcellus! The *real* Marcellus, I mean. He's a wizard on that accordion!

Ryan: You know, *some* people actually learn something at *their* music lessons.

Frank: Yeah, *some* people play actual music on *their* instruments.

Ish: *(mad)* Is that a dig?

Diego: Don't let them bother you. Just relax. Fish. *(takes off with Ish in pursuit)*

14

Revenge Served Cold

Summary

Tracie and Megan decide they're tired of the pranks their brothers, Crockett and Josh, keep playing on them. With the help of a friend, the girls plot their revenge. Now all they have to do is get the boys out of their room so they can put their plan into action!

Costumes/Props/Sets

All characters can wear contemporary clothing.

Seats or stools should be arranged in three groups: two together for the narrators, three together for the girls, and three together for the boys.

The use of actual props will give away some of the surprises in the play, so all props should be mimed.

Presentation

Mom and Dad should enter and exit as needed. Kennedy and Lane can enter when first needed, then remain on stage.

In Scene Three, the girls should pretend to plot together as the boys are talking in their room. Otherwise, when action is happening in one "room," the actors in the other room should freeze.

Supplemental Reading

Naylor, Phyllis Reynolds. *The Boys Start the War.* New York: Yearling Books, 2002.

———. *The Girls Get Even.* New York: Yearling Books, 2002.

———. *The Girls' Revenge.* New York: Yearling Books, 1999.

Spinelli, Jerry. *Who Put That Hair in My Toothbrush?* Boston: Little, Brown & Company, 2000.

Cast of Characters

Narrator 1 (girl)

Narrator 2 (boy)

Tracie and Megan, sisters
Crockett and Josh, their brothers
Mom
Dad
Kennedy, friend of Tracie and Megan
Lane, friend of Crockett and Josh

Revenge Served Cold

Scene One

Narrator 1: Some girls live happy lives. They smile. They laugh. They turn their faces to the sunshine and feel glad to be alive. These are the girls who don't have brothers.

Narrator 2: Oh, yeah? Well, there are happy boys in this world, too. You know, guys who get to use their own bathrooms once in a while. Guys who never have to look at cute little stuffed animals or listen to sickening love songs. Guys without sisters.

Narrator 1: Right. Anyway, this is the story of two of the *un*happy girls, sisters Tracie and Megan. Their brothers, Crockett and Josh, are ruining their lives.

Narrator 2: Crockett and Josh are *un*happy, too, because they have two sisters who are ruining *their* lives.

Narrator 1: Whatever. Our story begins on a rainy Saturday morning when Tracie and Megan are cleaning their room.

Tracie: Tell me, Megan: why do we let this place get so messy?

Megan: I guess we're slobs. I'll clean off the dresser if you check under the beds.

Tracie: Okay. Maybe I'll find my library book.

Narrator 1: Poor, innocent Tracie! She was just looking for a book. Instead, she found . . . horror!

Tracie: *(screams)*

Megan: What's the matter?

Tracie: Th-th-there's something under there! Something mushy!

Megan: What is it?

Tracie: I don't know! You look!

Narrator 1: Megan knelt down, lifted the bedspread, and looked under the bed.

Megan: Ew! That is disgusting!

Narrator 1: Carefully, Megan pulled out a slice of moldy pizza and threw it away.

Dad: What's going on in here?

Mom: Are you girls okay?

Tracie: No, we're not okay. Look in the wastebasket.

Dad: What in the world is that?

Megan: It's a slice of pizza that Crockett and Josh left under Tracie's bed.

Mom: Boys! Get in here!

Tracie: I am so sick of them doing stuff like that!

Megan: Me, too. They should be grounded for life.

Dad: Thanks for your advice, but your mother and I can make our own decisions.

Tracie: Well, I hope you decide to ground them for life!

Scene Two

Narrator 1: Crockett and Josh tried to look innocent as they walked into the room.

Narrator 2: Hey, maybe they *were* innocent!

Narrator 1: I doubt that.

Crockett: Did you call us, Mom?

Mom: Yes, I did. What do you know about this?

Josh: It's a trashcan.

Dad: None of your jokes, young man. How did that moldy pizza get under your sister's bed?

Crockett: Gee, Dad, how would we know?

Josh: Maybe Tracie left it there in case she wanted a snack later.

Crockett: Yeah, and then she forgot about it.

Tracie: I did not!

Mom: You girls did have pizza in here a couple of weeks ago, didn't you?

Megan: But we put the leftovers in the fridge, Mom.

Tracie: We never leave food in here any more. Not after the attack of the ants!

Crockett: *(to Josh)* That was so cool.

Josh: *(to Crockett)* Yeah.

Mom: Boys, do you promise me that you didn't put that pizza there?

Crockett: Yes, Mom.

Josh: We promise!

Dad: We-e-ell . . . all right.

Tracie: You mean you're not going to punish them?

Mom: Honey, you probably just forgot the pizza and left it there yourself.

Tracie: Yeah, sure.

Dad: Well, that's settled. Now I can get back to relaxing. Please—no more screaming.

Narrator 1: Everybody left Tracie and Megan alone in their room.

Tracie: I can't believe it! That's what always happens. They get away with everything!

Megan: Well, I'm tired of it! And I say we do something about it!

Tracie: Like what?

Megan: I say we get revenge. You know, teach them a lesson!

Tracie: Yeah! Maybe they'd stop bugging us if they knew their actions had consequences.

Megan: Ooh, impressive vocabulary! Now let's think this out and make a good plan.

Tracie: Revenge! *(evil laugh)*

Megan: Revenge! *(evil laugh)*

Scene Three

Narrator 1: They say that revenge is a dish best served cold.

Narrator 2: Like leftover pizza!

Narrator 1: So Tracie and Megan planned very carefully. They wanted to get back at their brothers . . .

Megan: Revenge! *(evil laugh)*

Narrator 1: But they wanted their revenge to be a total surprise.

Tracie: That way it will pack a really big punch.

Megan: Yeah, it'll shake them up so much that they'll never bother us again!

Tracie: Okay, so what do we do?

Megan: Hmmm . . . let me think.

Tracie: Hey! We could . . . we could . . . let me think, too.

Megan: We could leave some pizza under their bed!

Tracie: Yeah! We could give them back that moldy slice of pizza.

Megan: Good idea! Get it out of the wastebasket.

Tracie: I'm not touching it!

Megan: Well, neither am I.

Tracie: Okay, let's think of something else.

Megan: Okay.

Tracie: We could steal all their underwear and hide it.

Megan: Would they care?

Tracie: Probably not.

Megan and Tracie: *(think a minute)*

Tracie: You know . . . we're not very good at this evil scheming stuff, are we?

Megan: No, I guess not. If only there was someone to help us plan our revenge . . . someone with a devious mind and a cold heart . . . someone who—

Kennedy: Are you guys talking about me?

Tracie and Megan: Kennedy!

Narrator 1: Ever since Kennedy had moved in next door, she had been the sisters' best friend. Kennedy was friendly, nice, fun, and best of all, smart!

Kennedy: Why, thank you. *(to girls)* Your mom said to come on up. I hope that's okay.

Tracie: Okay? It's great!

Megan: We are so glad to see you!

Tracie: We really need your help with our big plan.

Kennedy: Would that be a devious and coldhearted plan?

Megan: Yep!

Kennedy: Okay, I'm in.

Scene Four

Narrator 1: Megan and Tracie told Kennedy how Crockett and Josh were ruining their lives. They even showed her the pizza sitting in the wastebasket.

Kennedy: Is that mold growing on those mushrooms?

Megan: Yes, it's mold.

Tracie: But I don't think those are mushrooms.

Kennedy: Ew!

Tracie: Can you help us?

Kennedy: You bet I can. I have some fantastic ideas for revenge.

Megan: Revenge! *(evil laugh)*

Tracie: Hey, enough of that already!

Megan: Excuse me! *(does evil laugh very quietly)*

Tracie: Megan!

Megan: Okay, okay! So, Kennedy, tell us your ideas.

Narrator 2: Meanwhile, the guys were in their room, enjoying a moment of quiet pride over their successful prank.

Crockett: *(shouting)* Awesome! We did it again!

Josh: *(shouting)* I can't believe it! That was great!

Crockett: The girls were so mad!

Josh: And Mom and Dad believed us—again!

Crockett: *(with fake sincerity)* You know, Josh, doesn't it seem almost too easy sometimes?

Josh: *(in the same tone)* I know what you mean. It's like there's no challenge anymore.

Crockett: Maybe we should just leave the girls alone. You know—give it all up.

Josh: Yeah, maybe we should.

Crockett and Josh: *(pause, then look at each other and burst out laughing)*

Dad: Hey, what's all the noise in here?

Josh: We were just joking around, Dad.

Dad: Well, stop it. I'm trying to relax, and I need some peace and quiet.

Crockett: Sorry, Dad.

Dad: Why can't you be quiet like your sisters?

Megan: *(evil laugh)*

Josh: *(sarcastic)* Sure, Dad. We'll be just as quiet as the girls.

Dad: You'd better! Don't make me come up here again. *(exit)*

Crockett: Hey, what was with that crazy laugh?

Josh: I don't know, but I didn't like the sound of it.

Crockett: Yeah, it sounded kind of . . . evil.

Josh: Do you think Megan and Tracie could be planning something?

Crockett: You mean, like something to get back at us?

Josh: Yeah.

Crockett: But they never did anything like that before.

Girls: *(burst of laughter)*

Josh: There's a first time for everything, I guess. Maybe we'd better be on our guard.

Crockett: Yeah, I guess you're right. Man! Sisters are such a pain!

Scene Five

Narrator 2: "Sisters are such a pain." How true! How true!

Narrator 1: Whatever. Back in the girls' room, everything was almost ready for the big revenge.

Megan: Okay, are we ready?

Tracie: Let's check the list.

Kennedy: Okay. Crackers?

Megan: Check.

Kennedy: Toothpaste?

Tracie: Check.

Kennedy: Hammer?

Megan: Got it.

Kennedy: Cookies?

Tracie: Right here.

Megan: Let me have one.

Kennedy: Hey, don't eat the cookies! We need them.

Tracie: We don't need the filling in the middle. We can eat that, can't we?

Kennedy: Yeah, I guess you're right. Go ahead. Now then—do we have the perfume?

Megan: Yep.

Kennedy: Potatoes?

Tracie: Check.

Kennedy: Well, I guess that's it then. We just have to wait for them to leave the house.

Megan: Then revenge will be ours.

Tracie: Please don't do that stupid laugh.

Megan: I won't. *(very quietly)* Heh. Heh.

Narrator 1: So the girls waited and waited, but the guys never left their room.

Tracie: They always go out on Saturdays.

Kennedy: So why are they still here?

Narrator 2: Crockett and Josh were still there because they weren't fools. They knew that something was up. They could feel it.

Crockett: Something is up.

Josh: Yeah, I can feel it.

Megan: We have to get them out of here!

Tracie: How?

Megan: I don't know! Any other Saturday they'd be gone all day.

Kennedy: I guess they don't want to go out in the rain.

Megan: What kind of wusses let a few drops of water keep them inside?

Tracie: Hey, maybe we can tell them that Lane called, and he wants them to meet him in the park.

Kennedy: But the phone hasn't rung.

Tracie: Oh, yeah. Wait! I know! You go down to the corner, Megan, and call the house. I'll answer the phone and pretend that it's Lane.

Megan: I'm not going out in that storm!

Tracie: *(coughs)* Wuss!

Megan: What was that?

Tracie: Just a little scratch in my throat.

Kennedy: You two need to learn some patience. Really good revenge takes time.

Megan: Okay. I guess we just have to wait.

Kennedy: We could prepare some of the stuff now. That way if they leave, even for a little while, we can get in and out quickly.

Tracie: Good idea! Give me the hammer!

Megan: And give me the cookies.

Scene Six

Narrator 1: The guys, big wusses that they were, got more and more worried about what the girls might do to them.

Narrator 2: They weren't worried! They were suspicious, being the smart guys that they were.

Narrator 1: Then why did they call Lane and ask him to come over?

Narrator 2: Since they didn't want to leave their room unguarded, they asked their friend to come to them. It makes perfect sense.

Narrator 1: Right.

Lane: So what's up you guys?

Crockett: Shh! We don't want Tracie and Megan to know you're here.

Lane: Why not?

Josh: Because . . . uh . . . why don't we want them to know, Crockett?

Crockett: Because we need his help, okay? And it might be best if his help was secret.

Lane: What's going on?

Narrator 2: The guys explained about their latest prank—and their feeling that something was up with their sisters.

Crockett: Something is up.

Josh: We feel it.

Crockett: They're going to do something to us.

Lane: But what would they—

(Pounding sounds are heard as Tracie mimes using a hammer.)

Crockett: What is that?

Josh: It sounds like they're building something.

Lane: Megan did get an A in Industrial Arts. She could probably build just about anything.

Crockett: Maybe they're just fixing a bookshelf or something.

Josh: I don't think so! They're making something . . . evil. I just know it!

(Pounding stops.)

Mom: *(enters yelling)* What is all the noise up here? *(in normal voice)* Oh, hi, Lane. *(yelling)* Can't you boys be quiet for just a little while so your father can get some rest?

Crockett: But, Mom, we weren't making any noise.

Josh: It was Megan and Tracie.

Mom: Don't try to weasel out of this. Just get quiet and stay quiet!

Crockett: Okay, Mom.

Josh: Yes, ma'am.

Lane: *(muttering)* I don't even live here.

Mom: What was that?

Lane: Yes, ma'am. We'll be as quiet as mice.

Mom: Good! *(exits)*

Josh: Man! I wish we knew what the girls are going to do to us. This waiting around and wondering is driving me nuts.

Lane: Well, they're not going to do anything as long as you guys are here.

Crockett: No kidding! That's why we're stuck in our room on a Saturday.

Lane: What I mean is: you have to leave so that they'll do whatever they're going to do.

Josh: Let's explain this again, and how about you listen this time, Lane?

Lane: No, you listen! You guys leave, see? And the girls think that the room is empty because they don't know that I'm here. I hide in the closet. They come in and do whatever. And I'm a witness!

Crockett: Hey, that's a good idea.

Josh: But don't let them get too far, okay?

Crockett: Yeah, just let them do enough to get themselves in big trouble.

Lane: Okay. Now let's clear a space for me to sit in your closet and keep watch.

Scene Seven

Narrator 1: After Lane was all settled in, Josh asked Mom for permission to go out, while Crockett knocked on his sisters' door.

Megan, Tracie, and Kennedy: *(singsong)* Who is it?

Crockett: Hey, who's in there with you?

Kennedy: Nobody here but us chickens. Buck! Buck!

Crockett: Funny, Kennedy. We're going to the gym for a while. You'd better stay out of our room while we're gone. I mean it! Don't you go in there. Stay out!

Megan: Okay, okay! Just go already.

Narrator 1: The girls watched out the window and made sure that their brothers really left the house. Then they hurried to the boys' room with all their revenge supplies.

Kennedy: We can be in and out of here in no time if we split up the work. Megan, you do the beds. Tracie, you do the drawers. I'll do the other stuff.

Narrator 1: Lane watched through a crack in the closet door, but he couldn't see too well. And things happened so quickly, that before he could decide to jump out and confront the girls, everything was done and they were hurrying out of the room.

Lane: Oh, no. I hope they didn't do too much damage.

Narrator 2: But when Lane looked around the room, he couldn't find any damage at all. In fact, it looked like the girls had cleaned things up!

Lane: I don't get it. They made the beds. I don't think I've ever seen those beds made. Maybe they put something in the dresser drawers . . . No. It looks like they straightened all the clothes up. And, gee, they sure smell good. And . . . and they left a plate of cookies. With a note. "We forgive you. Let's be friends." I just don't get it!

Narrator 1: Lane tried to figure things out while he waited for Josh and Crockett to return, but he couldn't make sense of the girls' strange behavior.

Narrator 2: Like anyone can make sense of girls' behavior.

Narrator 1: Finally, it hit him. Instead of taking revenge, the girls were trying to win their brothers over with kindness!

Lane: Man! What a mean thing to do!

Scene Eight

Narrator 1: When Crockett and Josh returned and found out what had happened, they agreed with Lane.

Josh: It's like they're trying to make us feel bad.

Crockett: I can't believe they'd do that to us!

Josh: Yeah, we're their brothers. Doesn't that mean anything to them?

Lane: I guess not.

Crockett: I never thought they could come up with a dirty scheme like this.

Lane: Hey, give me one of those cookies. I love sandwich cookies!

Crockett: We're not eating their stinking cookies.

Josh: Yeah!

Crockett: Let's put the beds back the way they were.

Josh: Okay.

Crockett: And our clothes.

Josh: Okay. I'll get the beds. You get the dressers.

Narrator 1: Crockett opened a drawer and started messing up the clothes inside.

Crockett: *(sniffs)* What is that smell? Hey, wait a minute! Our clothes smell like perfume.

Lane: Try the other drawers.

Crockett: They're all like that! They must have sprayed every piece of clothing with perfume. We can't wear any of this.

Josh: We'll have to wash everything.

Lane: Hey, check the beds.

Narrator 1: Josh ripped the covers back on his bed and discovered that the sheets were covered with some kind of crumbs.

Josh: What a mess!

Crockett: They're in my bed, too! That is so mean. We would have gotten into bed tonight, all unsuspecting, and wham! Crumbs all over! What is this stuff anyway?

Lane: It looks like crackers. Hey, they broke up a bunch of crackers.

Josh: With a hammer, maybe?

Crockett: I bet! And you thought they were building something!

Josh: That's what it sounded like.

Crockett: Still want one of those cookies, Lane?

Lane: I don't think so.

Josh: Go on. Try one.

Lane: No way!

Crockett: Look, Lane, you were supposed to stop them before they got too far.

Lane: I didn't have a chance!

Josh: You didn't do what you were supposed to do, so you owe us. Try a cookie and tell us what they did to them.

Crockett: Go on.

Lane: Let me smell one first. *(sniffs)* It smells okay.

Josh: Take a bite.

Lane: It tastes okay. Kind of minty actually. Try one.

Crockett: Maybe they stuck something in the middle. Let me open one up.

Josh: Hey, that doesn't look right.

Crockett: Lane! Stop eating that thing! This isn't cream filling. It's . . . it's toothpaste.

Lane: Gross!

Josh: You're not supposed to eat toothpaste!

Lane: Too late!

Crockett: They're trying to kill us! They're actually trying to kill us!

Scene Nine

Narrator 1: The guys rushed over to the girls' room, yelling and stomping the whole way. When they burst in the door, they found Megan, Tracie, and Kennedy calmly reading magazines.

Crockett: Are you trying to kill us?

Josh: You're not supposed to eat toothpaste!

Lane: It's not good for you!

Crockett: Yeah, you're only supposed to use a little bit on your toothbrush!

Josh: You're not supposed to eat it!

Lane: You could really make a person sick with a dirty trick like that!

Dad: *(enters)* Okay, I've had enough of you boys and all your carrying on! All I want is a little quiet on a Saturday. Is that too much to ask? Is it? Is it?

Mom: No, dear, it's not.

Dad: Is it?

Mom: *No*, dear.

Dad: Now I want to know: what is going on with you boys?

Narrator 2: Crockett looked at Josh. Josh looked at Crockett. Then they both looked at Lane.

Dad: Well?

Crockett: We were just playing around, Dad.

Josh: Yeah, we're sorry for being so noisy.

Lane: Really sorry.

Crockett: And we won't disturb you again.

Dad: Well, you'd better not. If your mother or I have to come up here one more time, you *will* be sorry.

All the kids: Yes, sir!

Dad: *(muttering as he leaves)* I work hard all week long. All I ask is to have a little . . .

Scene Ten

Narrator 1: For a moment, there was total silence as Tracie and Megan recovered from their shock. Then Tracie found her voice.

Tracie: Why didn't you guys tell on us?

Crockett: I don't know.

Josh: You could have gotten in really big trouble.

Megan: So? What do you care?

Crockett: *(nobly)* You *are* our sisters.

Kennedy: And anyway—if they told on you then you'd have to explain *why* you did what you did.

Tracie: Right! And since we don't usually play pranks, Mom and Dad would finally have to believe us about all the stuff the guys have been doing.

Josh: Still, you would have gotten into trouble if we told.

Lane: Yeah, you owe them!

Kennedy: Maybe this would be a good time to call a truce.

Lane: Great idea! End it here, why don't you?

Kennedy: No more pranks.

Lane: No more revenge.

Kennedy: And no telling!

Narrator 1: Tracie and Megan whispered together for a while, while Josh and Crockett did the same. Finally, they stopped talking and looked at each other.

Megan: We agree if you agree.

Crockett: Okay. We agree.

Josh: But what about our beds? And our clothes?

Tracie: We always have to clean up after your pranks.

Lane: She's right about that.

Josh: Okay. Just as long as this is the end of everything.

Megan: It is!

Narrator 1: So the guys went back and cleaned things up.

Lane: I wonder how they got the cream out of the middle of these cookies.

Crockett: Just throw them away and help me with these clothes.

Narrator 1: Isn't it nice when brothers and sisters make peace? From now on, they can all live happy lives of joy and harmony. They can smile! They can laugh! They can—

Narrator 2: Aren't you forgetting something?

Narrator 1: What?

Narrator 2: Remember the checklist?

Narrator 1: Yes. So?

Narrator 2: Where are those potatoes? And how long will it be before the guys find them?

Narrator 1: Ew! And what will they look like when they do?

Narrator 2: Now *that* is going to be funny!

Narrator 1: Hey, you're not getting any ideas, are you?

Narrator 2: Maybe.

Narrator 1: Mom! Dad! He's doing it again.

15

Scavenger Hunt

Summary

Whenever Chloe gives a party, it turns into a disaster, but she's determined to try one more time. For her latest get-together, she plans a scavenger hunt, which should be a lot of fun. So why does everything take such a strange turn?

Costumes/Props/Sets

All actors can wear contemporary clothing.

Props may be used if desired, but they are not necessary. The two groups might carry sacks for the hunt and mime all the props.

The actors can sit in a semicircle. If desired, the neighbors' seats could be set apart and the groups of scavengers could walk over to each one as needed.

Presentation

Adrian is annoyed and pouty about not getting to go to his sister's parties. He is angry about Chloe's halfhearted apology in the last scene. Danica has a superior attitude. She is suspicious of Chloe and infuriated that she would give them such an embarrassing list. Mrs. Kovak should play up her shock at the kids' request. In the last scene, the kids become more and more tickled as they tell about their adventures.

Supplemental Reading

Barry, Sheila Anne. *The World's Best Party Games*. New York: Sterling Publishing Company, 1987.

Smotherman, Chuck, ed. *Better Homes and Gardens' It's My Party: Twelve Great Parties You Can Make Yourself*. Des Moines, Iowa: Meredith Books, 2000.

Warner, Penny. *The Kids' Pick-a-Party Book: 50 Fun Themes for Happy Birthdays and Other Parties*. Minnetonka, Minnesota: Meadowbrook Press, 1997.

Cast of Characters

Narrator

Chloe

Jasmine, her best friend

Adrian, her younger brother

Danica

Oliver

Larry

George

Mrs. Fuentes

Mr. England

Mrs. Kovak

Mr. Brewer

Mom, Chloe and Adrian's mother

Scavenger Hunt

Scene One

Narrator: Chloe gives terrible parties. They're . . . disasters! Every single time Chloe has a party, some cloud of doom rolls in, making everything go wrong. Yet, she keeps having one party after another after another. Luckily, she has a good friend who cares enough to try to save her from herself.

Jasmine: Somebody has to tell you the truth, Chloe.

Chloe: About what?

Jasmine: Your parties.

Chloe: What about them?

Jasmine: I'm only telling you this because I care. Your parties are horrible! It's like you're cursed or something.

Chloe: Come on! It's not that bad.

Jasmine: *(to Adrian)* It is, too, isn't it, Adrian?

Adrian: How would I know? I'm just her one-and-only little brother. You know, the one who never gets invited to her parties.

Jasmine: Maybe you should be grateful for that.

Chloe: My parties are fun! Fun!

Jasmine: Oh, yeah? What about your Halloween party? You used wormy apples for bobbing.

Chloe: I didn't know they were wormy.

Jasmine: And neither did anybody else—until they bit into them.

Chloe: Only a few people did that. Pretty soon we realized that the apples were bad, and I stopped that activity.

Jasmine: Too bad the tub leaked and Larry slipped on the water and knocked over the jack-o'-lantern and caught the curtains on fire and—

Chloe: Okay, okay! The important thing is that people had fun.

Jasmine: For maybe fifteen minutes. Then they couldn't wait to get out of your house of horror.

Adrian: Ha! Good one!

Chloe: So one party bombed. Big deal.

Jasmine: One? What about the Valentine's Day party that you had on February 13th?

Chloe: That was a mistake on the invitations. It was supposed to be on the 14th. I wasn't ready when everybody showed up a day early.

Jasmine: That was sad, serving people oatmeal and tomato juice at a Valentine's Day party.

Adrian: I really like oatmeal. If only I had been invited . . .

Chloe: Give it a rest, pest.

Jasmine: And what about that cookout you had last summer? I never saw so many wasps in my life!

Chloe: I can't help it if wasps are attracted to pop.

Jasmine: I'm not saying that you can help any of this, Chloe. You're just doomed or something.

Chloe: No, I'm not. I've had a little bad luck, that's all. But everything is going to change with my next party.

Jasmine: Oh, no! Another one?

Chloe: Yes, another one. And this one is going to be fantastic because I have a great, really fun, awesome idea. People are going to remember this party forever!

Jasmine: That's what we're all afraid of.

Chloe: You'll see.

Adrian: Do I get to come?

Chloe: No!

Scene Two

Narrator: The first thing Chloe has to do is convince her friends to come to another party at her house. Not an easy task!

Chloe: Hey, everybody, take one of these invitations. Here you go, Jasmine. Larry. George, Oliver, and Danica.

Danica: I don't want one.

Chloe: Why not?

Danica: I'm busy that day.

Chloe: You don't even know when it is.

Danica: Yet amazingly I'm quite sure that I'm busy.

Oliver: Me, too.

Jasmine: I might be visiting my grandparents that day.

Chloe: In Hawaii?

Jasmine: Well . . . I . . . uh . . .

Larry: I'm going with her.

Chloe: You guys!

George: Sorry, Chloe. It's just that your parties are so . . . so . . . so . . .

Danica: Rotten.

Jasmine: See? I told you!

Chloe: It'll be different this time. I promise. We're going to have so much fun. My mother told me about how they used to have these really fun parties back in her day.

Danica: Hot diggity.

Chloe: Just listen! They had these scavenger hunts, see? They split into teams and each team got a list of stuff and they went around the neighborhood and asked people if they had any of the stuff and whoever finished their list first won. Doesn't that sound fun?

Jasmine: Hey, my sister did that at a party once. She said it was a blast.

Oliver: I don't know . . .

Chloe: Come on. Give it a try! Please?

Jasmine: You know I'll come. What are friends for?

Larry: I guess I can come, too.

George: What the heck!

Oliver: Okay, I'm in.

Chloe: Danica?

Danica: Oh, all right.

Chloe: Great! Thanks, you guys.

Narrator: *(to audience)* I guess some people never learn.

Chloe: Hey, just give me a chance, will you?

Scene Three

Narrator: The day of the party, an amazing thing happens. Everyone shows up.

Larry: Hi, Chloe.

Jasmine: Hey, the food looks great.

Danica: Are there apples in any of this stuff?

Chloe: No!

Adrian: Hi, everybody!

Chloe: What are you doing here?

Adrian: I'm just saying hi to everybody. Hi, everybody!

Jasmine: Hi, Adrian.

Chloe: Bye, Adrian.

Adrian: Come on, Chloe. Why can't I stay?

Chloe: Because . . . because . . . Because you'll make the teams uneven for the scavenger hunt.

Adrian: But—

Chloe: Okay, everybody, we have to split up into two teams. Who wants to be together?

Oliver: How about George, Danica, and me against you, Jasmine, and Larry?

Chloe: Okay. Now here are the rules. We each get a list of things to find. You have to leave the house to find the things on your list. You can ask the neighbors because my parents already checked with them. Or you can look for a thing outside somewhere. Or you can make a thing yourself if you can figure out how.

Danica: Gee, doesn't that sound fun?

Adrian: I think so.

Chloe: Now where are the lists?

Adrian: There they are on the refrigerator.

Chloe: Okay, Larry, you take this one. And here's your list, Oliver. When I say go, then everybody—

Narrator: But Oliver, George, and Danica take off as soon as Oliver has the list in his grubby, little hands.

Chloe: Hey!

Jasmine: They went left, so let's go right, okay?

Larry: Good idea. Let's go!

Adrian: I wish I could go along to see what happens.

Scene Four

Narrator: Danica, Oliver, and George run right up to Mrs. Fuentes's house next door and ring the bell.

Mrs. Fuentes: Yes? Oh, hello! Are you here for the scavenger hunt?

George: Yes, ma'am.

Danica: Do you have any . . . would you have a . . . hey, what's on that list anyway?

Oliver: The first thing is . . . oh, man!

Mrs. Fuentes: What do you need, dear?

Oliver: Do you . . . do you . . . do you have . . . a toenail?

Mrs. Fuentes: Well, of course, I do!

Danica: Can we have it?

Mrs. Fuentes: I'm afraid it's still attached to my toe.

Danica: Well, we need it.

Oliver: Would you mind clipping it off for us, ma'am?

George: We would really appreciate it.

Mrs. Fuentes: Well, all right. Let me find my nail clippers.

Narrator: Mrs. Fuentes goes inside for a while, then returns with a large toenail clipping in her hand.

Mrs. Fuentes: Here you go.

Danica: Take it, Oliver.

Oliver: You take it.

George: Maybe you could just drop it in the bag, ma'am.

Mrs. Fuentes: Okay, there! Good luck, kids!

George: Thanks!

Narrator: When they reach the sidewalk, Danica snatches the scavenger hunt list out of Oliver's hand.

Danica: This has to be the craziest list I ever saw. How are we supposed to find all this stuff?

George: I guess the list has to be tricky for the game to be fun.

Danica: Tricky? This is ridiculous! Hey, wait a minute. Do both teams have the same list?

Oliver: I didn't notice.

Danica: I bet Chloe gave us a hard list so we'd lose.

George: Chloe wouldn't do that.

Oliver: Yeah, she's too nice.

Danica: Whatever. Let's try the next house.

Scene Five

Narrator: Meanwhile, Chloe, Jasmine, and Larry knock on Mr. England's door.

Mr. England: Well, hello there, Chloe. I guess this is the day of your big party.

Chloe: Yes, Mr. England.

Mr. England: I hope we won't be having another visit from the fire department.

Chloe: No, sir.

Mr. England: So what are you kids looking for?

Larry: Let me check the list. Do you have . . . a grapefruit?

Chloe: A grapefruit? That can't be right.

Larry: That's what it says.

Jasmine: Didn't you make the list, Chloe?

Chloe: No, I had my mom make the lists. I didn't want anybody to say that the hunt was unfair.

Larry: So do you have a grapefruit, Mr. England?

Mr. England: I believe I do. Let me check.

Narrator: While Mr. England is gone, Chloe checks the rest of the list.

Chloe: I don't understand why Mom made a list like this.

Jasmine: It is kind of strange.

Larry: I guess she was just trying to make it fun.

Chloe: I guess.

Mr. England: Here you go—one pink grapefruit.

Chloe: Thanks, Mr. England.

Mr. England: Now, you're going to bring that back later, aren't you? I need it for my breakfast tomorrow.

Chloe: Uh . . . sure.

Mr. England: Okay, then. You kids have a good time.

Kids: Thanks!

Larry: Should we try that house next?

Chloe: Okay. But let's wait and ask for the gallon of milk last, okay?

Scene Six

Narrator: Danica, George, and Oliver stop at Mrs. Kovak's house next, and Danica rings the bell.

Danica: George, you ask her.

George: Not me!

Danica: It's your turn.

George: I don't care! I'm not asking anybody for—

Mrs. Kovak: Can I help you?

Danica: *(hissing)* Go on, George!

George: *(hissing back)* No!

Mrs. Kovak: I'm terribly busy, you know. What is it that you want?

George: *(mumbles)*

Mrs. Kovak: What was that, young man?

George: Pink panties.

Mrs. Kovak: What!

George: We need your panties.

Oliver: Not the ones you're wearing.

Danica: Unless they're pink.

Mrs. Kovak: I beg your pardon!

George: It's just for a game, ma'am. We'll bring them back.

Mrs. Kovak: I cannot believe you young people today. The nerve!

Narrator: Mrs. Kovak slams the door right in their faces. They hear her footsteps stomping away.

Danica: *(sighing)* Let's try next door.

George: Now it's your turn to ask, Danica.

Danica: How about we skip the panties for now and try the next thing on the list?

Oliver: Okay. Hopefully, people won't get so upset about moldy cheese.

Scene Seven

Narrator: Chloe's group is making good progress. They've already scavenged a loaf of bread, a pound of sugar, two tomatoes, and a can of dust spray to add to Mr. England's grapefruit.

Chloe: See? Isn't this so much fun, you guys?

Larry: Yeah, loads of fun.

Jasmine: This bag is getting heavy.

Chloe: Set it down a minute while I ring the bell.

Mr. Brewer: Oh, hello, Chloe.

Chloe: Hi, Mr. Brewer. We're here for the scavenger hunt.

Mr. Brewer: I remember how we used to do scavenger hunts when I was a kid. Isn't it fun?

Larry: Sure.

Jasmine: Right.

Mr. Brewer: So what do you need?

Chloe: A jar of pickles.

Jasmine: A small jar. A very small jar.

Mr. Brewer: Well, let me see what I have. Just a minute.

Chloe: You guys could have a better attitude, you know.

Jasmine: Sorry, Chloe, but this sack weighs a ton.

Chloe: I'll carry it next, okay?

Larry: How many more things do we have to get?

Chloe: Not many. Couldn't you at least try to enjoy this, Larry?

Larry: Hey, Chloe, I started out with an open mind. I really wanted to give you a chance to make up for my near-death experience at your Halloween party.

Chloe: I *told* you I was sorry about that.

Larry: I know, I know. But now I'm afraid of jack-o'-lanterns, and nothing is going to change that.

Chloe: Look, this is different. This is fun.

Mr. Brewer: Here you go!

Narrator: Mr. Brewer hands Chloe the largest jar of pickles she's ever seen.

Chloe: *(grunting)* Thanks.

Larry: Hey, Mr. Brewer, would you happen to have a gallon of milk, too?

Mr. Brewer: Sure thing! Hold on a minute.

Chloe: We were going to get that last, Larry.

Larry: Oh, really? I guess I forgot.

Chloe: Sure.

Larry: What a terrible mistake. Too bad it's your turn to carry stuff.

Scene Eight

Narrator: It's hard to believe, but an hour later, Danica's group only has one item left on their list. They've already scavenged a toenail, a hunk of moldy cheese, a jalapeno, a dirty sock, a can of carrot juice, a belly-button brush, a roll of toilet paper, a dead fly, and even the pink panties.

Danica: Who would have thought that sweet Mrs. Smith would wear a thong?

George: I couldn't believe it! I mean—she reminds me of my grandma.

Oliver: I'm really sick of this stupid game. Let's go back to Chloe's.

Danica: Just one more house and then we'll be able to quit.

Narrator: Since they've worked their way all around the block, they ring the bell at Mr. England's house.

Mr. England: Well, hello there. Are you part of the scavenger hunt?

Danica: Yes, sir. And we only need one more thing.

Mr. England: Oh, really? Well, I hope I can help you out. What do you need?

George: We need a tissue.

Oliver: A used tissue.

Mr. England: What kind of crazy hunt is this?

Danica: We're very sorry, sir, but we didn't make the list. You understand.

Mr. England: Oh, sure. Just wait here a minute.

Danica: I'm going to get that Chloe if it's the last thing I do. Making us ask for all this stupid stuff. She just did it to embarrass us.

George: I don't think she meant it like that, Danica.

Danica: Of course she did! And she's going to pay, let me tell you.

Mr. England: Here you go. It's not used, but it's the only tissue I have.

Danica: But it *has* to be used.

Mr. England: Young lady, that's all I have.

Danica: Well, couldn't you blow your nose on it?

Mr. England: I don't think so.

Danica: But—

Mr. England: I'm going inside now. Good-bye!

George: We can just crumple the tissue up and make it look used.

Oliver: But that would be cheating, wouldn't it?

Danica: Wait a minute! Chloe said we could make the things if we wanted to.

George: So?

Danica: So I'll just blow my nose . . . HONK! There! Now we have everything.

Scene Nine

Narrator: Danica, George, and Oliver rush back to Chloe's house with their sack of . . . uh . . . scavenge.

Danica: Ha! We win! We beat Chloe at her own devious game.

Adrian: Are you guys finished with the scavenger hunt?

Danica: Yep!

George: It wasn't easy, but we got everything.

Adrian: You did? Let me see.

Narrator: Danica is just opening the sack, when Chloe and the others come trudging in.

Danica: We were here first. We win!

Jasmine: *(flatly)* Yippee.

Larry: *(flatly)* What a thrill.

Chloe: Somebody take this sack before I drop it!

Mom: There you are! I just ran to the store for a minute and everyone disappeared. Where have you guys been?

Chloe: We were doing the scavenger hunt, Mom.

Danica: And we finished first. Here's our sack of stuff. We got the sock . . . the toilet paper . . . the toenail . . . the—

Chloe: We got all our stuff, too. See? We have the grapefruit . . . the milk . . . the pickles . . . everything on this list. Hey, wait a minute . . . This sounds like . . . I can't believe it! We were following a grocery list!

Danica: So you just accidentally got the wrong list? Right.

Chloe: No, it wasn't an accident. *Somebody* made sure I got the wrong list.

Adrian: Don't look at me!

Chloe: You told me the lists were on the refrigerator. You set me up!

Danica: He set *us* up. He made another list with all this weird stuff on it.

Adrian: I just *noticed* the lists on the refrigerator. I didn't *make* them!

Chloe: Oh, sure, Adrian. You ruined everything!

Mom: Now, Chloe, that's not true at all.

Chloe: He made us look like idiots out there. It was embarrassing to ask people for pickles and a grapefruit and a gallon of milk and—

Danica: You think that's embarrassing? Try asking a lady for her underwear!

Mom: Did someone actually give you those pink panties?

Oliver: Yes, Mrs. Smith did.

Mom: Oh, my!

Danica: And that repulsive toenail! Why . . . hey . . . hold on . . . I said we had to ask for underwear. I didn't mention pink panties.

Adrian: No, you didn't.

Jasmine: So how did you know, Mrs. Jackson?

Larry: Yeah, how?

Chloe: Mom? Mom! You didn't!

Scene Ten

Narrator: Mouths drop open. Eyes bug out. Everybody stares in shock at the person who is supposed to be the responsible adult.

Mom: Okay, you got me!

George: You mean *you* made those lists?

Mom: Yes, I did.

Adrian: See? You blamed me for nothing.

Chloe: So?

Adrian: So aren't you going to apologize?

Chloe: Sorry.

Adrian: Hey, don't get all brokenhearted or anything.

Chloe: What were you thinking, Mom?

Mom: Well, the stranger the list the more fun you have on a scavenger hunt!

Chloe: Is this really your grocery list?

Mom: *(laughing)* No! It wouldn't be very nice to take advantage of our neighbors like that. I was just having a little fun with you guys. I wondered if you'd notice that you had a grocery list.

Danica: You must have had a lot of fun making up our list.

Mom: I did! I never thought you'd find all that stuff.

Chloe: I bet this was the weirdest scavenger hunt ever.

Larry: Actually . . . it was so bizarre that it was kind of fun.

Oliver: And funny, too. You should have seen the look on Mrs. Kovak's face when George asked for her panties!

Jasmine: And can you believe that Mr. England wants his grapefruit back?

Danica: I wonder if he wants his tissue returned, too.

Oliver: Do we have to give back the toenail?

George: That was so funny! *(in a high voice)* "I'm afraid my toenail is still attached to my toe. Just let me clip it off for you."

Larry: Gross!

Adrian: Can I see the toenail?

Danica: It's in that sack.

Adrian: Where?

Danica: Right next to the moldy cheese. And the dead fly. See it?

Adrian: Cool!

Jasmine: Hey, how about those pickles? There's like a lifetime supply in that huge jar!

Mom: You know, Chloe, I think your friends are having a good time at this party.

Chloe: I think you're right. Wow! Thanks, Mom.

Mom: You're welcome.

Jasmine: Hey, Chloe, I'm sorry about that stuff I said. This is a greatest party ever!

Chloe: Thanks, Jasmine.

Mom: Time to eat, everybody!

Narrator: So it looks like Chloe's party curse has finally lifted. Everyone's having fun. There's no need for emergency services. And the food looks to be free of worms.

George: Man, this cheese is delicious.

Larry: Yeah, what is that flavor?

Mom: Cheese? I didn't put out any cheese.

Chloe: Hey, what's that white thing on top of the cake?

Oliver: What white thing?

Chloe: That little, white, curvy thing there. It looks like . . . Adrian! Adrian, where are you? I'm going to get you!

Danica: Please tell me that there were raisins in the cookie I just ate.

Chloe: Adrian!

16

Sherman and the Snakes

Summary

In "Sherman and the Snakes," Tyler feels like his trip to nature camp is being ruined by his classmate, Sherman. Sherman acts like he's never even *been* outdoors! He's terrified by night noises, scared of squirrels, and unable to tell an earthworm from a snake. Then an encounter with one of nature's creatures makes Tyler wonder: Who's the real nature-lover here?

Costumes/Props/Sets

All characters can wear casual attire appropriate to camping: jeans, T-shirts, shorts, etc.

Performers are seated in a semicircle. If desired, they can stand to read and act out their parts. Folded blankets or sleeping bags could be arranged on one side to serve as the cabin and the camping area. Tyler needs a stick for the final scene. Other props are not necessary.

A tape of sounds from nature can be used in Scene Three.

Presentation

Tyler becomes increasingly annoyed with Sherman throughout the play. Sherman is easily upset and excited by what he sees in nature, but he calms down and becomes interested and appreciative once he knows what he's dealing with.

Supplemental Reading

Danziger Paula. *There's a Bat in Bunk Five*. New York: PaperStar, 1998.

Harriott, Ray. *Stories for Around the Campfire*. Laurel, Maryland: Campfire Publishing Company, 1986.

McManus, Patrick F. *Kid Camping from Aaaaiii! to Zip*. Spokane, Washington: McManus Books, 1999.

Cast of Characters

Narrator

Tyler, who never dreamed he'd run into Sherman at nature camp

Amber, counselor at registration desk

Sherman, the biggest dweeb in Tyler's class

Ben, the counselor for Tyler's cabin

Russell, another camper in Tyler's cabin

Carlos, camper in Tyler's cabin

Mike, camper in Tyler's cabin

Josie, the lifeguard

Sherman and the Snakes

Scene One

Narrator: When Tyler signed up for nature camp, he thought that he'd be enjoying the great outdoors.

Tyler: Yeah, I thought I'd observe wildlife.

Narrator: Hike through the woods.

Tyler: Swim in the lake.

Narrator: Breathe fresh air.

Tyler: I thought I'd . . . well, have fun!

Narrator: But little did Tyler know what awaited him at Camp Who-what-to-how-about-that!

Amber: Welcome to Camp Who-what-to-how-about-that!

Tyler: Hi! Here's my registration form.

Amber: You're in Cabin Three, Tyler. Here's a list of all your activities. Have a great time!

Tyler: I will. Thanks!

Narrator: See? Everything started out just fine. But then . . .

Sherman: Tyler! Tyler! Tyler! Hey, Tyler!

Tyler: Oh, no! That's not—

Sherman:—Tyler! It's me! Sherman!

Narrator: Tyler couldn't believe it! Here he was at a camp—three counties away from home!—and Sherman Patterson had found him.

Tyler: What are you doing here, Sherman?

Sherman: It's a nature camp, Tyler. Where you learn about nature. Didn't you know?

Tyler: Of course, I knew! That's why I'm here.

Sherman: Me, too! I want to learn all about nature. I just *love* nature, don't you?

Tyler: Sure. Well, listen, I have to go find my cabin.

Sherman: Hey, what cabin are you in?

Tyler: *(with the voice of a doomed man)* Cabin Three.

Sherman: Oh, wow! So am I! This is so great!

Tyler: *(dully)* Yeah, great.

Sherman: Hey, let's go find our cabin and get unpacked!

Tyler: Yeah, let's.

Scene Two

Narrator: Sherman skipped happily to Cabin Three while Tyler trudged along behind him.

Tyler: How can this be happening to me?

Narrator: When they reached the cabin, they found that all the beds had been taken, except two. Which were right next to each other!

Tyler: Oh, no!

Ben: Hi, guys! Welcome to Cabin Three. I'm your counselor, Ben. This is Russell, Carlos, and Mike.

Russell, Carlos, and Mike: Hi.

Sherman: Hi! I'm Sherman, and this is my friend, Tyler.

Tyler: Hey, wait, that's not right!

Ben: You're not Tyler?

Tyler: Yeah, but . . . never mind.

Ben: You guys can bunk here.

Sherman: Hey, look, Tyler. We can have beds right next to each other.

Tyler: *(sarcastic)* Oh, goody.

Sherman: Isn't that lucky? I can't believe I'll be right here by my buddy!

Tyler: Sherman, I've never even laid eyes on you outside of school!

Sherman: Until now!

Tyler: *(to other guys)* I hardly even know the guy.

Russell: Yeah, right.

Carlos: Sure.

Mike: Uh-huh.

Ben: We'll all be friends by the time you go home.

Russell: Yeah, right.

Carlos: Sure.

Mike: Uh-huh.

Sherman: Fantastic! That is so fantastic! Did you hear that, Tyler?

Tyler: I heard.

Narrator: Things seemed pretty bad to Tyler, but then, he didn't know how terrible things could really get! There was a reason he never saw Sherman outside of school. *Nobody* ever laid eyes on Sherman outside of school. That was because Sherman never spent much time outside at all!

Tyler: How could I have known that the guy had no personal contact whatsoever with nature? After all, we were at a *nature* camp!

Narrator: But that night, Tyler found out the truth about Sherman.

Scene Three

(Russell, Carlos, and Mike snore lightly in the background.)

Narrator: Tyler was sound asleep, dreaming that he was floating above the lake and woods, when . . .

Sherman: Tyler! Tyler! Wake up!

Tyler: *(groggy)* Wh-what?

Sherman: Wake up!

Tyler: What do you want?

Sherman: *(scared)* What's that noise?

Tyler: I don't hear anything.

Sherman: Listen! *(pauses)* Oh, no! There it is again!

Tyler: What are you talking about?

Sherman: Don't you hear that? And that? And, oh, no, what in the world was that? Tyler, I'm too young to die!

Tyler: Sherman, all I hear are some frogs. And crickets. And maybe an owl.

Sherman: Th-that's all?

Tyler: Yep! Well, except for that snoring. Who *is* that? Hey, quiet down, will you?

Sherman: So there's nothing out there that's dangerous or anything?

Tyler: *(disgusted)* No, of course not!

Sherman: Oh. *(pauses and listens)* Gee, it sure is noisy out there!

Tyler: Whatever.

Sherman: You know what, Tyler? It's kind of like a song, isn't it?

Tyler: Yeah, it's music to my ears. Now go to sleep!

Narrator: After Sherman settled back down, Tyler lay awake for a while, listening to the night sounds. He'd never paid much attention to them before, but now he noticed them all. Finally, he fell asleep just like he did when he listened to CD's at bedtime.

Scene Four

Narrator: Cabin Three's first activity the next morning was gardening. Ben showed the guys how to turn the soil and how to weed. Then he made a big mistake.

Ben: Watch out for snakes, guys.

Sherman: S-s-s-snakes?

Ben: Sometimes we find one in the garden.

Sherman: S-s-s-snakes?

Ben: So let's get to work!

Narrator: For a few minutes, everything was peaceful.

Tyler: Man, it's great, being outside like this!

Sherman: Snake! Snake! Snake! Snake! Snake! Snake! Snake!

Narrator: All the guys dropped their hoes and hurried over to see—what was it? Oh, yeah, the snake. Tyler was the first to arrive.

Tyler: Where is it?

Sherman: *(pointing)* There! Snake!

Narrator: Tyler was just in time to see a big earthworm burrowing into the ground.

Ben: Where is it?

Russell: Let's catch it!

Tyler: *(disgusted)* It was just a worm.

Carlos: A worm!

Mike: What's the matter, Sherman? Did the big, old, nasty worm scare you?

Russell: Yeah, you have to watch out for those killer worms!

Ben: You guys get back to work. *(turns to Sherman)* Don't worry, Sherman. Earthworms won't hurt you. And actually, most snakes won't either. We'll be learning about them later.

Narrator: As Ben went back to work, Tyler shook his head at Sherman.

Tyler: I can't believe you!

Sherman: I could swear I heard rattles.

Tyler: *(muttering)* Maybe it was your brain rattling around in your head!

Sherman: *(pointing)* Look, Tyler! There it is again!

Tyler: It's just another worm!

Sherman: You're sure it's not a snake?

Tyler: *(picking up worm)* Positive! It's perfectly harmless. It even helps improve the soil.

Sherman: It does?

Tyler: Sure! Earthworms eat their way through the dirt and leave behind waste that makes the soil richer.

Sherman: Really? Amazing! Let me hold it. Look how its rings bunch together then spread apart! It sure can move for something with no legs.

Tyler: I guess I never thought about that before.

Russell: Did you find another snake over there?

Carlos: Be careful, you guys!

Tyler: *(to Sherman)* So it moves! Big deal! It's just a worm!

Narrator: Tyler walked off, rolling his eyes so that everyone could see he thought Sherman was a big doofus.

Scene Five

Narrator: After their work in the garden, it was Cabin Three's turn to swim in the lake. Everyone jumped into the cool, refreshing water. Tyler floated peacefully near the lifeguard's raft.

Tyler: Aaah, this is so relaxing!

Sherman: Shark! Shark! Shark! Shark! Shark! Shark!

Josie: Sherman, calm down!

Sherman: I'm too young to die!

Narrator: The lifeguard, Josie, had to dive in and pull Sherman to shore. As soon as he hit dry land, he checked himself all over to make sure nothing was missing.

Sherman: I think I'm okay.

Josie: Sherman, there are no sharks in the lake.

Sherman: But I felt something touch my leg!

Josie: Sometimes a little fish will brush up against you. Or maybe you felt an underwater plant.

Sherman: There are plants under there?

Josie: Yes.

Sherman: Poisonous plants?

Josie: No, Sherman. The plants in the lake can't hurt you. And neither can the fish. The lake is perfectly safe, okay?

Sherman: Okay.

Narrator: Josie went back to her station, and Sherman swam over to talk to Tyler.

Sherman: Did you see that?

Tyler: Yeah, I saw it.

Sherman: I thought I was being attacked by sharks! Wasn't that funny?

Tyler: *(flatly)* Yeah. Real funny.

Russell: Hey, Sherman, I think I just saw the Lake Who-what-to-how-about-that Monster swimming around!

Carlos: Yeah, you better get out of the water while you still can!

Mike: Take your buddy Tyler with you!

Tyler: Real funny.

Sherman: There's no monster in this lake! *(pause)* Is there, Tyler?

Tyler: Of course not! Now go away, will you?

Sherman: *(laughing)* You're a riot, Tyler!

Narrator: Over the next few days, Sherman was terrified by killer squirrels, tripped by evil tree roots, and chased by venomous butterflies! Each time, he was very interested to learn about whatever had frightened him, but he never seemed to actually adjust to being out in nature.

Tyler: And he hung around me! Every! Single! Minute!

Narrator: By the time Cabin Three had their overnight campout, Tyler was really sick of Sherman.

Tyler: Well, he's ruining everything! I really love all this nature stuff, but I can't enjoy any of it with Sherman around all the time! He is so annoying! And totally useless!

Narrator: Maybe he'll be different at the campout!

Tyler: As if!

Scene Six

Narrator: At the campsite, Ben told the guys that they could set out their sleeping bags anywhere in the clearing. Tyler moved his several times when he thought Sherman wasn't looking, but Sherman always noticed and moved his sleeping bag right next to Tyler's.

Tyler: You don't have to keep moving your sleeping bag, Sherman.

Sherman: But you keep moving yours so I have to move mine or I won't be next to you anymore because yours isn't where it used to be which was next to mine but it isn't there anymore so—

Tyler: Okay, okay, I get it!

Ben: Who wants to go back to the mess hall with me and help carry our food?

Tyler, Russell, Carlos, and Mike: Sherman!

Ben: *(warning)* Come on, guys.

Mike: Okay, I'll go.

Narrator: After Ben and Mike left, the guys sat around, feeling bored.

Russell: I thought campouts were supposed to be fun.

Tyler: It will be better when Ben makes the fire.

Sherman: *(nervously)* You know, they say the woods can be dangerous at night.

Russell: It's still daylight!

Sherman: But what if Ben doesn't come back?

Tyler: Sheesh! We can see the mess hall through those trees!

Sherman: Oh, yeah. *(pauses)* I can't believe we're going to sleep right out in the open.

Carlos: I know. All kinds of creatures come out at night.

Tyler: Like bats.

Russell: And snakes.

Narrator: Sherman was looking scared, but Tyler was so tired of him that he decided to really rattle his bones!

Tyler: Sometimes things crawl into your sleeping bag with you.

Sherman: Th-th-they do?

Tyler: Have you checked inside your sleeping bag recently?

Sherman: No.

Russell: You'd better do it now. Before anything gets comfortable in there!

Sherman: *(in a small, frightened voice)* Okay.

Narrator: Sherman cautiously approached his sleeping bag and carefully checked inside.

Tyler: *(whispering to other guys)* At least we're rid of him for a minute.

Sherman: Snake! Snake! Snake! Snake! Snake! Snake!

Russell, Carlos: *(laughing)* What an idiot!

Tyler: *(angry)* Man, I cannot believe him!

Sherman: Tyler! It's a *sna-a-a-a-a-ake!*

Narrator: Tyler couldn't take it any more! He jumped up and stomped over to Sherman.

Tyler: What is your problem? You are ruining this whole—

Narrator: But Tyler shut up the second he saw the huge, mean-looking snake coiled up inside Sherman's sleeping bag.

Scene Seven

Sherman: It's big, isn't it?

Tyler: Shhh! Don't talk, Sherman. And don't move!

Narrator: Tyler signaled to Carlos and Russell with his hand. One look at his face, and they came running!

Carlos: Man, that thing is huge!

Sherman: I'm going to move closer and get a better look. It might just be a—

Carlos: It's moving!

Tyler: Oh, no! It's headed for my sleeping bag! *(he snatches up a stick)*

Sherman: *(shrieking)* What are you doing?

Tyler: What does it look like I'm doing? *(he starts to swing downwards)*

Sherman: *(grabs end of stick, stopping Tyler)* Don't, Tyler!

Tyler: Let go, Sherman. Oh, great! Now I have a killer snake *inside* my sleeping bag thanks to you, you big dweebix!

Sherman: It's not a killer. It's a blacksnake like we learned about in Nature Study. It's harmless.

Tyler: That's easy for you to say. It's not waiting to get you!

Carlos: Kill it!

Narrator: V-e-r-y carefully, Tyler unzipped his sleeping bag and flipped it open with the stick. The snake was curled up near the bottom of the bag.

Tyler: Where it can bite my toes off!

Russell and Carlos: Kill it! Kill it!

Sherman: No! You can just scare it away!

Narrator: Tyler took a good look at the snake. Sherman was right—it *was* a blacksnake.

Tyler: It actually looks kind of cool.

Russell: Kill it!

Narrator: But Tyler was thinking. Maybe Sherman had started out with a stupid attitude about nature, but he *was* learning. And who really appreciated nature: a guy who hardly noticed the sounds and sights around him and then was ready to pulverize a harmless creature? Or a guy like Sherman?

Carlos: What are you waiting for?

Tyler: Sherman is right. It would be stupid to kill it.

Narrator: Tyler gently poked at the snake until it slithered off. Then he tossed the stick away.

Ben: Hey, guys, we're back!

Russell: I'm going to tell him about the snake.

Carlos: No, I am!

Narrator: They went off to fill Ben and Mike in on what they'd missed. Sherman turned to Tyler.

Sherman: I don't think this campout is such a great idea.

Tyler: You'll have a good time.

Sherman: Ben says it's really cool, sleeping out under the stars. Have you ever done that before?

Tyler: Well, I've camped out a lot of times, but I'm not sure that I really looked at the stars when I did. But I'm going to this time. It's going to be great.

Sherman: Yeah, I bet you're right. I'm sure glad . . . what's that noise?

Narrator: A woodchuck appeared at the edge of the clearing. Tyler and Sherman stared at the woodchuck. The woodchuck stared back.

Tyler: Don't worry, Sherman. It's just a—

Sherman: I *know* what it is! *(turning to others)* Bear! Bear! Bear! Bear! Bear!

17

The Sick Soda Contest

Summary

In "The Sick Soda Contest," Kevin's friends all know that he has a sensitive stomach. They're always teasing him, and they even *try* to make him sick! When one of the guys suggests a contest to see who can make the worst tasting drink, no one expects Kevin to "survive." But Kevin is determined to show his friends what he's made of, no matter how nauseous he feels!

Costumes/Props/Sets

All characters can wear normal, contemporary attire.

Four seats are needed for the "living room." If props are going to be used, a small table might be added where dishes can be set. A "kitchen" could be set up to one side with a table stacked with various cups, glasses, pitchers, bottles, and utensils for miming the concoction of the sodas.

Presentation

Throughout the play, Kevin should display nausea by swallowing hard, gagging, putting his hand over his mouth, choking, and the like. He should become more and more nauseated as the play progresses.

Until the end of the play, Tran seems totally unaffected by the sick sodas. Throughout the play, Parker and Maleek slowly become more sickened but not to the degree that Kevin is.

At the end of the play, each of Kevin's friends can run from the stage at the appropriate moment. Kevin's parent can enter the kitchen area.

Supplemental Reading

Dahl, Roald. *Roald Dahl's Revolting Recipes*. New York: Puffin, 1997.

Horvath, Polly. *Everything on a Waffle*. New York: Farrar, Straus, and Giroux, 2001.

Masoff, Joy. *Oh, Yuck! The Encyclopedia of Everything Nasty*. New York: Workman Publishing, 2000.

Rockwell, Thomas. *How to Eat Fried Worms*. New York: Yearling Books, 1973.

Thomas, John E., Danita Pagel, and Danita Thomas. *The Ultimate Book of Kid Concoctions: More than 65 Wacky, Wild, and Crazy Concoctions*. Strongsville, Ohio: Kid Concoctions Company, 1998.

Cast of Characters

Narrators 1, 2, and 3

Kevin, known among his friends for his weak stomach

Tran, the "brains" behind the Sick Soda Contest

Parker and Maleek, other friends

Parent, Kevin's mom or dad

The Sick Soda Contest

Scene One

Narrator 1: Kevin had a weak stomach.

Kevin: A *very* weak stomach!

Narrator 2: He couldn't stand the smell of garbage.

Narrator 3: And spicy food made him nauseous.

Narrator 1: And the merry-go-round?

Kevin: I guess you could say it's my favorite ride.

Narrator 2: As long as it's standing still!

Narrator 3: Of course, Kevin's friends were *so* understanding about his problem.

Narrator 1: They were always teasing Kevin about his weak stomach.

Narrator 2: They even *tried* to make Kevin sick!

Kevin: Yeah, like the time we went to the fair.

Maleek: Come on, Kevin! It's just the kiddie roller coaster!

Tran: Yeah, there's a reason they call it "The Turtle"!

Parker: What kind of big chicken are you?

Kevin: Well, Parker . . . *(makes chicken noise)* The biggest!

Narrator 3: But he let them talk him into riding "The Turtle."

Narrator 1: Afterwards, he had to lie on a bench for two hours!

Kevin: And when I finally felt better . . .

Tran: Hey, let's get some fried sausages!

Parker: With onions and peppers!

Maleek: And mustard and ketchup and sauerkraut . . .

Kevin: *(moaning)* Oh, man!

Narrator 2: Kevin's friends were, of course, quite sympathetic when he ran for the bathroom.

Parker: Hey, what's the matter with you?

Tran: Good going, Maleek! I think it was the sauerkraut that got him!

Narrator 3: But none of his friends' tricks prepared Kevin for "The Sick Soda Contest."

Scene Two

Narrator 1: One day when the guys were just sitting around in Kevin's living room, Tran dreamed up something . . . terrible!

Narrator 2: Disgusting!

Narrator 3: Nauseating!

Maleek: So what do you want to do?

Parker: I don't know.

Maleek: This is boring!

Kevin: We can go up to my room and play a game.

Maleek, Tran, and Parker: *(moan)*

Kevin: Well, what do you want to do?

Tran: I know! We'll have a contest! It'll be . . . it'll be . . . I know! It'll be "The First Annual Sick Soda Contest!"

Parker: Sick soda?

Tran: Yeah! See here's what we do: we take turns going into the kitchen and making the most putrid drink we can come up with! And everybody has to drink it! And then at the end, we'll vote on which one was the best . . . I mean, the worst!

Maleek: Yeah!

Parker: Great idea!

Kevin: I don't know, Tran. That doesn't sound very safe.

Tran: Of course, it's *safe*! Because the rule is that you can only use *safe* ingredients that are *safe* for people to consume . . . *safely*! Okay, Kevin?

Maleek: Come on, Kevin. It'll be fun!

Parker: Yeah! What are you afraid of?

Kevin: Nothing!

Tran: Well, then, let's get started. You go first, Parker.

Scene Three

Narrator 1: Parker went to the kitchen and started making his sick soda. From the living room, the guys could hear cabinet doors slamming, the refrigerator opening, and Parker humming happily. Tran and Maleek flipped through some comic books while they waited, but Kevin just sat there, looking sick already!

Tran: Hey, Parker! Hurry up in there! Kevin's thirsty!

Kevin: Real funny, Tran!

Narrator 2: Parker returned to the living room, carrying several glasses on a tray. He set the tray on the coffee table.

Parker: Ta da!

Tran: Hey, wait a minute! There are only three glasses!

Parker: Yeah, so?

Tran: You have to drink it, too!

Maleek: Yeah!

Parker: But . . . but . . . but there's not any left!

Tran: No problem!

Narrator 2: Tran went to the kitchen and came back with a fourth glass. Carefully, he poured a little from each glass into the fourth one. Then he handed around the glasses.

Tran: There you go! Everybody, drink up!

Narrator 3: Nobody took even a sip. They were all too busy peering into their glasses.

Kevin: What's in this?

Parker: It's my secret recipe! Try it!

Kevin: You try it!

Maleek: This smells funny.

Kevin: It disgusting! It smells like . . .

Narrator 1: Kevin covered his mouth, too nauseated to finish the sentence!

Maleek: Mustard! I can't drink this if it has mustard in it! I'm allergic to mustard!

Kevin: *(mutters)* Why didn't I think of that?

Tran: No, you're not! Sheesh, Maleek, you put a gallon of mustard on every hot dog you eat! Right on top of the sauerkraut, right, Kevin?

Kevin: *(moaning)* Don't talk about sauerkraut!

Parker: Let's just get this over with! Come on—on the count of three! One, two, three!

Narrator 2: Gagging and making faces, they all gulped down their sick sodas.

Narrator 3: Even Kevin!

Kevin: That was the worst thing I ever tasted!

Maleek: Wait until you taste my special recipe!

Scene Four

Narrator 1: Maleek took the tray to the kitchen, leaving the used glasses behind. As Maleek worked on his sick soda in the kitchen, Tran held one of the empty glasses right under Kevin's nose.

Tran: Hey, Kevin! There's still a little bit left in this glass. Want it?

Narrator 2: Kevin had to swallow a few times before he could answer!

Kevin: *(with a choking sound)* No thanks!

Narrator 3: Maleek soon returned with four fancy glasses on the tray.

Maleek: Here you are, gentlemen!

Kevin: Hey, those glasses are for company!

Parker: So what are we?

Kevin: We're not allowed to use those! I knew this was a big mistake! Let's just stop this right now and—

Tran: So we'll wash them! Relax!

Maleek: Yeah, relax and have a nice, refreshing soda!

Narrator 1: Maleek handed around the glasses, and everyone carefully examined the new drink.

Parker: This is green.

Maleek: Yes, it is, isn't it?

Kevin: And . . . and . . . *(swallows hard)* chunky-looking!

Maleek: Mm-hmm.

Parker: So what are those chunks?

Maleek: *(mocking)* It's my secret recipe!

Tran: Come on, come on! On the count of three . . . one, two, three!

Kevin: Wait!

Narrator 2: Everyone froze, each with a fancy glass near his mouth.

Tran: What?

Kevin: I think I'm allergic to . . . to . . . to . . . chunks!

Maleek: *(makes chicken noise)*

Kevin: I'm not scared!

Parker: So drink it then!

Tran: Go on!

Narrator 3: As his friends watched, Kevin slowly raised the drink to his lips. Then in one sudden and impressive movement, he drained the glass! After he took the glass from his lips, he had to chew for awhile.

Maleek: Way to go!

Tran: Okay, let's do it, guys. One, two, three!

Narrator 1: The others drank and chewed up their sodas. Just watching them, made Kevin feel sick himself. He wanted to suggest that they declare Maleek the winner and end the contest right then, but he was afraid that if he opened his mouth something besides words would come out!

Tran: That was nothing, Maleek! My sick soda is going to be really disgusting!

Scene Five

Narrator 2: Tran took the empty tray to the kitchen, and the guys slouched on the furniture, holding their stomachs and moaning.

Parker: Is that the blender?

Maleek: *(groans)* Who knows what he's grinding up in there?

Parker: What's that beeping? Is he using the microwave?

Kevin: *(moaning)* Oh, man!

Maleek: Hey, Kevin! You're not getting sick, are you?

Kevin: *(through gritted teeth)* No!

Narrator 3: Tran returned to the living room with coffee cups on the tray. After he passed around the cups, everyone bent down and sniffed.

Kevin: Hey, wait a minute! This is . . . this is . . . warm! Sodas aren't warm!

Parker: Yeah! This isn't soda!

Tran: The first ingredient was grape pop, so it counts. Everybody ready? One, two—

Narrator 1: Suddenly Tran jumped up, a look of horror on his face as he peered into his cup.

Tran: It's alive! Alive!

Kevin: Oh, real funny, Tran. Ha. Ha. Ha.

Parker: Ha. Ha.

Maleek: Yeah, real funny.

Narrator 2: Kevin, Parker, and Maleek peered into their cups ve-e-ery closely, swishing their drinks around. Kevin even stuck a finger in and poked around.

Tran: You guys are such wusses! Now, on the count of three—

Kevin: Wait! We can't drink this fast! It's . . . it's . . . it's . . .

Maleek: Hot!

Parker: Yeah, hot!

Tran: It's not hot! Kevin just stuck his finger in it!

Maleek: Thanks, Kevin!

Tran: It's a little warm, that's all. So get ready: one, two, three!

Narrator 3: Everyone drank. Afterwards, Kevin just lay there, swallowing and shuddering!

Parker: That was disgusting!

Maleek: Gross! I'm going to die!

Tran: That was the worst one yet, wasn't it? So what do you say, Kevin? Just want to forfeit? There's no way you can beat me!

Narrator 1: Kevin tried to sit up, but he felt so nauseous that he couldn't do anything but moan.

Tran: *(in a baby voice)* What's the matter, Kevin-Wevin? Is your tummy upset, wittle fellow?

Parker: *(weakly)* Oh, just leave him alone, Tran.

Tran: I guess I win! He can't even sit up! What a loser!

Narrator 2: Somehow, Kevin managed to struggle into an upright position.

Kevin: It's not over yet, Tran!

Scene Six

Narrator 3: Kevin dragged himself to his feet, picked up the tray, and staggered into the kitchen. When he walked into the room, his mouth dropped open.

Kevin: My parents are going to freak if they see this mess! It looks like there's been a huge food fight! It looks . . . oh, man!

Narrator 1: Kevin put one hand to his stomach and one over his mouth. Then he slowly lowered the top half of his body to the table, turning his head to rest on one cheek. He couldn't help moaning.

Maleek: *(calling to Kevin)* Hey, what's taking so long?

Tran: He's probably on the floor, sick as a dog!

Kevin: I am not!

Parker: He can't help it! Leave him alone.

Narrator 2: Kevin raised his head and pushed himself up.

Kevin: Hey, I don't need people feeling sorry for me! I'm going to show those guys what I'm made of. I'll make the sickest sick soda of all time!

Narrator 3: You wouldn't believe everything Kevin put in that drink!

Narrator 1: Steak sauce!

Narrator 2: Yogurt!

Narrator 3: Peanut butter!

Narrator 1: Oregano!

Narrator 2: Olive oil!

Narrator 3: Bananas!

Narrator 1: Pepper!

Narrator 2: Cocoa!

Narrator 3: Orange Juice!

Kevin: And a hundred other secret ingredients!

Tran: Hurry up!

Kevin: I'm almost ready!

Narrator 1: Kevin looked into the pitcher and fought off nausea for a moment. Then when he had control of himself, he poured his drink into glasses, set them on the tray, and went to the living room.

Kevin: Here you go, guys! This is the worst sick soda *(swallow)* you ever *(swallow)* tasted!

Parker: It smells like something died in there!

Maleek: What's in this stuff?

Kevin: Wouldn't you like to know? Or maybe you wouldn't!

Tran: Is that . . . is that . . . is that . . . corn?

Kevin: Yep! And that's garlic. And that brown thing is a chocolate chip. And I think that pink chunk is bologna.

Narrator 2: Tran slowly set his glass down and carefully got to his feet. Then he dashed from the room.

Kevin: Gee, I guess he's not feeling too well.

Maleek: Neither am I!

Narrator 3: Maleek ran off, holding his stomach.

Parker: Buh-buh-buh-buh-bologna?

Narrator 1: Parker took off, too!

Narrator 2: So Kevin became the winner of the First Annual Sick Soda Contest!

Narrator 3: Kevin's sick soda was so revoltingly, disgustingly, nauseatingly putrid that his friends declared him the winner without even tasting it!

Kevin: And the really great thing is that no one wants to make me sick any more. My friends and I are going to be doing lots of nice, calm, nonsickening things together. Just as soon as we're ungrounded.

Narrator 1: See, the guys were too sick to clean up the kitchen.

Narrator 2: And when Kevin's dad (mom) got home . . .

Parent: What in the world? Kevin? Kevin! *(bellowing) Ke-e-e-e-evin*!!!!

Kevin: Oh, man, I don't feel so great.

18

Survival

Summary

When Outback Ollie, the World-Famous Bumble-bee Hunter, sets out to observe humans, he expects their behavior to be as predictable as animal behavior. He figures that his subject, Elena, will do anything to survive as part of the "in" group. But Elena has a different kind of survival instinct.

Costumes/Props/Sets

Outback Ollie's face, arms, etc. can be covered with red spots. He can wear khaki clothing that resembles a safari outfit. Everyone else should wear contemporary clothing. Destiny should have long fingernails.

Eight stools should be placed on the stage with one sitting alone for Ollie, two sitting together for Elena and Andrew, and five for Destiny, her friends, and later Elena. The heckler should be seated somewhere in the back of the audience.

Props can be mimed, but if props are desired, students can have books, pencils, and notebooks. Elena could wear a CD player and headphones in the first scene. Food items could be used in the cafeteria scene. Outback Ollie pretends to catch and wrestle the bumblebee.

Presentation

Outback Ollie speaks with an Australian accent. He should use a quiet, nature-film-narrator voice when making observations. He is insecure, emotional, and sympathetic, but he tries to hide all that.

The heckler is annoying and sarcastic at first, but, as the play goes on, he becomes concerned about Elena.

Abbie, Mio, and Tyler follow Destiny like zombies. They say what she wants them to say in robotic voices. They even laugh without emotion.

Supplemental Reading

Farrell, Juliana, and Beth Mayall. *Middle School: The Real Deal from Cafeteria Food to Combination Locks*. New York: HarperCollins Juvenile Books, 2001.

Haynes, Betsy. *Blackmailed by Taffy Sinclair*. New York: Bantam Books, 1987.

Irwin, Steve and Terri. *The Crocodile Hunter: The Incredible Life and Adventures of Ste.‿ and Terri Irwin*. New York: New American Library Trade, 2002. (For older students.)

Maynard, Thane. *Working with Wildlife: A Guide to Careers in the Animal World*. New York: Franklin Watts, 1999.

Cast of Characters

Outback Ollie, the World-Famous Bumblebee Hunter

Heckler, an annoying member of the audience

Elena, who desperately wants to be part of the "in" group

Andrew, Elena's friend

Destiny, a popular girl

Abbie, Mio, and Tyler—Destiny's group

Survival

Scene One

Outback Ollie: G'day! G'day, mates! Hello, there! Great to meet you! Hello! Sorry, love (mate), no time for autographs! Well then, I guess you all know who I am. You don't? Crikey! It's me! I'm Outback Ollie, the World-famous Bumblebee Hunter! In person!

Heckler: Watch out, Ollie! There's a wasp!

Outback Ollie: *(terrified)* Where? Where?

Heckler: Got you!

Outback Ollie: Listen, mate, the venomous wasp is no joking matter. Though the sting of the wasp is not deadly, it hurts! As you can see, folks, I am an expert on all kinds of animal life, not just bumblebees. I've observed animals all over the world, and I've got the scars, scratches, bumps, bruises, tooth-marks, gashes, and rashes to prove it! Today, however, I'm here to observe human behavior. You know, humans can be just as interesting as animals!

Heckler: Or as boring as watching paint dry!

Outback Ollie: *(glares at heckler, then addresses audience)* So let's observe the human called "Elena" in her natural habitat.

Elena: *(enters, moving head and body to music on CD player)*

Outback Ollie: Notice the rhythmic movements of the Elena: the back-and-forth motion of the head, the up-and-down movement of her feet, the—

Elena: *(removes headphones)* Who are you?

Outback Ollie: *(hides behind script)*

Elena: Hey, who are you?

Heckler: It's Outback Ollie, the *Bumbling* Hunter.

Outback Ollie: Shhh!

Elena: Whatever! *(takes seat)*

Outback Ollie: Now let's observe how the Elena interacts with other members of her species.

Destiny, Abbie, Mio, and Tyler: *(enter, whispering and laughing)*

Elena: *(watches them sadly)*

Andrew: *(enters and sits)* Hi, Elena! What's up?

Elena: Nothing.

Andrew: *(notices others)* Not again! Elena, what does it matter if you're not in their group? Who cares?

Elena: That would be me. I know that I shouldn't care, Andrew, but I just do, okay? Just once in my life I'd like to be "in." Just once!

Andrew: Like that's going to happen!

Elena: Well, thanks for your support.

Andrew: I just meant that Destiny and her group are never going to be friends with someone like you.

Elena: Someone like me? Gee, thanks again.

Andrew: Wait a minute. That didn't come out right. What I really meant was . . . um . . .

Elena: Hey, don't overwork your brain cells, Andrew.

Andrew: Um . . . um . . . um . . . wait, I almost have it! Okay! Here goes. *(stilted)* What I meant was that Destiny and her friends are too self-absorbed to ever appreciate your superior intellect and charming personality. There! How's that?

Elena: Thanks, Andrew. I just wish . . . oh, never mind.

(Bell rings. Everyone takes seats.)

Outback Ollie: Crikey! It appears that the Elena is some kind of outcast human. Sad, idn't it? Mother Nature can be so cruel.

Destiny: *(approaches Elena)*

Outback Ollie: What's this? I'm afraid we're in for some aggressive behavior, folks. Notice the sharp claws and vicious fangs! This could be quite horrible! Let's watch.

Destiny: Hi!

Elena: Uh . . . hi, Destiny.

Andrew: Hi there, Destiny!

Destiny: Hello, Adam.

Andrew: That's Andrew.

Destiny: Of course it is. Listen, Elena, I'd like to talk to you after this class, okay?

Elena: Uh . . . okay.

Destiny: Meet me by the lockers.

Elena: Uh . . . okay.

Andrew: What about me?

Destiny: What about you? *(returns to seat)*

Elena: What do you think that's about?

Andrew: Who knows? It apparently doesn't involve me.

Elena: I'll tell you everything afterwards.

Andrew: *(brightening)* Okay!

Outback Ollie: Hmmm . . . why have sharp claws and vicious fangs if you're not going to use them?

Heckler: You have a brain that you don't use!

Outback Ollie: Listen, mate, how about using that big mouth of yours a little less? Or else!

Heckler: Or else what?

Outback Ollie: You just . . . you better . . . you can just . . . Look! It's the rare and beautiful can't-see-um! Right there! See it? No, not there! Now it's over there! And now—well, it's gone now! But we still have these humans to observe!

Scene Two

Elena: *(nervously waiting)*

Destiny: *(approaches with her friends)* Hi, Elena!

Elena: Uh . . . hi . . . uh . . . Destiny.

Destiny: Everybody, say hi to Elena.

Abbie, Mio, and Tyler: Hi, Elena.

Destiny: Aren't you going to say hi to everybody?

Elena: Oh, yeah! Hi, everybody!

Abbie, Mio, and Tyler: Hi, Elena.

Destiny: That was kind of impersonal, Elena. Don't you know everybody's names?

Elena: Sure!

Destiny: So?

Elena: Oh! Hi, Abbie and Mio and Tyler. Hi!

Destiny: Now that's the way to treat your friends!

Elena: Uh . . . friends?

Destiny: Well, we're not your enemies, are we?

Elena: No, but . . . well . . . we haven't been exactly close!

Destiny: *(laughs)*

Abbie, Mio, and Tyler: Ha. Ha. Ha.

Destiny: Really, Elena, your simple honesty is *so* refreshing. Isn't it?

Abbie, Mio, and Tyler: Yes, refreshing.

Destiny: Listen, Elena. *(pulls Elena to one side and whispers to her, her voice becoming more and more like a buzz)*

Outback Ollie: Crikey! Did that wasp come back? Oh, it's that Destiny creature. Hmm . . .

there's something . . . predatory . . . about her. I have the feeling that Elena could get stung!

(Destiny and friends leave.)

Andrew: So what did she say? What did she say?

Elena: She wants to be friends.

Andrew: Who with?

Elena: With me, of course!

Andrew: You?

Elena: You don't have to act so surprised.

Andrew: But, Elena . . . it's just that . . . who'da thunk . . . I mean . . . *(stilted)* I never thought that Destiny would ever appreciate your charming intellect and superior personality.

Elena: Well, she does!

Andrew: Are you sure?

Elena: Of course I'm sure!

Andrew: Okay then. Well, let's go to lunch.

Elena: Um . . . see, Andrew . . . the thing is . . . I promised to eat lunch with Destiny and everybody.

Andrew: Oh.

Outback Ollie: Oh!

Elena: You know, to get to know them all a little better.

Andrew: Hey, maybe I should get to know them, too.

Elena: I don't know, Andrew. Maybe later. Like after I really know everybody and all that. Maybe then I can sort of introduce you. Maybe . . . later . . . maybe . . .

Andrew: Oh. Sure. I understand. Well, see you later.

(Andrew sits alone. Elena sits with Destiny and her friends. They mime talking and eating lunch.)

Outback Ollie: Well, I never! He's her friend! How can she just dump him like that? I hate it when people do that! Just dump you like a bag of garbage! Like you don't have any feelings whatsoever! Sure, they say they'll see you later, but they don't mean it! They just—

Heckler: Earth to Ollie! Earth to Ollie!

Outback Ollie: Huh? Oh! Heh, heh. Not that anything like that has ever happened to me, you know. Crikey! I'm a world-famous and well-loved celebrity, I am. And manly, too! Here! Just watch me as I courageously wrestle that bumblebee right down to the ground. Mmph! Grunt! Ungh! There! I got the little stinker! How many blokes can do that?

(looks down at bee in hand) Aw . . . they're so cute when they look at you with those big, old compound eyes.

Heckler: Give me a break! Could we get on with the play?

Outback Ollie: All right! All right! Go on home now, little buddy! *(releases bee)*

Heckler: Puh-lease!

Outback Ollie: Well, then, mates. Let's get back to observing our humans.

Scene Three

(Elena gets up, starts to walk past Andrew.)

Andrew: Hi, Elena!

Elena: Hi, Andrew.

Andrew: So what are you doing?

Elena: Oh, nothing! It's just that Destiny forgot to get a drink, so I'm going back in the lunch line to get something for her.

Andrew: How do you forget to get a drink?

Elena: She just did, okay? *(walks past, returns with drink, gives it to Destiny, sits)*

Andrew: *(to Ollie)* I don't like this.

Outback Ollie: Me neither.

(Elena heads past Andrew again.)

Andrew: Now what?

Elena: Nothing!

Andrew: They don't sell "nothing" in the lunch line.

Elena: I'm just getting some ice cream.

Andrew: For yourself?

Elena: *(mumbles)*

Andrew: Was that a yes?

Elena: No!

Andrew: Don't tell me you're getting ice cream for Destiny.

Elena: Okay, I won't! *(walks on, returns with ice cream, gives it to Destiny, sits)*

Andrew: *(to Ollie)* I really don't like this.

Outback Ollie: I hear you, mate! But in nature, this kind of behavior isn't unheard of. Ants gather food and feed it to their queen. So do honeybees and other insects.

Andrew: Destiny isn't a queen!

Outback Ollie: She seems to exert some kind of power over other members of her species. See?

(Elena makes another trip, ignoring Andrew.)

Andrew: This is terrible!

Outback Ollie: Yes, it is, idn't it? But that's the way it is with Mother Nature. You can't fight it, mate!

Andrew: I have to try, dude, I have to try.

Outback Ollie: Dude?

Scene Four

(Bell rings, everyone faces front as if in classroom, pretending to work.)

Outback Ollie: I've studied animals the world over. I can predict which flower will attract a butterfly. I can watch the movements of a honeybee and tell you where its hive is located. I can interpret the howls of a wolf from far, far, far . . . far away. I can tell the difference between a photograph of an alligator and a photograph of a crocodile . . . most of the time. I can—

Heckler: So what's your point?

Outback Ollie: My point is that animals always behave in certain ways. That's why you can predict their future behavior. Humans have patterns of behavior, too. Based on my observations, I'd say that they'll do almost anything to improve their social position. It's a matter of survival, pure and simple. Andrew isn't going to be able to overcome that instinct in Elena.

Heckler: *(seriously)* Do you think it's really so hopeless?

Outback Ollie: I'm afraid so.

Andrew: Hey, Elena, you have to help me with math this afternoon, okay? I know we were going to study for that science test, but I am totally lost on fractions and percents and decimals and all that.

Elena: Well, actually, Andrew, I can't study with you today.

Andrew: Why not?

Elena: I have other plans, okay?

Andrew: But *we* had plans.

Destiny: *(looks their way)*

Elena: *(turns away from Andrew and pretends to work)*

Destiny: *(goes back to work)*

Andrew: It's safe to talk to me now—no one's looking.

Elena: Look, you don't have to get mad! I have a good reason why I can't study with you today.

Outback Ollie: Yeah, right!

Andrew: So what's this good reason?

Elena: Well, I have to help somebody do something.

Outback Ollie: Oh, really? And who would that somebody be, I wonder?

Everyone: *(looks at Ollie)*

Outback Ollie: Don't mind me. Just an observer, you know. Go on about your business.

Andrew: Oh, really? And who would that somebody be, I wonder?

Elena: *(mumbles)*

Andrew: What was that?

Elena: It's Destiny, okay?

Andrew: And just what is it that you're helping her with?

Elena: What does that matter? She needs my help and she's my friend and so I'm helping her and that's all there is to it!

Andrew: Whatever!

(Bell rings. As Destiny's group leaves, Destiny stops to speak to Elena.)

Destiny: See you after school, Elena.

Elena: Yeah, see you!

Destiny: Don't forget your math book. I am so confused about those fractions! *(exits)*

Outback Ollie, Andrew: Fractions!

Elena: She asked me first, okay?

Andrew: About the fractions maybe! But we were supposed to stay after and study together today, and you can't talk your way out of that!

Elena: Whatever.

Andrew: I just can't believe you! *(exits)*

Outback Ollie: *(to audience)* See? I told you.

Heckler: But the play isn't over yet.

Outback Ollie: No, it's not. But let's face it, mate. Everything doesn't always come out happy in the end, does it?

Scene Five

Elena: *(to Ollie)* I don't know what Andrew is so mad about. Do you?

Outback Ollie: I . . . uh . . . well . . . uh . . .

Heckler: Hey, what's your problem?

Outback Ollie: I'm an observer. It's not right for me to interfere.

Heckler: Isn't wrestling with critters interference?

Outback Ollie: Not really! I always return them to their natural habitats, unharmed. Wish I could say the same thing for myself!

Elena: Excuse me! Are you going to help me or not?

Outback Ollie: Sorry, love. This is your habitat and your life. I'm just here to watch and learn.

Elena: Gee, thanks!

Outback Ollie: You're welcome.

Elena: I think Andrew's jealous—that's what I think.

Outback Ollie: Maybe.

Elena: He just can't handle it that I'm making new friends.

Outback Ollie: Could be.

Elena: He can't stand it that I'm getting to be so popular.

Outback Ollie: You might be right.

Elena: Well, I can't help it if he has a problem, can I?

Outback Ollie: Don't ask me.

Elena: You know, it's sad how much Andrew has changed.

Outback Ollie: *Andrew's* changed? I mean, oh, really?

Elena: I guess that happens sometimes. People change. Friends outgrow each other. Life goes on.

Outback Ollie: That it does!

Elena: Well, I have a friend to help. That's the kind of person I am!

Destiny: *(enters)* Hi, Elena!

Elena: Hi! Ready to get to work on that math?

Destiny: Have you done the assignment yet?

Elena: Yes, I finished it in study hall.

Destiny: Great! Then this won't take long. Let me see your paper.

Elena: Why?

Destiny: So I can copy it, of course!

Outback Ollie: What? Well, I never!

Elena: Copy it? But I thought you wanted me to help you with the assignment.

Destiny: Duh! How much more helpful could you be? Give me your paper.

Outback Ollie: I can't stand this!

Elena: But . . . but . . . but that would be cheating.

Destiny: Not really. Weren't you going to explain it all to me and help me work the problems?

Elena: Yes.

Destiny: And then in the end, I would have gotten them all right, right?

Elena: Yes.

Destiny: So we're just saving time, okay? We're all going to the mall this afternoon, and I was hoping that you could go with us, Elena. So the sooner we get the work done, the sooner we can go.

Elena: I don't know, Destiny.

Destiny: Do you want to be my friend or not?

Elena: Sure I do! But—

Destiny: Friends help friends, don't they?

Elena: Yes, but—

Destiny: This is getting really boring, Elena! Just let me have your paper.

Outback Ollie: Crikey! This is worse than watching a lion bring down an antelope. You know that the antelope's demise is unetivable . . . inetivable . . . inevibuh . . . you know you can't do one thing about it! But still, it just breaks your heart, dudn't it?

Elena: I can't do it, Destiny. It just isn't right.

Destiny: What kind of friend, are you? *(exits)*

Elena: Not a very good one, I guess. That's probably what Andrew thinks.

Scene Six

Outback Ollie: I can't believe it! I thought that the survival instinct would be so strong that Elena would do anything Destiny wanted. Anything!

Heckler: See? It wasn't inevitable.

Outback Ollie: That's easy for you to say.

Heckler: And you said there wouldn't be a happy ending.

Outback Ollie: I was wrong, wadn't I? Totally, completely . . . Hey! Wait a minute. Elena doesn't look any too happy. What's the matter, sweetheart?

Elena: Oh, nothing much. It's just that I'm an idiot who let herself be used by someone posing as a friend while at the same time I mistreated a real friend and ruined a fantastic friendship and now I wish I could crawl under a rock, that's all.

Outback Ollie: Oh, all right then. As long as it's nothing . . . oh, I see! Well, you know I'm just an observer here and I'm not supposed to interfere in the natural scheme of things, but I'll say one little thing.

Elena: What?

Outback Ollie: I think you could still work out a happy ending here.

Elena: I could?

Outback Ollie: You certainly could! And here's your chance?

Andrew: *(enters, "casually" ignoring Elena)*

Elena: Hi, Andrew.

Andrew: Where's your new little friend?

Elena: She left.

Andrew: Oh? Well, I'm getting ready to leave, too. See you.

Elena: Andrew! Wait!

Andrew: Why?

Elena: Because . . . because I want to tell you that I'm sorry.

Andrew: You are?

Elena: Yes, really sorry! You've always been a good friend, and you don't deserve to be treated the way I've been treating you. That Destiny—like she doesn't know what real friendship is. But you do! I'm sorry I didn't appreciate that.

Andrew: Do you really mean that?

Outback Ollie: She does, mate!

Elena: I really do. Can you forgive me?

Andrew: Sure!

Elena: Great!

Andrew: So can you help me with my math?

Elena: You bet! *(they pretend to work together)*

Outback Ollie: This is brilliant, just brilliant!

Heckler: She survived!

Outback Ollie: She did! She's still . . . Elena . . . only stronger, I'd say.

Heckler: So I guess you don't know everything.

Outback Ollie: Not about humans, I don't! Obviously I need to make further observations of this fascinating species. Maybe I'll start with the humans right here. I wonder what they'd do if I said the play is over.

Heckler: Gee, I wonder.

Outback Ollie: *(watching audience intently)* The play is over!

19

Would I Lie to You?

Summary

When Sophie falls into the habit of lying, her friends lose their trust in her. Even worse, they start to avoid her. Who wants to listen to someone tell such ridiculous stories? Somehow, Sophie has to get her friends to give her another chance!

Costumes/Sets/Props

All actors can wear contemporary clothing. If a costume change is desired for Sophie, she can add a skirt or dress over her clothes and wear glasses.

Actors should sit on stools arranged in a semicircle, with a stool for the narrator to one side. The adults could enter and exit for their short scenes.

Sophie could use a prop cell phone in the last scene.

Presentation

Sophie desperately tries to make her stories sound interesting to the other kids. Jacob is skeptical all along. He is unimpressed with Sophie's stories, and he speaks in a sarcastic tone. He becomes more and more frustrated and upset as people refuse to believe his theory about Esther's true identity. Esther speaks calmly and pleasantly, but she adopts a sorrowful tone as she tries to lay a guilt trip on Sophie's friends. The friends become more emotional as they decide they miss Sophie.

When the bell rings in the last scene, everyone should exit except Sophie, Leila, and the Narrator. The Narrator exits later in the scene when Sophie wants to speak to Leila privately. Esther's part in the last scene should be taped ahead of time and replayed from offstage. Or if desired, Sophie can exit immediately after giving Leila the phone and she can do Esther's lines from offstage, leaving Esther's existence in doubt.

Supplemental Reading

Choldenko, Gennifer. *Notes from a Liar and Her Dog*. New York: Putnam, 2001.
Fletcher, Ralph. *Spider Boy*. New York: Clarion Books, 1997.
Hawkins, Laura. *The Cat That Could Spell Mississippi*. Boston: Houghton-Mifflin, 1992.
Korman, Gordon. *Liar, Liar, Pants on Fire*. New York: Scholastic, 1997.

Rocklin, Joanne. *Jace the Ace*. New York: Macmillan, 1990.
Warner, Sally. *Dog Years*. New York: Alfred A. Knopf, 1995.

Cast of Characters

Narrator

Sophie/Esther

Leila, Sophie's best friend

Jacob, who doubts Sophie from the start

Megan

Toby

Bryce

Mrs. (Mr.) Austin

Mom (Dad), Sophie's parent

Would I Lie to You?

Scene One

Narrator: Sophie's problem starts out small. Very small. She's just talking to her friends about visiting her dad in Florida.

Sophie: So we get on this strange boat with a big fan that blows you across the water.

Leila: Weird!

Sophie: No kidding. And we zoom along so fast that my dad's hat flies off his head.

Jacob: Wow. Really fascinating. So who's going to the game tonight?

Sophie: Hey, I wasn't finished.

Jacob: Go ahead then.

Sophie: Anyway . . . sometimes the boat would pop up in the air and we'd . . . like . . . scream . . . and . . . well, it was really scary.

Jacob: Wow. Be still, my beating heart.

Sophie: Wait—there's more. We . . . we saw this alligator. But we didn't see it until too late, and the guide couldn't turn the boat, so we hit the alligator!

Toby: Whoa!

Bryce: So then what happened?

Sophie: The boat flew into the air, and then it splashed down real hard, and we all got soaked.

Megan: What about the alligator?

Sophie: The guide drove back and checked. The alligator was just fine.

Leila: Wow! That was lucky.

Jacob: Yeah. Amazingly lucky.

Narrator: Okay, so most of Sophie's story is true. She did ride in an airboat. Her dad did lose his hat. Oh, and they did see an alligator. Way, way off. That's all. But Sophie figures: what's the harm in exaggerating a little?

Sophie: *(to herself)* I'm just making the story a little more interesting. It's not really lying.

Narrator: That's what Sophie told herself. But that turned out to be a lie, too.

Scene Two

Narrator: The kids go on to Science, where the subject of reptiles comes up.

Leila: *(excited)* Mrs. Austin, Sophie had a run-in with an alligator while she was in Florida.

Mrs. Austin: Tell us about it, Sophie.

Sophie: Oh, it was nothing, really.

Jacob: Really.

Bryce: Tell the story, Sophie.

Narrator: Sophie knows that her story is a big, fat lie, but she likes the way that everybody's looking at her like they can't wait for her to speak. So she tells her tall tale again.

Mrs. Austin: What a fascinating story! Were you scared?

Sophie: I . . . uh . . . not really. It all happened so quickly that I didn't have time to be scared. But after a few minutes, I started shaking. Like a delayed reaction, I guess. So my dad took off his jacket and wrapped it around me.

Jacob: Good thing that didn't blow off with his hat.

Sophie: He was wearing the jacket. How could it blow off?

Jacob: Stranger things have happened. I mean, who would believe that a boat could hit an alligator and become airborne? But you say that happened.

Sophie: I don't just say that it happened. It did happen.

Jacob: Whatever.

Mrs. Austin: Let's get back to our lesson now.

Jacob: *(muttering)* Yeah, let's get back to reality.

Scene Three

Narrator: Lies are funny things, you know. They start out small, but soon they grow. Hey! I'm a poet! *(turns to others)*

Rest of Cast: *(stares at him)*

Narrator: *(to audience)* Anyway . . . Sophie's story about the alligator grows every time she tells it.

Sophie: And not only was the alligator alive and well—he was wearing my dad's hat!

Leila: You didn't say that before.

Sophie: I guess I forgot.

Jacob: Hey, who wouldn't forget a detail like that? It's not like there's anything unusual about a reptile with headgear.

Narrator: It doesn't take long for everybody to get tired of the alligator story, and they stop paying attention to Sophie. For a few days, she tries to drum up some interest by talking about ordinary things.

Sophie: Last night there was this cool show on about—

Jacob: Saw it.

Sophie: Oh. Did anybody else have trouble with that grammar exercise?

Jacob: Nope.

Sophie: Oh. Hey, I'm getting some leather pants.

Jacob: Wow. On to a more interesting topic: how about that gravity?

Narrator: One day Sophie even tries to revive the alligator story.

Sophie: Did I tell you guys how big that alligator was? That alligator that we hit in Florida, you know? He was longer than the boat!

Bryce: Come on, Sophie.

Sophie: Would I lie to you?

Jacob: Do alligators have sharp teeth?

Narrator: No matter what Sophie talks about, no one is interested in listening to her any more. She really misses the attention that the alligator story got her, so she starts lying again.

Sophie: *(to herself)* It's not really lying. It's just . . . just creative storytelling.

Narrator: Whatever! It certainly isn't the truth!

Scene Four

Narrator: First, Sophie tells everyone this big tale about seeing a famous singer at the mall.

Sophie: So she goes, "Why don't we go to the food court?" And I go, "Sure!" And she goes—

Narrator: By the time Sophie finishes that story, everyone's eyes are glazing over.

Leila: *(daze)* Uh-huh. Uh-huh. Uh-huh.

Bryce: She's not talking anymore, Leila. She went to class.

Leila: Uh-huh. Uh-huh. Uh-huh.

Narrator: Another time, Sophie makes up this long story about finding a wallet in the grocery store and looking for the owner who just happens to be a rich guy and blah, blah, blah . . .

Sophie: And he gave me a hundred-dollar bill for a reward!

Jacob: Right. Millionaires spend a lot of time in grocery stores.

Sophie: I'm telling the truth.

Toby: Oh, sure.

Narrator: The less that people want to listen to Sophie, the more she tries to impress them with her stories. After a while, Sophie has lied so much that everyone's sick of her. When her friends see her coming, they hurry off in another direction. Leila's the only person who will sit next to her at lunch. And if Sophie calls anybody . . .

Megan: *(making static)* Screech . . . something's wrong . . . screech . . . signal's breaking up . . . bye!

Sophie: That's weird. We weren't on cell phones.

Narrator: Sophie finally sees that she's made a big mess of her life. But how can she fix things?

Sophie: Everybody hates me.

Leila: That's not true. It's just that your stories are a little . . . kind of . . .

Sophie: What you're trying to say is that no one believes a word I say any more. If only I could start over! I would do everything right if I had a second chance.

Leila: People will give you a second chance, Sophie. All you have to do is—

Sophie: Could you be quiet for just a minute, Leila? I'm trying to think.

Leila: Sorry.

Sophie: So . . . everybody thinks I'm a big fat liar . . . and they don't trust me . . . how can I get a second chance? How can I . . . Hey, I know!

Narrator: That's when she thinks of the biggest lie of all.

Scene Five

Narrator: That weekend Sophie works out every detail of her second-chance plan. By the time Monday morning rolls around, she's on her way to a new life. Meanwhile, her friends are standing around in front of school, totally unaware of the big change.

Jacob: Aah . . . Sophie's not here yet. We can all enjoy a few moments of truth.

Leila: You're so harsh! Sophie realizes her mistake, and she says she's not going to lie any more.

Bryce: Are you sure she was telling the truth when she said that?

Toby: Ha! Good one.

Megan: There's Sophie now! At least, I think that's Sophie.

Narrator: Everyone turns and stares. The girl walking their way looks just like Sophie except that she's wearing glasses, which Sophie doesn't wear, and a dress, which Sophie would never wear.

Leila: Sophie! You look so different.

Esther: I'm sorry. You've mistaken me for my twin sister. My name is Esther.

Jacob: Yeah, right. Good one, Sophie!

Esther: Let's try this again. I am not Sophie. I am Sophie's twin sister, Esther.

Leila: Sophie never mentioned a twin sister.

Megan: Yeah!

Esther: I'm not surprised. I rarely speak of Sophie myself. It's . . . it's just too painful.

Toby: What do you mean?

Esther: You see, when our parents broke up all those years ago, Dad took me and Mom took Sophie. I see my dear sister only once or twice a year. It's really hard on us—and we miss each other so much.

Leila: That's so sad!

Jacob: It's sad all right. Come on, Sophie. You can come up with a better story than that.

Esther: I assure you, I am telling the truth.

Bryce: Sounds pretty fishy to me!

Megan: Me, too.

Esther: I understand your skepticism, but as you get to know me, I'm sure you'll accept the truth. Instead of uselessly proclaiming my identity over and over, I'd like to find out about Sophie's problem.

Jacob: Which one?

Leila: Jacob!

Esther: As I understand it, Sophie's having a problem with honesty. She telephoned me in Florida and told me all about it.

Toby: Florida?

Esther: Yes, I live there with our father.

Jacob: I just bet you do! And I suppose that Sophie came down there and visited you, didn't she?

Esther: Yes, she did. It was so nice to see her! *(moved to tears)*

Leila: There, there, Esther.

Toby: Don't cry!

Esther: I'm sorry, everyone. Just remembering her visit reduces me to . . . *(cries again)*

Jacob: This is ridiculous, Sophie!

Esther: But I'm not—

Jacob: Do you think we're stupid?

Esther: No, I'm just trying—

Jacob: Talk about lame!

Bryce: Hey, be quiet, Jacob.

Toby: Let Esther talk.

Jacob: You guys are nuts!

Leila: Go on, Esther. What about Sophie visiting you in Florida?

Esther: Oh, we had a lovely time. Dad even took us on a guided airboat tour of the Everglades.

Jacob: Let me guess. His hat blew off.

Esther: Why, yes, how did you know?

Jacob: And the boat ran over an alligator and then the guide drove back and found out that the alligator was wearing your dad's hat.

Esther: My. Someone has quite an imagination.

Jacob: That's the story that you told us!

Leila: He means that Sophie told us.

Esther: Oh, I see. Sophie didn't go into great detail about her problem, but it must have been quite serious if she was making up stories like that. No wonder she felt so awful.

Megan: She did? I mean, you did? I mean . . . whatever!

Esther: Oh, yes! She said she would give anything to take it all back and regain everyone's trust, but she knew that was impossible. So she begged me to switch places with her.

Leila: Poor Sophie!

Esther: Dad and I talked, and then he called Mom and suggested the switch. So Sophie could get a new start among people who did not know her shame.

Megan: I guess we were kind of rough on . . . uh . . . Sophie.

Toby: I feel like such a worm.

Leila: What a lousy friend I was!

Esther: If only you had appreciated Sophie's good qualities and—

Jacob: Oh, come on. Just stop it, Sophie. Stop it!

Esther: I'm Esther.

Jacob: We don't believe you.

Leila: I believe her.

Toby: We all do.

Megan: We-e-ell . . . I don't know.

Esther: I appreciate your honesty, Megan.

Jacob: What about you, Bryce?

Bryce: I just don't know what to think.

Jacob: Well, I do! She's a fake!

Scene Six

Narrator: Jacob feels sure that Sophie's cover will be blown in science class. After all, won't "Esther" need some kind of paperwork?

Mrs. Austin: I didn't know you were getting glasses, Sophie.

Leila: She's Esther—Sophie's twin sister.

Toby: She's going here now.

Megan: While Sophie lives with her dad in Florida.

Jacob: Supposedly.

Megan: Yeah. Supposedly.

Mrs. Austin: I don't understand. Sophie has a twin sister?

Jacob: It came as quite a shock to all of us, too. Shouldn't "Esther" have some kind of registration form, Mrs. Austin? A note from home? A birth certificate? Something?

Mrs. Austin: Of course. Where is your registration card, Esther?

Esther: Mom couldn't come in this morning, but she called and the principal said I could start today.

Mrs. Austin: I'll just call down to the office and check on that.

Jacob: Ha! She's calling the office. What do you think of that?

Esther: It sounds like a very good idea.

Jacob: That's what—huh?

Leila: Look, Jacob, you already drove Sophie away. Why don't you do the right thing and be friends with her sister?

Jacob: That is not her sister. It's Sophie, I'm telling you! Sophie!

Mrs. Austin: Okay, Esther. You're all set for now. But Mr. Martinez says that your mother needs to get in here tomorrow and take care of things.

Esther: Yes, ma'am.

Jacob: You mean . . . she's really Sophie's sister?

Mrs. Austin: Yes, apparently she is.

Leila: See, you guys.

Bryce: Well, all right. I guess an okay from the office is good enough for me.

Megan: Me, too. Welcome to our school, Esther!

Esther: Thanks!

Narrator: But Jacob is still skeptical. And determined to expose Sophie's big lie to the world!

Scene Seven

Narrator: All morning long, teachers accept Esther with open arms. So do the other kids.

Jacob: Just look at her, people. That's Sophie!

Narrator: But no one will listen. By lunchtime, Esther is on her way to becoming popular. Everyone wants to sit with her in the cafeteria.

Esther: You're all so kind, but I'd like to sit with my sister's friends and get to know them better.

Jacob: Lucky us.

Leila: So how do you like our school so far, Esther?

Esther: It's very nice, but I miss—

Jacob: Hey, remember that time we all did that skit about the Presidents?

Megan: Sophie was hilarious doing that Abraham Lincoln rap.

Jacob: Yeah, you were great, Sophie.

Esther: Thanks, but I'm Esther.

Toby: Nice try, Jacob. You can't trick her because she's really Esther.

Jacob: No, she's not, and I'm going to prove it.

Bryce: How?

Jacob: By . . . because . . . I'll . . . she's . . . I don't know! All I know is that she's Sophie and she's lying to everyone again and you're all fools to fall for it.

Esther: If it will make you feel any better, test me. Ask me something that only Sophie would know, and if I don't know it, then you'll know that I'm not Sophie.

Leila: Good idea! What did I give Sophie for her last birthday?

Esther: Hmmm . . . I don't know.

Leila: See, Jacob?

Jacob: She's just saying that. She really does know *(shouting)* because she's Sophie!

Narrator: But Jacob can't figure out how to prove his theory. For the rest of the lunch period, he sits there, racking his brain, while "Esther" gets everyone talking about how great Sophie is.

Bryce: She makes good chocolate chip cookies.

Megan: She helped me with my math.

Toby: She lent me a pencil.

Leila: She was the best friend I ever had.

Jacob: She was a big liar!

Leila: Jacob, she felt really bad about that. She was really, really sorry.

Jacob: Was she? She never said she was sorry.

Esther: Maybe she was afraid that no one would forgive her.

Megan: Aaw . . .

Toby: Poor Sophie!

Bryce: *(getting emotional)* She had such a nice smile, didn't she? It was like . . . sunshine!

Leila: Why did she have to go?

Jacob: You're talking about her like she died. She's right here in front of you.

Leila: Look Jacob—

Esther: Just let it go, Leila. You know, each of us grieves in our own special way.

Leila: I know. I just wish she'd come back.

Others, except Jacob: Me, too! Yeah! etc.

Esther: Maybe I could talk her into returning.

Toby: Can you call her in Florida tonight?

Esther: Well . . . not exactly. I hate to say this after all that you've been through, but I haven't been totally honest with you guys.

Jacob: Aha!

Esther: Sophie is not in Florida.

Jacob: Aha!

Esther: She's still here in town, staying at a motel with Dad. They're not leaving for Florida until tomorrow.

Jacob: A-huh?

Leila: Where? Can we talk to her?

Esther: You'd better leave that up to me. I'll go over there tonight and tell her all the wonderful things you've said, and—if we're lucky—she'll be back at school tomorrow.

Kids, except Jacob: Great! Wonderful! etc.

Jacob: *(way sarcastic)* Gee, I wonder if Sophie will come back.

Leila: Oh, I hope so!

Scene Eight

Narrator: The next morning, Leila is so excited to see if Esther's plan worked that she bikes all the way to Sophie's house and knocks on the door.

Mom: Oh, hi, Leila. My, aren't you up early?

Leila: Hi, Mrs. Torelli. Is Sophie here?

Mom: Of course! She's upstairs getting dressed for school.

Leila: Great! That's the best news I ever got.

Mom: It doesn't take much to make you happy, does it? Go on up if you want.

Leila: Thanks.

Mom: Just a little warning, okay? Yesterday she decided that she wants to be called "Esther."

Leila: *(smile fades)* Esther?

Mom: Go figure!

Leila: I . . . uh . . . forgot something. I'd better go back home.

Mom: Do you need a ride?

Leila: No, thanks. I have my bike.

Mom: But that's a long way, Leila. We can put your bike in the trunk, and I'll give you a lift.

Leila: That's okay. I can just—

Sophie: Leila! What are you doing here?

Leila: I came to talk to my best friend, but she doesn't live here anymore. Does she, "Esther"?

Sophie: I . . . uh . . . listen, Leila—

Leila: I'm leaving now. Good-bye!

Mom: What's going on, Sophie?

Sophie: I think I just made the biggest mistake of my life, Mom. And I don't know how to fix it.

Scene Nine

Narrator: By the time Leila rides her bike to school, she is steaming mad.

Leila: Just wait until I tell everyone what Sophie did! Nobody will ever be her friend again.

Narrator: The other kids are waiting in front of the school, hoping for Sophie's return.

Megan: Is Sophie coming back, Leila?

Jacob: She can't come *back* because she was never *gone*.

Toby: Give it a rest, Jacob.

Leila: He's right.

Toby: Thanks, Leila.

Leila: No! I mean that Jacob's—

Bryce: There she is now!

Megan: Sophie! We missed you.

Leila: I'm going in.

Sophie: Wait, Leila! Just listen to me for a minute.

Leila: Why should I listen to a big liar like you?

Megan, Toby, and Bryce: *(gasp dramatically)*

Sophie: Please give me a chance. I want to apologize. I should have been honest with you. With everybody. See, I . . . I have a split personality.

Megan, Toby, and Bryce: *(gasp)*

Leila: Oh, brother. Don't you ever speak to me again!

Sophie: Wait! See . . . uh . . . my mom has this twin sister, and my cousin and I look exactly alike.

Megan, Toby, and Bryce: *(gasp)*

Leila: If you value your lives, stop making that stupid noise. *(to Sophie)* Why can't you just be honest for once?

Sophie: I am being honest!

Leila: I'm out of here.

Jacob: Me, too.

Sophie: Okay, okay, don't go! I'll tell the truth.

Narrator: Finally Sophie admits her whole devious plan. Pretending to move so that everyone feels sorry. Calling school and claiming to be her own mother to get one day as "Esther." Posing as her twin sister and working on everyone's emotions until they miss Sophie and forgive her.

Sophie: I'm so stupid. I had a bunch of good friends, and just because I wanted more attention, I went and ruined everything. I'm so sorry.

Leila: You should have said *that* a long time ago.

Jacob: Yeah. Like right after that stupid alligator story.

Bryce: That's all you had to do—just apologize.

Sophie: *(eagerly)* So you guys forgive me?

Others: No!

Sophie: *(sadly)* Oh.

Leila: We have to see if you mean what you say first.

Sophie: I mean it. I really do.

Toby: We'll see. It'll take a while before we can trust you again.

Sophie: I understand. But just wait—I'm going to prove myself to you.

Jacob: *(sarcastic)* And listen, everybody, don't worry. I forgive you for not believing me.

Leila, Bryce, Toby, and Megan: *(mutter something)*

Sophie: Can you forgive *me*, Jacob? Some day?

Jacob: *(seriously)* Maybe some day, Sophie. *(bell rings)* But right now I have to get to class.

Narrator: As everyone heads off to first period, Sophie stops Leila.

Sophie: Wait a minute, Leila. Can we talk? *(looks at Narrator)* Privately?

Narrator: *(shrugs and exits, too)*

Sophie: I want to apologize again. You're my best friend, and it's just terrible that I wasn't honest with you.

Leila: Whatever.

Sophie: All these years, you thought we were really close, and I'm sorry that it wasn't true.

Leila: "All these years?" Have you been lying to me for years?

Sophie: No, but I haven't told you everything. That's going to change, okay? From now on, my life is an open book. I'm not keeping anything from you any more, no matter how painful it is.

Leila: What do you mean?

Sophie: I don't have time to explain right now. I have to go talk to the principal about what I did yesterday. But I have an idea! Take my cell phone and speed-dial three.

Leila: *(dials phone while Sophie watches)*

Esther: *(offstage)* Hello?

Leila: Who is this?

Esther: This is Esther.

Leila: What?

Sophie: See? *(exits)*

Esther: Hello? Hello?

Leila: Are you really Esther?

Esther: Yes, of course, I am.

Leila: It can't be! Esther? I can't believe it! Esther! The real Esther? Wow!

Esther: Listen, whoever-you-are, I could chat like this for hours, but I can't be absent today. No way I'm missing a field trip to the Kennedy Space Center. Bye!

Leila: What the . . . but that means . . . she didn't lie about . . . *(exiting)* Sophie! Sophie!